# *How to Grill*
# VEGETABLES

## Also by
# STEVEN RAICHLEN

*The Brisket Chronicles*

*Project Fire*

*Project Smoke*

*Barbecue! Bible® Sauces, Rubs, and Marinades, Bastes, Butters & Glazes*

*Man Made Meals*

*Planet Barbecue!*

*Barbecue! Bible® Best Ribs Ever*

*Indoor! Grilling*

*BBQ USA*

*Beer-Can Chicken*

*How to Grill*

*The Barbecue! Bible®*

*The Caribbean Pantry*

*Miami Spice*

# How to Grill
# VEGETABLES

## The New Bible for Barbecuing Vegetables over Live Fire

## STEVEN RAICHLEN

Workman Publishing
New York

Library of Congress Cataloging-in-Publication Data is available.
ISBN 978-1-5235-0984-3 (paperback)

Design by Becky Terhune
Photography by Randazzo & Blau (except as noted below)
Food styling by Nora Singley
Prop styling by Bette Blau
Author photo by Roger Proulx

Workman books are available at special discounts when purchased in bulk for premiums and sales promotions as well as for fundraising or educational use. Special editions or book excerpts can also be created to specification. For details, contact the Special Sales Director at specialmarkets@workman.com.

Workman Publishing Co., Inc.
225 Varick Street
New York, NY 10014-4381
workman.com

WORKMAN is a registered trademark of Workman Publishing Co., Inc.

Printed in the United States of America
First printing April 2021

10 9 8 7 6 5 4 3 2 1

## PHOTO CREDITS

**COURTESY OF AUTHOR:** Title Page: Nancy Loseke • **GEAR PHOTOS: Adobe Stock:** Wilding, pg. 5 (firewood); **Matthew Benson/*Project Fire*:** pg. 6 (grill basket, grilling pan), pg. 7 (tiered fire, plancha), pg. 9 (indirect grilling), pg. 10 (wood smoking), pg. 12 (heat check); **Matthew Benson/*Project Smoke*:** pg. 5 (charcoal), pg. 8 (smoker pouch steps), pg. 11 (smoker pouch step), pg. 12 (air flow in wood fire); **Big Green Egg:** pg. 4 (Green Egg); **Bradley:** pg. 5 (electric smoker); **Companion Group:** pg. 6 (gloves); **Guacho Grills:** pg. 4 (wood-fired grill); **KUDU:** pg. 4 (open-fire grill); **Lodge:** pg. 4 (hibachi); **Pit Barrell** pg. 4 (Pit Barrel Cooker); **Shutterstock.com:** Alekseykolotvin, pg. 6 (foil pan); Anthony DiChello, pg. 5 (propane tank); Anton Mykhailovskyi, pg. 6 (metal skewer); nito, pg. 6 (bamboo skewers); **Weber:** pg. 4 (charcoal grill, gas grill), pg. 5 (water smoker), pg. 6 (grill tongs); **Kenneth Yu:** pg. 6 (grill brush), pg. 7 (grill wok), pg. 7 (thermometer) • **ADDITIONAL STOCK PHOTOS: Alamy:** Hera Food, pg. 170; Valentyn Volkov, pg. 27. **Shutterstock.com:** Africa Studio, pg. 307 (left); AJCespedes, pg. 311 (bottom right); BestPix, pg. 307 (right); Binh Thanh Bui, pg. 309 (top right); Brian Chase, pg. 310 (middle); Vilaiporn Chatchawal, pg. 305 (bottom left); Cozine, pg. 305 (middle); Chris Curtis, pg. 6 (top left); D_M, pg. 309 (bottom right); Darat2018, pg. 312 (top right); Kim Tae Eun, pg. 309 (left); EvergreenPlanet, pg. 307 (top middle); Jiang Hongyan, pg. 305 (right); Rasul Iskandarov, pg. 63; Kenishirotie, pg. 314 (right); Kovaleva_Ka, pg. 304 (middle); KungCrayfish, pg. 309 (middle); llepet, pg. 237; Mongolka, pg. 310 (left); Nataly Studio, pg. 308 (top middle), pg. 311 (middle); New Africa, pg. 305 (top left); oksana2010, pg. 54; Nipaporn Panyacharoen, pg. 116; paulista, pg. 307 (bottom middle), pg. 308 (bottom middle); Phototribe, pg. 215; Pineapple studio, pg. 306 (left); PosiNote, pg. 312 (bottom right); ravl, pg. 311 (top right); Sakuoka, pg. 312 (middle); Dmitrij Skorobogatov, pg. 313 (right); Danny Smythe, pg. 312 (left); Irina Solatges, pg. 314 (left); SoloEfrain, pg. 47; SOMMAI, pg, 304 (right), pg. 308 (right); Akepong Srichaichana, pg. 310 (right); Tiger Images, pg. 303, pg. 313 (left); Tim UR, pg. 306 (middle); Hong Vo, pg. 304 (bottom left); vvoe pg. 306 (right); Kelvin Wong, pg. 311 (left); xpixel, pg. 190; zcw, pg. 304 (top left). **StockFood:** Johnér, pg. 284; The Picture Pantry, pg. 3.

*To Nancy Loseke,*
*Inspired assistant, true friend*

# Acknowledgments

The cover of this book lists as its author Steven Raichlen. But I couldn't have written it without the generous help of my extended barbecue family.

Godmother (den mother?) of that family is my longtime assistant, Nancy Loseke—dotter of i's, crosser of t's, whose tireless efforts enable me to stay focused while multitasking. That's no easy feat and it simply wouldn't happen without her.

Workman Publishing has been my publisher for 27 years, and there I'm guided by my brilliant editor Kylie Foxx McDonald, photo director Anne Kerman, art director Becky Terhune, executive director of marketing and publicity Rebecca Carlisle, and director of publicity Chloe Puton. Molly Kay Upton, Moira Kerrigan, and Cialina Temena-Husemann keep our website and social media humming, while Carolan Workman, Susan Bolotin, Suzanne Rafer, Dan Reynolds, Page Edmunds, Sarah Curley, Kate Karol, Barbara Peragine, Doug Wolff, and many others are always there when I need them. We all labor under the inspiration of the late Peter Workman, our founding publisher, mentor, and friend.

If you like the photos in this book as much as I do, you'll join me in thanking food stylist Nora Singley and food stylist assistants Alyssa Kondracki and Sami Ginsberg, prop stylist Betty Blau, photographer Steven Randazzo, and photo assistant Nick Mehedin.

And if you like my TV show, *Project Fire Season 3*, which is largely based on this book, you'll join me in acknowledging Matt Cohen, Ryan Kollmorgan, and Gwenn Williams of Resolution Pictures; plus Steven Schupak, Anna Trapani, Stuart Kazanow, Frank Batavick, Mike English, Donna Hunt, and many other friends at Maryland Public Television. I'd also like to thank our fire wrangler Steve Nestor; chef Chris Lynch (love that fire cider); and Craig Reed just for being himself.

I have been fortunate to have a small army of first-rate recipe testers, including Evan Atkinson, Steven Carne, Nick Clark, Gerald Dlubala, Todd Evans, Timothy Hibbard, Rob Kettenring, Jake Klein, JP Lavoie, Max Lavoie, Freddy Leong, Steve Nestor, Derick Thielbar, and Glenn Tiede.

Material support for the photo shoot came from Big Green Egg, The Companion Group, Fire Magic, Kai USA, KUDU, Lodge Cast Iron, Southbay Forgeworks, Staub, Weber, and YETI.

Last, but certainly not least: Thanks to my immediate family—Ella, Mia, Julian, Betsy, and Jake, grilled vegetable lovers all—who add sparks to my fire and a spring to my step. And above all, thanks to my wife, Barbara—longtime counselor, collaborator, partner, and best friend. Happy anniversary, honey! I couldn't have done it without you.

—Steven Raichlen
Miami, Florida

# CONTENTS

# Introduction

Somewhere between the wood fire–blistered tomato toasts I ate at a Yotam Ottolenghi restaurant in London, and the shiitake "bacon" pioneered by visionary vegan chef Rich Landau, vegetables hit the grill big time.

Vegetables we love to cook over live fire, like peppers, corn, and zucchini.

Vegetables we would never have dreamt of grilling, such as okra and brussels sprouts on the stalk.

Vegetables that use edgy grilling techniques traditionally reserved for animal proteins, such as ember-grilling, salt-slab grilling, and hay-smoking.

Meatless proteins, like Cambodian grilled eggs, smoked "ham" that is really tofu, and "cheesesteaks" made with grilled seitan and rutabaga "cheese." Really.

Veggies for hardcore carnivores who value the health and environmental benefits of incorporating more plant foods into their diets, or simply want killer accompaniments for grilled meats.

Veggies for anyone—omnivore, flexivore, pescatarian, vegetarian, vegan—who delights in the smokiness and supernatural sweetness live fire imparts to plants.

It's enough to make you envy your vegetarian and vegan friends who have known for years what some meat eaters are just now discovering: the gustatory thrill of grilling vegetables, fruit, breads, cheese, eggs, and meatless proteins.

Never have so many forward-thinking grill masters and chefs brought so much creativity to what for decades was relegated to side dishes.

And never has the man who brought you *The Barbecue! Bible* and *The Brisket Chronicles* been more excited about writing a grill book that focuses on plant foods with nary a T-bone or sparerib in sight.

Welcome to *How to Grill Vegetables*.

Grilling has evolved a lot in the two-plus decades since I wrote *The Barbecue! Bible*. *How to Grill Vegetables* covers the grilling basics, of course, but also includes the new grilling and smoking techniques used by cutting-edge chefs around the world to bring vegetables from the periphery to the center of the plate. For vegetables possess an astonishing range of colors, textures, and tastes—especially when grilled or smoked. Whether you're a carnivore or omnivore looking for electrifying new flavors, or a vegetarian/vegan looking to up your grill game, this book has you covered.

Think out-of-the-box hay-smoked lettuce, caveman grilled squash, flatbread cooked directly in the coals, and more. Think traditional world vegetarian barbecue classics, such as Brazilian grilled cheese skewers (see page 259), Vietnamese-style grilled eggs (see page 249), grilled vegetable paella cooked over live fire (see page 206), and grilled corn salad inspired by Mexican elote (see page 144). Yes, there will be flaming pineapple and cedar-planked hasselback apples for dessert.

If you've read my books or watched my TV shows, you know that vegetables have *always* been part of my grill world—from the earliest days of *The Barbecue! Bible*. But this is the first time I've brought them together in a single book, putting them center stage, as it were, and emphasizing the *new* ways in which people are firing up their grills and smokers to cook plant and dairy foods.

I wrote this book to celebrate the incredible flavors these foods have to offer the griller and smoke master. True, most of the recipes in this book are meatless (which will make our vegetarian friends happy), but there are plenty of recipes that contain a bit of meat or seafood to elevate the flavors of a dish—for example, smoked German-style potato salad (see page 88), Grilled Asparagus with Bagna Cauda (see page 28), and sizzling zucchini braciole (see page 203). This book is not about ideology. It all boils down to (or maybe I should say grills up to) great eating and good taste.

## CHAPTER 1

# HOW TO GRILL VEGETABLES LIKE A PRO IN 9 EASY STEPS

...................................................................................................

**G**rilling plant and dairy foods draws on the same skill set used for grilling meat, seafood, or pretty much anything. You choose your grill, fuel, and tools, and fire them up. You master the basic grilling techniques, target temperatures, and how to recognize doneness. You practice good grill management and hygiene, of course, with safety at the top of your list. In short, you follow the advice covered extensively in many of my previous books, such as *Project Fire*, *Project Smoke*, and *The Barbecue! Bible*. So, here's a quick refresher, with a more in-depth look at what you need to grill vegetables, eggs, cheese, and so on.

# Step 1:
# SELECT YOUR GRILL/ SMOKER

The first thing you need to grill vegetables, of course, is a grill. Your choice is almost unlimited these days: gas grill or charcoal, pellet grill or kamado, wood-burner or smoker, and more.

- A **charcoal grill** (like a Weber kettle) offers the greatest versatility, enabling you to direct grill, indirect grill, smoke, spit-roast, or grill in the embers. Burns charcoal, obviously.

- A **gas grill** offers the convenience of push-button ignition and turn-of-a-knob heat control. Perhaps that's why it's the grill of choice for 68 percent of American households. Look for a gas grill with at least 2 burners, preferably 3 to 6 (so you can shut 1 burner off for indirect grilling). Other desirable features include a rotisserie attachment (for spit-roasting) and a smoker box (for adding wood chips or chunks), although if the truth be told, it's

difficult to produce a significant smoke flavor on a gas grill. Use for direct and indirect grilling and spit-roasting. Burns gas.

- **Hibachis** and other grills without lids burn hot, but limit you to direct grilling—good for smaller, tender vegetables and satays and other small kebabs. The hibachi's small size eliminates large whole vegetables, like cabbage, onions, cauliflower, or winter squash. Great for entertaining (put it in the center of the table and let everyone grill their own food). Burns charcoal.

- A **wood-burning grill** (like a KUDU or Argentinean- or Santa Maria–style grill) delivers the most smoke flavor (not to mention the mesmerizing flicker of a wood fire), but restricts you to direct grilling and ember-grilling (caveman grilling). Burns wood.

- A **rotisserie grill** (like the Kalamazoo Gaucho) is great for spit-roasting large vegetables, like whole cabbages or stalks of brussels sprouts. Some have grates for direct grilling as well. Burns charcoal, wood, or gas.

- A **kamado grill/cooker**, an ovoid ceramic (or sometimes metal) cooker (like the Big Green Egg, Akorn, and Kamado Joe). Works well for direct grilling, indirect grilling, smoking, and ember-grilling. Some models come with a rotisserie attachment. Burns charcoal (but a few models are gas-fired).

- A **drum grill** (like the Pit Barrel Cooker) does a fine job with direct and indirect grilling and smoking, but it's a little awkward for ember-grilling (caveman grilling). Burns charcoal.

- A **pellet grill** (like the Green Mountain Grill and Traeger) works well for indirect grilling and smoking. In general, it's less effective for high-heat direct grilling, but a few models, like the Memphis Wood Fire Grill (which has a removable burn chamber cover and perforated grill plate), do have direct grilling and searing capability. Note: When working with a pellet grill, you get the most smoke when you run it at lower temperatures (between 180°F and 275°F). Burns wood, or more precisely, compressed sawdust pellets.

- This brings us to **smokers**, which come wood-fired (**offset smokers**, like the Horizon and Lang); charcoal-fired (**water smokers**,  like the Napoleon and Weber Smokey Mountain); and **gas** and **electric smokers** like Masterbuilt and Bradley. (You can also smoke on a charcoal grill with a lid, or a kamado or pellet grill.) Most smoking is done at a low temperature (225°F to 250°F). Bradley sells a **cold-smoking** attachment,  which lets you smoke delicate foods, like leaf lettuce, and melt-prone foods, such as cheese, without actually heating or cooking them.

## STEP 2:
# FIND YOUR FUEL

Depending on the grill or smoker you choose, you'll burn gas, charcoal, or wood. Wood is my favorite fuel for grilling because it produces both heat and a smoke flavor.

- **Gas** takes the form of **propane** (sold in 18-pound cylinders) or **natural gas** (piped in by your local utility company). I always keep an extra propane cylinder on hand;

there's nothing worse than running out of gas halfway through a grill session. Note: If using natural gas, make sure your grill has burners specifically designed for it.

- **Charcoal** comes in two forms: **briquette** and **lump**—the former taking the familiar form of compact black pillows composed of coal dust, wood scraps, binders, sand, and other additives that enable it to burn at a hot, consistent temperature for 45 minutes or more. Most briquettes contain petroleum binders and borax, which burn off when the coals are lit, but which purists may not want directly under their food. Royal Oak and Original Natural Charcoal make eco-friendly briquettes using natural starch binders with nary a petroleum product in the mix.

    The charcoal I use is lump, consisting of charred hardwood and nothing more. Recent years have seen the rise of single wood variety charcoals, like quebracho from South America, maple from Quebec, and mesquite from the American Southwest. Each burns differently—for example, mesquite burns the hottest, shooting out sparks you will find exciting or disconcerting, depending on your temperament. Quebracho charcoal burns hot and consistently, as do maple, oak, and hickory. (Note: The

Charcoal briquettes (left) and natural lump charcoal (right)

flavors produced by the various charcoals are pretty similar.) When buying lump charcoal, look for uniform-size pieces and bags with minimal pulverized charcoal dust at the bottom. Oh, and avoid "lump" charcoal with sharp corners and straight edges: It probably came from leftover flooring or the furniture industry.

- **Wood** should be hardwood—either from a fruit tree, like apple or cherry; a nut tree, like hickory or pecan; or other hardwoods, like alder or mesquite. Use split logs that have been seasoned (dried) in a kiln or the open air. While you're at it, load up on kindling and small logs to help you get your fire going.

Split hardwood logs ready to meet flame

# STEP 3:
# GATHER YOUR GEAR

Here's the basic tool set any griller needs:

- A **chimney starter** for lighting a charcoal grill.

- A **smoker box** for generating wood smoke (primarily used on gas grills). This is a metal box or cylinder with holes in the top or sides or wire mesh. Fill it with wood chips, pellets, or sawdust (depending on the model) and light it following the manufacturer's instructions.

- A **long-handled, stiff wire brush** or wooden grill scraper for cleaning the grate. Note: When buying a wire brush, look for one with bristles firmly anchored in a twisted wire armature or twisted into a steel wool–like cluster, not inserted directly into a wood or plastic head. This reduces the rare but documented risk of a stray metal bristle winding up in your food.

- Long-handled, spring-loaded **tongs** for handling the food.

- An **offset grill spatula** with a thin blade for moving small, fragile, or stick-prone foods.

- **Leather or Kevlar gloves** for handling hot grates.

- **Insulated rubber food gloves** for handling large hot foods, like spit-roasted cauliflower.

- A slender **metal skewer** for testing doneness (unlike when grilling meats or seafood, you don't really need an instant-read thermometer for vegetables).

- **Wooden toothpicks** for testing doneness and pinning together small vegetables, such as asparagus stalks, onion wedges, and garlic cloves.

- A variety of **bamboo skewers** for making kebabs (ideally, this will include some flat bamboo skewers, which reduce slippage).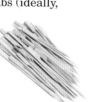

- **Flat metal skewers**, the traditional skewer for grilling vegetables in the Middle East and Mediterranean. The metal conducts the heat from the fire to the center of the vegetable, so it cooks both from the outside in and the inside out.

- A large supply of **disposable aluminum foil drip pans** (9 × 13 inch). Use them for marinating; transferring food to and from the grill (you don't have to worry about cross-contamination with most vegetables); pan-grilling and pan-smoking; as drip pans under the food; and so on. You can't have too many of these.

In addition, you'll need some specialized tools for vegetable grilling, including:

- **Vegetable grilling grid.** This looks like a sheet pan perforated with holes or slits to let through the smoke and fire. It's useful for grilling small vegetables, like green beans or okra, and chopped or sliced vegetables, like mushrooms, peppers, or broccoli florets.

- **Wire mesh grill basket.** Useful for grilling small vegetables, like snow peas and green beans. Place it on the grate for direct grilling. For even more flavor, position the basket directly on the hot charcoal or wood embers.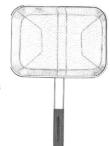

- **Grill wok.** A round or square wok-like metal bowl with holes or slits designed for "stir-grilling." The perforations allow the fire and smoke to reach the vegetables.

- **Plancha.** I consider this heavy cast-iron griddle indispensable for vegetable grilling. Excellent for searing squash and eggplant slices and grilling small vegetables, like okra. A plancha also enables you to toast bread or fry eggs for grilled breakfasts or sandwiches. You'll also need a metal scraper, like a clean paint or putty scraper, for cleaning the plancha.

- A **frying thermometer** for frying vegetables prior to smoking or grilling (used infrequently but handy nonetheless!).

- **Egg spoon.** Popularized in America by Alice Waters (and more recently, by *Project Fire* on public television), this cool tool enables you to fry an egg in a deep pool of olive oil (for maximum crispness) in your fireplace or over a campfire.

Burning logs = wood smoke, which flavors the eggs as it cooks them. The Alice Waters hand-forged version can be found at Permanentcollection.com; less expensive models can also be found online through Etsy.com.

# STEP 4:
# MASTER THE BASIC GRILLING AND SMOKING TECHNIQUES

There are five basic grilling and smoking techniques (six if you count smoke-roasting separately), plus several specialized grilling techniques (see page 9). Master them and you can grill virtually anything that grows in a garden or field or comes from a dairy—and beyond.

**Direct grilling.** This is what most of Planet Barbecue does when it grills. In a nutshell, you cook foods quickly and directly over a hot fire. Direct grilling (generally over high heat) works great for high-moisture vegetables such as asparagus and zucchini; tender vegetables, like eggplants and mushrooms; small vegetables, such as okra and snow peas; and tofu,

bread, and cheese. You can also direct grill denser vegetables, like artichokes and sweet potatoes, but work over a moderate fire.

> **GRILLING HACK:** When direct grilling, build a tiered fire, with a hot zone in the back (or on one side) for searing, a medium zone in the center for cooking, and a fire-free safety zone in the front (or on the opposite side) for dodging flare-ups or keeping food warm. Use a spatula to rake out the coals.

Making a tiered fire

**Indirect grilling.** In this method, you grill large or dense vegetables next to rather than directly over the fire. On a charcoal grill, rake the coals into two mounds at opposite sides of the grill and do your cooking in the center. On a 2-burner gas grill, light one side and indirect grill on the other. On a gas grill with 3 or more burners, light the outside or front and rear burners and do your grilling in the center. Note: Indirect grilling is always done with the grill lid closed.

# SO HOW MUCH WOOD SHOULD YOU USE FOR SMOKING?

When **indirect grilling or smoke-roasting**, you use hardwood chunks or chips to generate smoke. How much you use depends on your grill or smoker, and of course, on the size of the wood. For a typical kettle grill, I use 1 large chunk, 2 medium chunks, or 3 to 4 small chunks every hour. There is no need to soak chunks. Or use 1 to 1½ cups wood chips and soak them for 30 minutes in cool water to cover, then drain well before adding them to the coals. (This slows the rate of combustion.) For quick smoking (for example, for smoked cheese or the shiitake "bacon" on page 26), use 1½ cups chips and don't bother soaking them—you want to generate smoke hard and fast.

When **enhancing a gas grill fire with wood**, place 1 large, 2 medium, or 3 or 4 small wood chunks under the grate over one or more of the burners. Heat until you see smoke, then add your food. Alternatively, make a couple of aluminum foil smoker pouches and place them under the grate directly over the burners: Wrap soaked, drained wood chips in heavy-duty foil to make a flat pillow shape, pleating the edges to seal the pouch. Poke holes in the top with the tip of a bamboo skewer to release the smoke. Place the pouch under the grate over one of the burners. Run the grill on high until you see smoke, then dial the heat back to the desired temperature.

## HOW TO MAKE A SMOKER POUCH

1. Place 2 cups wood chips in the center of a sheet of heavy-duty aluminum foil.

2. Bring two sides of the foil up over the top of the chips and fold it closed.

3. Pinch closed and pleat the two sides.

4. Pierce the top of the smoking pouch with a sharp implement to make holes to release the smoke.

Indirect grilling

**GRILLING HACK:** Indirect grilling is often done with food placed inside of or over an aluminum foil drip pan. See pan-grilling on page 11.

**Smoke-roasting.** A variation on indirect grilling, this is a technique used often in Raichlendia generally and in this book specifically. To smoke-roast on a charcoal grill, set up your grill for indirect grilling (see above) and add wood chunks or chips to the coals. On a gas grill, place the wood in the smoker box (if your grill has one) or under the grate directly over the burners. Or use an auxiliary smoker box or smoker pouch (see box, facing page—where you'll also find more on wood quantities for smoke-roasting).

**Smoking.** Lower the temperature (to around 250°F) and pump up the smoke, and you arrive at a technique practiced widely in the American barbecue belt: smoking (aka barbecuing). Indispensable for cooking Texas-style brisket and Kansas City–style ribs, smoking works well with wet vegetables,

such as cut tomatoes or onions. It's also used to cook baked beans and dense vegetables, such as rutabagas and beets. To smoke on a charcoal kettle grill, use half or a third as much fuel as you normally would. (With a full chimney of charcoal, your grill will get too hot for true smoking.) Otherwise, use a smoker (as opposed to a grill)— see page 5.

**SMOKING HACK:** When smoking foods prone to wilting or melting (like lettuce or cheese, respectively), place the food on a wire rack over a pan of ice. Or use a cold smoke generator, like an A-Maze-N Smoker Maze or PolyScience Smoking Gun. For even more effective cold smoking, invest in a cold smoker, like a Little Chief, or a cold smoker attachment for your Bradley or Masterbuilt smoker. Several pellet grill manufacturers, such as Traeger and Louisiana Grills, also offer cold smoker attachments.

Spit-roasting cauliflower on a charcoal grill

**Spit-roasting.** Some years ago, I was in Brazil, where I witnessed a singular way to grill onions: on a spit in a charcoal-burning rotisserie. (The same restaurant served spit-roasted pineapple for

dessert.) A gentle reminder that, while most of us normally don't spit-roast fruits and vegetables, the rotisserie can be a highly effective cooker for produce. See the Rotisserie Brussels Sprouts with Turmeric Oil and Curry Leaves (page 178) and the Volcano Pineapple (page 279).

**Ember-grilling (aka caveman grilling).** This is the most ancient way of grilling and one of my favorite ways to cook vegetables. There's nothing like direct contact with live embers to caramelize the natural plant sugars in onions or peppers, for example, imparting an intoxicating smoke flavor you just can't achieve otherwise. Sicilians grill artichokes in the embers (see page 214), and this is how people roast eggplant throughout the Middle East. To ember-grill, let a charcoal or wood fire burn down to glowing coals. Fan them with a folded newspaper to dislodge any loose ash, then lay the vegetables

**GRILLING HACKS**

• To ember-grill green beans, snow peas, sugar snap peas, and other small vegetables, place them in a wire mesh grill basket and lay the basket directly on the coals.

• You can't really practice ember-grilling on a gas grill, but you can approximate the effect by cranking it up as high as it will go, then direct grilling veggies until the skins are charred. You can also do this on a very hot plancha.

on the embers. (Generally speaking, the process is quick enough that you shouldn't need refueling, but if you do, light more coals in a chimney starter, or arrange fresh charcoal on the current bed of embers and wait for them to ignite.)

# STEP 5:
# MASTER THE SPECIALIZED GRILLING AND SMOKING TECHNIQUES

Once you've mastered the basic grilling techniques (see page 7), add some specialized grilling techniques to your repertoire. The following are especially effective for veggies.

## GRILLING HACKS

- Season a plancha as you would a cast-iron skillet—by scouring it with coarse salt and vegetable oil, then oiling it and indirect grilling or baking it at 350°F for 1 to 2 hours.

- To gauge whether a plancha is hot enough, sprinkle a few drops of water on its surface. If the water evaporates in a second or two, the plancha is ready. After using (but while still hot), scrape it clean with a metal spatula and re-oil it. The more you use it, the better it gets. (Note: I try to avoid washing a plancha with soap.)

Charring a grilling plank

**Plank grilling.** Most of us know this method of grilling through the cedar planks used for cooking salmon. But plank grilling is excellent for cheese (see the Planked Brie with Fig Jam and Walnuts, page 262) and tomatoes and eggplant (see the Cedar-Planked Eggplant Parmigiana, page 188). It imparts a subtle smoke flavor and, in the case of cheese, prevents it from melting between the bars of the grate. Cedar is the plank most people use, but you can grill on any untreated hardwood plank, from alder to hickory. Choose a plank that is ¼ to ½ inch thick.

**Plancha grilling.** The plancha (heavy griddle) has become one of my favorite tools for grilling—great for slender foods, such as scallions or asparagus; flammable foods, like bacon-wrapped squash or onion rings (or pretty much anything wrapped in bacon); and of course, foods you might not normally grill, such as eggs and sandwiches. I'm partial to a cast-iron plancha: Once you season it properly, it acquires

a nonstick surface. Sure, you could use it on your stove, but what I like about plancha cooking on a grill is that you can infuse the food with wood smoke by adding chunks or chips to the fire. Just cover the grill for a few minutes after you add the wood to hold in the smoke. (Don't have a plancha? Use a large cast-iron skillet.)

**Salt-slab grilling.** Grilling on pink salt slabs became fashionable a few years ago, and there's more to it than the obvious cool factor. A salt slab delivers a mild, even heat suited to delicate foods, and the salt imparts a subtle flavor to veggies (like winter squash—grill cut side down so the flesh absorbs some of the salt flavor), and even desserts. Fresh pineapple, for example, is awesome roasted on a salt slab.

## GRILLING HACKS

- It's important to heat the salt slab gradually and never directly over the fire (set up your grill for indirect grilling at a medium to medium-high heat). Likewise, never use it when it's really cold outside (i.e., if you can see your breath when you exhale, it's too cold). Sudden changes in temperature may cause it to crack or even explode.

- Yes, you can reuse a salt slab. Scrape it clean with a metal scraper while still hot. Once cool, store it in a sealed plastic bag to keep the humidity in the air from dissolving the salt. Do not wash it or you'll dissolve the salt.

**Steam-grilling.** Use this technique for grilling large dense vegetables, like cauliflower and rutabaga. Place the vegetable on a large sheet of heavy-duty aluminum foil with 3 or 4 tablespoons of water. Tightly wrap it in foil, pleating the edges to make a hermetic seal. Direct grill or indirect grill at high heat so the water boils and steams and softens the vegetables. Then unwrap and discard the foil, and direct grill the veggie to create a dark flavorful crust.

**Pan-grilling.** I use this technique often for grilling firm root vegetables, like parsnips, carrots, and potatoes (whole if small, like fingerlings; cubed if large). Set up your grill for indirect grilling and heat to medium-high. Place the vegetables in an aluminum foil drip pan or in a cast-iron skillet with butter or olive oil and salt and pepper. Indirect grill until browned and crisp outside and cooked through, stirring every 10 or 15 minutes. The last 3 to 5 minutes, slide the pan directly over one of the grill's burners to sizzle and crisp the crust.

**GRILLING HACK:** Feeling daring? Grill the vegetables in the aluminum foil drip pan directly over the fire. You'll need to use more olive oil or butter and stir more often than you would in a heavier pan. But the crisp crust and meltingly tender center are worth the effort.

**Foil grilling (hobo pack grilling).** Campers call this configuration a hobo pack. I'd never really taken it seriously as a grilling method—until I met Pat Martin of Martin's Bar-B-Que Joint in Nashville. Pat wraps okra, onions, peppers, and Cajun spices (a few slices of kielbasa help, too) in aluminum foil and lets the resulting steam and searing work their magic (see the recipe on page 182).

**GRILLING HACK:** Use heavy-duty foil for making hobo packs. Often, I double it up. Pleat the seams to seal in the steam. And take great care opening the hobo pack (do it with a knife and not your fingers): The escaping steam is hot!

**Leaf grilling.** Long before there were pots and pans, people wrapped food in leaves and grilled them in or next to the fire. (Think of this as the precursor of the tamale.) We still use this ancient technique today. For a great application of leaf grilling, wrap goat cheese, honey, and thyme in fresh or pickled grape leaves and direct grill or grill in the embers.

**Hay- or straw-smoking.** I first encountered this method in southern Italy, where smoldering hay or straw is used to smoke delicate melt-prone foods, like mozzarella. (Hay is a grass; straw is a stalk—the smoke flavor is pretty similar.) Light a bunch of hay or straw on one side of your grill (or place it at the bottom of your smoker). Position the food to be smoked as far away from it as possible. Cover the grill or smoker to hold in the smoke. This is a very quick process— 3 to 5 minutes will do it.

**GRILLING HACKS**

• To straw-smoke eggs or lettuce (and other delicate leaves), place them on a wire rack over an ice-filled metal pan to keep the food cool.

• When smoking cheese this way, move it with a spatula. Don't pick it up with your fingers, or you'll rub off the smoke film and leave fingerprints.

**Vegetable skin–smoking.** Here's one of the world's most dramatic methods for smoking, and you don't even need a smoker. Char eggplants, peppers, or other thin-skinned vegetables over or in a hot fire. As the skin burns, the smoke penetrates the vegetable's flesh.

That's the secret to great baba ghanoush (see page 55) or a proper roasted pepper salad (see page 78). You can skin-smoke on a grill set up for direct grilling (it should be screaming hot), but I prefer to do it directly on the embers. I once smoked a pumpkin by roasting it on the embers, for example, then turned it into pumpkin pie. Now *that* was a dessert.

> **GRILLING HACK:** Once you're done skin-smoking the vegetable, shake it to dislodge any live embers and let it cool on a rimmed metal sheet pan. (Never place it on a plastic or wood platter lest a stray ember burn it.)

## STEP 6:
# FIRE IT UP

If you bought this book, chances are you know how to fire up a grill. Here's a quick refresher.

**Gas grill.** Easy, right? You simply turn on the gas and push the igniter button. Well, actually, there's a little more to it than that. First, always have the lid open when you light a gas grill. (This prevents a potentially dangerous accumulation of gas.) Turn on the burners in the manufacturer's recommended sequence. (Some grills won't work if you light the burners out of order.) Push or turn the igniter and listen and look for the "whoosh" that lets you know your grill is lit. Then—and this is very important—hold your hand about 3 inches above the burner after about 60 seconds to make sure it's really lit. At that point, it's safe to close the lid and heat the grill to the desired temperature.

> **GRILLING HACK:** On many gas grills, there's a battery (usually AA or AAA) behind the igniter button that powers the spark mechanism. If your grill fails to ignite, try replacing the battery.

Hold your hand over the fire (4 inches above the grate) to gauge the heat.

**Charcoal grill.** It's simple: Use a chimney starter. Place a paraffin fire starter or some crumpled newspaper in the bottom of the chimney starter (make sure it's resting on a heatproof surface) and add charcoal or chunks of wood to the top. Light the fire starter or newspaper. When the coals glow red (this will take 15 to 20 minutes), carefully dump them into the firebox (the bottom of your grill). Let the grill grate heat for a few minutes before beginning to cook. The beauty of a chimney starter is this: clean ignition without the need to resort to lighter fluid or other petroleum products.

> **GRILLING HACK:** Some kamado grill manufacturers recommend using an electric starter to light the coals (it's a little cumbersome to squeeze a chimney into the bottom). Others direct you to fill the firebox with lump charcoal, then nestle a paraffin starter under a couple of coals at the top and light it. This gives you a top-down burn—the preferred fire for low-slow cooking on a kamado.

**Wood fire.** Channel your inner Boy or Girl Scout: Build a Lincoln Log–cabin-like structure with small split logs, then larger split logs, placing crumpled newspaper and kindling in the center and one log across the top. Leave plenty of space between the logs to allow for good airflow. (Good airflow gives you a clean fire.) Light the paper and kindling and you're in business.

There are two ways to grill over a wood fire once it's lit. You can grill over it while the wood is still flaming, which gives you

A log-cabin-like structure maximizes airflow in a wood fire.

a more pronounced smoke flavor. Or you can let the fire burn down to glowing embers, which reduces the smoke flavor but gives you a steadier searing heat. (The latter gives you more control, which is why I prefer it for most vegetables.)

**Wood-enhanced fire.** In the beginning, all vegetables were grilled over a wood fire. In many parts of the world, they still are. A wood fire remains the best way to grill vegetables, imparting an inimitable smoke flavor that's lighter than that achieved by smoking, but that nonetheless radically transforms the taste of grilled vegetables. If you grill over a campfire or own a wood-burning grill like a Grillworks or KUDU, it's easy to grill veggies over a wood fire. If you don't, here are several ways to enhance your fire with wood:

**On a charcoal grill:**

- Light hardwood chunks instead of charcoal in your chimney starter (see the Grilling Hack below).

> **GRILLING HACK:** There's a super easy way to make a wood fire in a kettle grill. Fill your chimney starter with wood chunks instead of charcoal. Light as you normally would charcoal, and when the embers glow red, pour them into the firebox. Note: Wood chunks burn faster than charcoal, so be prepared to add a second lit chimney. And never cover a wood fire with a lid or your food will become unbearably smoky.

- Place hardwood chunks or wood chips (the latter usually soaked and drained) directly on the lit charcoal.

**On a gas grill:**

- Add wood chunks or chips to your grill's smoker box (if it has one).

- If your grill does not have a built-in smoker box, place wood chips or smoking pellets in a freestanding smoker box.

- Place wood chunks under the grate directly over the burners.

- Use a smoker pouch (see box, page 8).

**Smoker.** These come in so many different configurations (offset, water, barrel, box, and more) and burn so many different fuels (wood, pellets, gas, electric) that it's best to consult the manufacturer's instructions for firing them up and operating them.

# STEP 7:
# DIAL IN THE RIGHT TEMPERATURE

One of the keys to successful grilling is heat control. (Or as one wag puts it, control the fire, don't let it control you.) As you cook your way through this book, you'll be working at six key temperatures. (For simplicity's sake, the recipes in

this book use verbal descriptors—e.g., low or high—instead of specific temperatures.) Master them and you can grill anything!

- **100°F and below:** Cold smoking. Used for smoking foods without actually cooking them. The smoked lettuce salad recipe on page 72 calls for this technique.

- **250°F (low):** Smoking/barbecuing. This is the temperature used for true barbecue—to cook brisket, pork shoulders, and ribs to perfection. You're going to use it to barbecue onions, cabbages, and other large, whole round vegetables.

- **300°F (medium-low):** This is the temperature at which you direct grill large, dense vegetables, like potatoes and winter squash.

- **350°F (medium):** This is the temperature at which you direct grill moist root vegetables, like sweet potatoes and yams, and at which you indirect grill large vegetables, like onions and beets.

- **400°F (medium-high):** This is the temperature at which you direct grill firm green vegetables, like broccoli and artichokes. I also use it for indirect grilling potatoes and pan-grilling carrots and sunchokes.

- **500°F and up (high):** This is the temperature you use for direct grilling high-moisture vegetables, like zucchini and tomatoes. You need a high heat to keep them crisp (at lower temperatures, they get soggy).

# STEP 8:
# PRACTICE GOOD GRILL MANAGEMENT

The rules for grilling vegetables are pretty much the same as those for grilling meat or seafood: Keep it hot. Keep it clean. Keep it lubricated. In other words, you want to start with a hot clean grate that you oil right before the food goes on. Heat your grill grate well, then scrub it with a stiff wire brush or scrape it clean with a wooden scraper.

To oil it, fold or roll a paper towel into a tight pad, then clasp it in long-handled tongs. Dip it into a small bowl of vegetable or olive oil, and rub it across the grate in the direction of the bars. In addition to oiling the grate, this has the added advantage of giving the grate one last clean (and catching any stray brush bristles). Re-oil the grate as cooked vegetables come off and new ones go on. Note: When grilling smooth-skinned vegetables, like whole eggplants and bell peppers, it is not necessary to oil the grate. But it doesn't hurt—and it helps put a better nonstick finish on your grate if you do.

And when you're done, brush and oil the grill grate one final time so your grill is clean and lubricated for your next grill session.

When grilling multiple vegetables (or smaller vegetables or bread or tofu slices), arrange them in orderly sequential rows, starting in the back, working your way forward. That way, you know where you started and which piece to turn when.

Always leave at least 25 percent of your grill grate food-free (and preferably fire-free beneath it). This is your safety zone, where you can move the vegetables if they start to burn or if the fire gets too hot.

So how do you know when a particular vegetable is done? Unlike with grilling and smoking meat, I rely less on internal temperature and more on look and feel to gauge doneness.

- For small skinny veggies, like scallions and asparagus, when the outside is blistered and darkened, the vegetable is cooked. Ditto for sliced vegetables, like eggplant or zucchini.

- For small round or pod vegetables, like tomatoes or okra, use the pinch test: Pinch it between your thumb and forefinger. When squeezably soft, it's cooked.

- For larger vegetables, like squash or potatoes, use the skewer test: When you can easily pierce the vegetable with a slender metal skewer or cake tester, it's cooked.

# STEP 9:
# KEEP IN MIND HOW GRILLING VEGETABLES IS DIFFERENT

Many vegetables are grilled the same way as animal proteins. You direct grill a portobello mushroom cap, for example, just as you would a steak. (In fact, grilled portobellos are often served as "steaks.") Indirect grilling a whole squash or head of cauliflower is no different than indirect grilling a chicken.

But there are a few key differences between meat and vegetables, first and foremost of which concerns fat.

**Fat.** All animal proteins contain fat; some, like pork shoulders or ribs, contain a lot of fat, which helps keep them succulent during grilling or smoking. Vegetables contain no intrinsic fat, so you have to add fat to keep them moist. That fat can take the form of olive oil in a marinade, butter in a baste, or a strip of bacon or pancetta wrapped around a jalapeño pepper, an ear of corn, or a wedge of acorn squash.

**Moisture.** All animal proteins contain water (roughly 75 percent per pound). Vegetables are mostly water, too, but the water content varies. On the high end, you have tomatoes and peppers (roughly 95 percent); dense root vegetables, like parsnips and rutabagas, contain around 80 percent. High-moisture vegetables lend themselves to quick, high-heat direct grilling, whereas lower-moisture vegetables require the gentle prolonged heat of indirect grilling. The same is true for dense vegetables, like beets and kabocha squash.

**Smoke.** Vegetables absorb wood smoke very differently than meats. Smoke penetrates the moist, porous surface of meat easily, which is why Texas brisket and Kansas City–style ribs acquire such a delectable flavor (and smoke ring) with prolonged smoking. This is not the case with hard vegetables, like turnips and beets. The smoke tends to stay on the surface, which is why many smoked vegetables wind up smelling like ashtrays rather than barbecue. Moisture-rich vegetables, like tomatoes and onions, do best with straight smoking. Denser, drier veggies, such as turnips and rutabagas, should be blanched or boiled before smoking.

**Boiling is not a dirty word.** One of the canons of carnivorous barbecue is that you should never, *ever* boil ribs (or other meats, like chicken or brisket). Yet many vegetables contain a hard, fibrous, insoluble substance called cellulose, which makes it difficult to achieve tenderness and moistness solely by direct or indirect grilling. For this reason, I sometimes call for blanching (briefly immersing a vegetable in boiling water) or parboiling (partially cooking a vegetable in boiling water) prior to cooking. This is especially true for hard or dense vegetables, such as artichokes or cauliflower. Note: The water should be well salted and rapidly boiling for green vegetables. (This keeps them bright green.) When cooking root vegetables such as potatoes and rutabagas, start them in cold water, then gradually bring them to a boil. This allows the starches to expand slowly, minimizing a mealy texture.

**Crunch and crust.** Grilling is my favorite cooking method for vegetables (surprise!), searing (even charring) the exterior, caramelizing the natural plant sugars (which gives grilled vegetables a supernatural sweetness), and gently infusing the vegetables with the flavor of wood smoke. The one thing grilling can't do is give you a crisp crust (the sort that results from sautéing eggplant slices dredged in flour, for example, or frying sweet potatoes in tempura batter). But there is a way to give grilled vegetables that crunch, and that's by topping them with toasted or sautéed breadcrumbs or nuts, or crumbled slices of grilled bread.

**Size.** Finally, there's the question of size. Most meats (with the exception of chicken wings and shrimp) are at least single-portion serving size. Many vegetables come in bite-size or smaller pieces (the short list includes green beans, asparagus stalks, edamame, and brussels sprouts). So, you need to group small vegetables together for grilling. One method is to thread them onto skewers to make kebabs or rafts. Another is to grill them on a vegetable grid or in a wire-mesh grill basket (see page 6).

So, now you know the basics and fine points of grilling vegetables. It's time to fire up your grill!

# CHAPTER 2

# STARTERS & PASS-AROUNDS

**B**ruschetta. Poppers. Grilled vegetables with flavorful dips. What better way to round out cocktails or start a meal than with veggies smokily charred over a hot fire? This chapter has you covered with the likes of Tuscan "edamame" (fava beans grilled in the pod), crispy grilled kale, and wood-grilled avocados served with two unconventional salsas. And speaking of smoke, how about spiced, smoked chickpeas or crisp shiitakes smoked like bacon? The French Renaissance writer François Rabelais called these small bites "spurs of Bacchus" (how's that for a metaphor?), and when it comes to getting a meal off to a lively start, these grilled and smoked starters and pass-arounds are as timely now as then.

# RECIPES

# BUFFAQUE BROCCOLI
## WITH BLUE CHEESE DIP

**YIELD** Serves 4 to 6 as a starter

**METHOD** Smoke-roasting (indirect grilling with wood smoke)

**PREP TIME** 20 minutes

**GRILLING TIME** 20 to 30 minutes

**GRILL/GEAR** Can be grilled over charcoal, gas, or wood. You'll also need hardwood chunks or chips (soaked), see page 8; 2 aluminum foil drip pans (9 × 13 inches) or a 10- to 12-inch cast-iron skillet.

**WHAT ELSE** You can certainly direct grill the broccoli, and if you do it over a wood or wood-enhanced fire, you'll get a haunting smoke flavor. But I prefer to smoke-roast (indirect grill) the broccoli in a foil pan— it cooks up a little crisper and you still get plenty of smoke thanks to the wood chunks or chips you add to the fire.

The Buffalo wing burst upon the American food scene in 1964 at the Anchor Bar in Buffalo, New York. It took the country—and the world—by storm. Since then, a great many foods have been Buffaloed, from shrimp to ribs to brussels sprouts, and the original cooking method (deep-frying) is often replaced, at least in barbecue circles, by cooking on a grill or barbecue pit. The result: bold flavors, reduced fat, and a satisfying smokiness. Which brings me to this Buffaque Broccoli. No, it's not a chicken wing; it will never be a wing. But it is a vegetable you can proudly serve—even to carnivores—at your next tailgating party. The Blue Cheese Dip is optional.

## INGREDIENTS

**FOR THE BROCCOLI**

2 heads broccoli

Extra virgin olive oil

Coarse salt (sea or kosher)

Freshly ground black pepper

Onion powder

Hot red pepper flakes

**FOR THE "WING" SAUCE**

6 tablespoons (¾ stick) unsalted butter

½ cup sriracha

3 to 4 tablespoons Thai sweet chili sauce (one good brand is Mae Ploy), or to taste

2 tablespoons Louisiana-style hot sauce (such as Crystal or Frank's RedHot)

Blue Cheese Dip (optional; recipe follows)

1 tablespoon finely chopped fresh chives (optional)

Celery ribs, for serving (optional)

**1.** Set up your grill for indirect grilling and heat to medium-high.

**2.** Peel the broccoli stems with a paring knife. Cut the broccoli into large florets (each should be 2 to 3 inches in length and include a portion of the stem). Cut the remainder of the stems into finger-size strips. Arrange the broccoli in a single layer in the foil pans. Drizzle with olive oil and stir to coat. Sprinkle with the salt, pepper, onion powder, and hot red pepper flakes (I leave the quantities open to your taste). Stir to mix.

**3.** Place the foil pans with the broccoli on the grill away from the fire. If enhancing a charcoal fire, add the wood chunks or chips on the coals; if enhancing a gas fire, place the chunks or chips in your grill's smoker box or place chunks under the grate directly over one or more burners. Close the lid and indirect grill the broccoli until sizzling, lightly browned, and crisp-tender, 20 to 30 minutes.

**4.** Meanwhile, make the "wing" sauce: Melt the butter in a small saucepan over medium heat. Stir in the sriracha, Thai sweet chili sauce, and hot sauce. Simmer for about 3 minutes.

**5.** Move the foil pans directly over the fire the last 3 to 5 minutes, stirring so the broccoli browns and crisps evenly. Stir in half the "wing" sauce and cook for 1 minute.

**6.** Arrange the broccoli on a platter. Pour the remaining "wing" sauce over it. Spoon or squirt the Blue Cheese Dip over the broccoli or serve alongside (if using). Sprinkle with chives (if using). Serve at once, with celery (if using).

# BLUE CHEESE DIP

**YIELD** Makes 1½ cups

Tell me you saw this one coming. Buffalo wings have been served with blue cheese sauce ever since that fateful day in 1964. The Raichlen twist? Bolster the smoke flavor by adding a smoked blue cheese like Smokey Blue from Rogue Creamery in Oregon.

## INGREDIENTS

3 ounces smoked blue cheese or Roquefort or Gorgonzola

½ cup mayonnaise, preferably Hellmann's or Best Foods

¼ cup sour cream

Freshly ground black pepper to taste

2 to 4 tablespoons heavy cream or milk

Place the cheese in a food processor and grind to a coarse paste. Add the mayonnaise, sour cream, and pepper and process until smooth, running the machine in short bursts. Work in enough cream or milk to obtain a creamy pourable sauce. Transfer it to small bowls for dipping or drizzle it over the broccoli from a squirt bottle or with a spoon.

# SPICY SMOKED CHICKPEAS

If this were a vegetarian grill book (which it's not), smoked chickpeas would be the equivalent of bacon bits. These spice-crusted chickpeas possess smoke flavor that makes them irresistible for snacking—not to mention for churning into Smoked Hummus (page 53) and adding to paella (see page 206). Kill two birds with one stone: Smoke one batch for munching and a second batch for using later.

## INGREDIENTS

2 cans (15.5 ounces each) chickpeas

3 tablespoons extra virgin olive oil

1 teaspoon smoked or sweet paprika

1 teaspoon each coarse salt (sea or kosher) and freshly ground black pepper

½ teaspoon ground cumin

½ teaspoon Urfa pepper, cayenne pepper, or hot red pepper flakes

**1.** Set up your grill for indirect grilling and heat to medium-high.

**2.** Meanwhile, drain the chickpeas in a colander. Arrange them on an aluminum foil drip pan spread with clean kitchen towels. Blot dry with more towels. Remove the towels and add 1½ tablespoons olive oil, the paprika, salt, pepper, cumin, and Urfa pepper to the chickpeas. Mix well.

**3.** If enhancing a charcoal fire, add the wood chunks or chips to the coals; if enhancing a gas fire, place the chunks or chips in your grill's smoker box or place chunks under the grate directly over one or more burners. Place the chickpeas in their drip pan on the grate away from the heat.

**4.** Close the lid and indirect grill until the chickpeas are smoky, 15 to 20 minutes, stirring once or twice so they smoke evenly.

**5.** Add the remaining 1½ tablespoons olive oil to the chickpeas and stir to coat. Move the chickpeas directly over the fire and direct grill until crisp, 2 to 4 minutes, stirring often.

**6.** Let the chickpeas cool to room temperature before serving. The chickpeas can be stored in an airtight container or resealable plastic bag in the refrigerator for up to 3 days. Re-crisp them on the grill (set up for indirect grilling) or in a 400°F oven, if necessary, before serving.

**YIELD** Makes 2 cups, enough to serve 4, and can be multiplied as desired

**METHOD** Smoke-roasting (indirect grilling with wood smoke)

**PREP TIME** 10 minutes

**GRILLING TIME** About 20 minutes

**GRILL/GEAR** Can be cooked over gas or charcoal enhanced with wood, but for the best smoke flavor, use charcoal. You'll also need hardwood chunks or chips (soaked), see page 8.

**WHAT ELSE** The purist will wish to start with dried chickpeas (garbanzo beans), soak them overnight, refrigerated, in water to cover, then boil them until soft. For the rest of us, cooked chickpeas in a can or jar (preferably organic or imported from Italy or Spain) will work just fine. Urfa pepper (Urfa biber) is a dried hot pepper from Turkey that acquires its distinctive flavor from being dried on the vine before grinding. Order it online or substitute French Espelette pepper, hot paprika, or cayenne.

# PADRÓN PEPPER POPPERS

Poppers, those cheddar-stuffed, bacon-wrapped jalapeño peppers, are common currency on the American barbecue trail. These come with a decidedly Spanish twist, using Padrón peppers, tangy Manchego cheese (a sheep's milk cheese from the La Mancha province in Spain), musky-sweet membrillo (quince paste—any fruit jam or preserve will do), and smoky pimentón (Spanish smoked paprika). I've made the jamón Serrano (Spanish ham) optional; if unavailable, you could use prosciutto, speck, or bacon—or simply omit the meat entirely. The result: a popper like you've never experienced.

## INGREDIENTS

12 large Padrón or shishito peppers (hand-select them when you're shopping)

6 ounces (1½ cups) Manchego cheese, shredded or finely grated

⅓ cup mayonnaise, preferably Hellmann's or Best Foods

1 scallion, trimmed, white and green parts thinly sliced

2 teaspoons pimentón (Spanish smoked paprika) or sweet or hot paprika

Vegetable oil for oiling the grill grate

2 tablespoons quince paste (membrillo), guava paste, or other fruit preserve (optional), cut into matchstick slivers

3 ounces thinly sliced jamón Serrano or other cured ham, or 6 strips bacon

**1.** Cut the Padróns in half lengthwise. Scrape out the seeds with a small metal spoon or grapefruit spoon.

**2.** Place the Manchego, mayonnaise, scallion, and pimentón in a bowl and stir to mix. Spoon the mixture into the Padrón halves. Top each with a sliver of quince paste (if using).

**3.** If using jamón Serrano, cut it into strips 1 inch wide and 4 inches long. If using bacon, cut it in half widthwise.

Wrap each popper crosswise with a strip of ham or bacon, securing it with a toothpick. The poppers can be prepared several hours ahead to this stage, covered, and refrigerated.

**4.** Meanwhile, set up your grill for indirect grilling and heat to medium-high. Brush or scrape the grill grate clean and oil it well. If enhancing a charcoal fire, add the wood chunks or chips to the coals; if enhancing a gas fire, place the chunks or chips in your

**YIELD** Serves 4

**METHOD** Smoke-roasting (indirect grilling with wood smoke)

**PREP TIME** 15 minutes

**GRILLING TIME** 15 to 20 minutes

**GRILL / GEAR** Can be grilled over charcoal or gas but tastes best grilled over wood or a wood-enhanced fire. If you're enhancing a charcoal or gas fire, you'll also need hardwood chunks or chips (soaked), see page 8. You'll also need wooden toothpicks.

**WHAT ELSE** Padrón peppers (named for a municipality in northwest Spain) and their Japanese cousins, shishitos (the two are similar in flavor, but Padróns are larger and easier to stuff), are slender peppers about the size and shape of your index finger. Dark green in color with dimpled contours, they have a gentle, herbal, almost grassy flavor that lies midway between a poblano and a green bell pepper, but milder than either. Unless, that is, you happen to get one with capsicum hellfire—which occurs randomly in one of every ten or so peppers. That's what makes eating Padróns, er, exciting. Look for them at Whole Foods or your local farmers' market, or order them online from Melissas.com.

grill's smoker box or place chunks under the grate directly over one or more burners. Arrange the poppers on the grate over the drip pan away from the heat (it helps to have them on a wire rack or grilling grid for efficient transport to and from the grill).

**5.** Close the grill lid. Indirect grill the poppers until the cheese mixture and ham are sizzling and browned and the sides of the peppers are soft, 15 to 20 minutes.

**6.** Transfer to a platter, remove the toothpicks, and serve.

# TUSCAN "EDAMAME"

**YIELD** Serves 2 or 3

**METHOD** Direct grilling

**PREP TIME** 5 minutes

**GRILLING TIME** 8 to 12 minutes

**GRILL/GEAR** Can be grilled over charcoal or gas, but tastes best grilled over a wood or wood-enhanced fire. If you're enhancing a charcoal or gas fire, you'll also need hardwood chunks or chips (soaked), see page 8.

**WHAT ELSE** Look for fresh fava beans in Italian markets and the produce section of upscale supermarkets. (Whole Foods carries them in season, usually late March through early May.)

Every spring, fresh fava beans come to market, their large green pods looking like edamame on steroids. My stepson, Jake Klein, who is a chef, likes to grill them in the pods seasoned with olive oil, fresh thyme, and sea salt. Grilling delivers a firmer texture than boiling, and imparts interesting herbal smoke flavors. To keep your fingers clean, you may want to wear gloves when peeling the charred pods.

## INGREDIENTS

1 pound fresh fava beans in their pods

2 tablespoons extra virgin olive oil

Coarse salt (sea or kosher) and freshly ground black pepper

2 teaspoons fresh thyme leaves

**1.** Set up your grill for direct grilling and heat to high. If enhancing a charcoal fire, add the wood chunks or chips to the coals; if enhancing a gas fire, place the chunks or chips in your grill's smoker box or place chunks under the grate directly over one or more burners. (There's no need to oil the grill grate.)

**2.** Brush the fava bean pods on both sides with olive oil and season with salt, pepper, and the fresh thyme leaves.

**3.** Arrange the fava bean pods on the grate and grill until the pods are blistered and blackened, 4 to 6 minutes per side. Transfer the pods to a platter and serve. To eat the favas, break open the pods and pluck out the beans inside.

# GRILLED RADISHES
## WITH ROQUEFORT BUTTER

When I was a student in Paris, we ate at a cheap homey bistro in the Latin Quarter called Le Petit Saint Benoît. Fancy and sophisticated it was not. Appetizers ran from champignons à la grecque (pickled mushrooms) to poireaux à la vinaigrette (boiled leeks with vinaigrette sauce—for an interesting grilled version, see page 85) to the most exquisitely barebones French bistro dish of all: radis au beurre (fresh radishes with sweet butter and sea salt). There was something about the contrast of textures and flavors—crisp, peppery radishes, soft sweet butter, crunchy crystals of salt—that was so much more than the sum of the parts. As for grilling radishes? That's something the French would *never* do, but grilling adds a gentle smoke flavor, while mellowing the radish-y bite. I like to grill the radishes on bamboo skewers, which makes them perfect for dipping. I also like to mix the butter with Roquefort cheese—a congenial way to supply the salt.

**YIELD** Serves 4

**METHOD** Direct grilling

**PREP TIME** 20 minutes

**GRILLING TIME** 4 to 6 minutes

**GRILL/GEAR** Can be grilled over charcoal, gas, or wood. You'll also need small bamboo skewers and a sheet of aluminum foil (12 × 18 inches) folded into thirds, shiny side out, like a business letter (this will be your grill shield).

**WHAT ELSE** Radishes (from the Latin word *radix*, meaning "root") come in many varieties: cherry belle (the common round red radish), watermelon radish (large and round with a red center), and fire and ice (the elongated radish with a red top and white bottom so beloved by the French), to name a few. All are great for grilling. I like to cut the radish in half to expose more surface area to the fire, but you can also grill the radishes whole.

## INGREDIENTS

**FOR THE ROQUEFORT BUTTER**

2 ounces Roquefort cheese, at room temperature

4 tablespoons (½ stick) unsalted butter, at room temperature

**FOR THE RADISHES**

1 bunch radishes, stemmed and scrubbed

Extra virgin olive oil

Coarse salt (sea or kosher) and freshly ground black pepper

Vegetable oil for oiling the grill grate

**1.** Make the Roquefort butter: Force the Roquefort through a mesh strainer into a mixing bowl. (Alternatively, mash it to a paste with the back of a spoon.) Stir in the butter. Place the Roquefort butter in 1 or 2 small bowls. Note: The Roquefort butter can be made up to 3 days in advance. Store it, refrigerated, in a small covered container. Let warm to room temperature before serving.

**2.** Cut the radishes in half widthwise on the diagonal. Skewer on bamboo skewers, 2 radish halves to a skewer, leaving ¼ inch between each. Lightly brush with olive oil and season with salt and pepper.

**3.** Set up your grill for direct grilling and heat to high. Brush or scrape the grill grate clean and oil it well.

**4.** Arrange the radish kebabs on the grill, sliding the foil grill shield under the exposed part of the skewers to keep them from burning. Grill until the radishes are browned on both sides, 2 minutes per side or as needed.

**5.** Serve the radishes on the skewers with the Roquefort butter for dipping.

# SHIITAKES CHANNELING BACON

**YIELD** Serves 4 as an appetizer

**METHOD** Smoking

**PREP TIME** 10 minutes

**SMOKING TIME** 5 to 30 minutes (depending on your grill or smoker)

**GRILL/GEAR** Charcoal grill, smoker, or handheld smoker. You'll also need hardwood chunks or chips (unsoaked), see page 8; or hardwood sawdust for an indoor smoker; a frying thermometer (optional); and a wire rack or a grill basket.

Most vegetable charcuterie involves several days of curing and smoking. Here, shiitakes channel bacon in a recipe that can be made from start to finish in less than an hour. (The active time is only about 15 minutes.) The recipe comes from a terrific vegan restaurant in Washington, DC, called Fancy Radish. You'll love the crisp crunch and rich bacon-y mouthfeel. You'll also love the earthy smoke flavor—similar to bacon, but more mushroom-like. Make shiitake bacon for snacking in its own right, or for serving with smoked eggs (see pages 245 and 246). Which just goes to show that everything tastes better with bacon—even if that bacon contains no meat.

## INGREDIENTS

8 ounces fresh shiitake mushrooms (pick the largest caps you can find)

1 cup grapeseed or canola oil, or as needed, for frying

Vegetable oil for oiling the grill grate

Coarse salt (sea or kosher)

**1.** Use a sharp knife to cut off the mushrooms' fibrous stems flush with the caps. (Unlike most varieties of mushrooms, shiitake stems are unpalatable.) Thinly slice the shiitake caps crosswise on a mandoline or by hand. The slices should be no more than ⅛ inch thick.

**2.** Set a wire rack over a rimmed sheet pan or line a plate with paper towels. Pour the oil into a 10-inch frying pan to a depth of ½ inch and place over medium-high heat. When the oil starts to shimmer, add a shiitake slice; when the temperature is right, bubbles will dance around it. (The temperature on a frying thermometer will be 350°F.) Add the shiitake slices, working in batches as needed to avoid crowding the pan, and fry until golden and crisp, 2 to 3 minutes, stirring with a slotted spoon. Transfer the fried shiitakes to the wire rack to drain. Let the fried shiitakes cool to room temperature.

**3.** If using a grill to smoke the shiitakes, set it up for indirect grilling and heat

it to medium. Brush or scrape the grill grate clean and oil it well. Add wood chunks or chips to the coals. If using an outdoor smoker, set it up following the manufacturer's instructions and heat it to 250°F. Add wood as specified by the manufacturer. If using a stovetop or handheld smoker, follow the manufacturer's instructions.

**4.** Arrange the fried shiitake slices on a wire rack or in a grill basket and place it on the grill or in the smoker. Smoke the shiitakes long enough to apply a discernible smoke flavor, 5 to 8 minutes for a grill, 20 to 30 minutes for a smoker (the smoking time is longer because the temperature is lower), 5 to 10 minutes with a handheld smoker.

**5.** Let the shiitake "bacon" cool to room temperature, then season with salt. It tastes best served immediately or within a few hours of smoking. Store in an airtight container in the refrigerator if you plan to keep it longer.

**WHAT ELSE** Fresh shiitakes are available in the produce section of most supermarkets, not to mention, quite likely at your local farmers' market. The flavor is off-the-charts delectable—musky and aromatic, with natural umami flavors that may remind you of smoke. Choose large caps, 3 to 4 inches if you can find them, to maximize the length of the "bacon" strips. Note: Shiitake "bacon" involves a two-step process—and one that's the exact opposite of making pork bacon. First, you fry thinly sliced shiitakes to make them crisp. Then you smoke them to make them taste like bacon. To keep the cooking entirely outdoors, you could do the frying on your grill's side burner. You can do the smoking in your smoker or on a charcoal grill or indoors with a handheld or stovetop smoker.

# GRILLED ASPARAGUS
## WITH BAGNA CAUDA

**YIELD** Serves 2 to 4 and can be multiplied as desired

**METHOD** Direct grilling

**PREP TIME** 20 minutes

**GRILLING TIME** 6 to 8 minutes

**GRILL/GEAR** Can be grilled over charcoal, gas, wood, or a wood-enhanced fire. If you're enhancing a charcoal or gas fire, you'll also need hardwood chunks or chips (unsoaked), see page 8. You'll also need wooden toothpicks or small bamboo skewers.

**WHAT ELSE** Anchovies come in at least three forms: pickled (e.g., boquerones), salt-packed, and in oil. You want the latter for this recipe. Bagna cauda is olive oil–based, but you can also simmer the garlic and anchovies in heavy cream, which gives you an even richer dip. If you're feeling fancy, you can peel the ends of the asparagus stalks with a vegetable peeler instead of snapping them off. Note: This recipe calls for asparagus, but any crisp slender vegetable, from okra to carrots, is great for grilling and dipping in bagna cauda.

Bagna cauda, literally "hot bath," is a specialty of the Piemonte in northern Italy where crisp vegetables (the French would call them crudités) are dipped in a warm sauce of anchovies, garlic, and cream or olive oil. In other words, just the sort of starter that's ripe for a live-fire makeover. To grill the asparagus, I call for a technique popular in Japan, pinning the stalks with toothpicks into rafts, which are easier to grill than individual stalks. For the hot bath, I offer two alternatives—the traditional anchovy bagna cauda (here, olive oil–based), and a vegan variation flavored with miso.

## INGREDIENTS

### FOR THE ASPARAGUS

1 pound asparagus, preferably thicker stalks

Extra virgin olive oil

Coarse salt (sea or kosher) and freshly ground black pepper

Vegetable oil for oiling the grill grate

### FOR THE ANCHOVY BAGNA CAUDA

½ cup extra virgin olive oil

2 cloves garlic, peeled and minced

1 tin (2 ounces) oil-cured anchovies, drained, blotted dry, and finely chopped

½ teaspoon freshly and finely grated lemon zest

Freshly ground black pepper

Vegetable oil for oiling the grill grate

**1.** Holding an asparagus stalk by the base in one hand, bend the top half over to snap it at its natural point of tenderness. Repeat with the remaining stalks. Discard the fibrous stems.

**2.** Pin the asparagus stalks together side by side with toothpicks to form rafts, 4 or 5 stalks per raft.

**3.** Lightly brush the asparagus rafts on both sides with olive oil and season with salt and pepper.

**4.** Meanwhile, make the bagna cauda: Heat the ½ cup olive oil in a small saucepan over medium-high heat. Add the garlic and cook until lightly browned, 1 to 2 minutes, stirring. Stir in the anchovies, lemon zest, and pepper to taste, and simmer, stirring

often, until the anchovies disintegrate, about 5 minutes. Keep warm.

**5.** Set up your grill for direct grilling and heat to high. Brush or scrape your grill grate clean and oil it well. If enhancing a charcoal fire, add the wood chunks or chips to the coals; if enhancing a gas fire, place the chunks or chips in your grill's smoker box or place chunks under the grate directly over one or more burners.

**6.** Arrange the asparagus rafts on the grate and grill until darkly browned on both sides, turning with tongs, about 3 minutes per side. Alternatively, you can grill the stalks on a hot vegetable grid or in a grill basket.

**7.** Arrange the asparagus rafts on a platter or plates, and remove and discard the toothpicks. Serve with bowls of warm bagna cauda on the side, using your fingers for dipping. Alternatively, arrange the grilled asparagus on plates and spoon the bagna cauda over them. You can eat these with a knife and fork.

# MISO BAGNA CAUDA

YIELD ¾ cup

Miso gives this bagna cauda the rich, salty, umami flavors of anchovies— for people who don't like or eat this big-flavored fish. Use white miso (made with cultured soybeans and rice), red miso (a long-fermented soybean and grain version), or awase miso (a combination of the two).

## INGREDIENTS

1 clove garlic, peeled and minced

½ teaspoon freshly and finely grated lemon zest

2 tablespoons miso, or to taste

2 tablespoons fresh lemon juice

2 tablespoons hot water

6 tablespoons extra virgin olive oil

Coarse salt (sea or kosher) and freshly ground black pepper

Place the garlic and lemon zest in a small mixing bowl and mash to a paste with the back of a spoon. Add the miso, lemon juice, and hot water and whisk until the miso dissolves. Whisk in the olive oil. Correct the seasoning, adding salt and pepper to taste. No cooking required. In the unlikely event you have any left, store it in a covered container in the refrigerator, where it will keep for at least 3 days. Let warm to room temperature before serving.

# GRILLED AVOCADOS TWO WAYS

Call it Old World–New World fusion. Call it a cross-cultural culinary mash-up. It starts with a New World fruit that most of us treat as a vegetable, and that until recently, few of us would have dreamed of grilling. That would be avocado—most readily consumed as guacamole, but whose sweet creamy flesh is mystically transformed by wood smoke.

## GRILLED AVOCADOS
## WITH CATALONIAN FIRE-ROASTED TOMATO AND ALMOND SAUCE

From the Old World—from Tarragona in Catalonia, Spain, to be precise—comes a tangy and spicy tomato sauce called salbitxada (sometimes written salvitxasa and pronounced sal-beet-chada), based on two other New World foods (tomatoes and peppers) and made nutty by the addition of almonds and sherry vinegar. Together they form a starter that's as irresistible as it is unexpected. Note: In Spain salbitxada is traditionally served with grilled calçots (Catalonian second-growth onions that resemble small leeks), or asparagus or artichokes—alternatives I heartily endorse.

**YIELD** Serves 4 to 8

**METHOD** Direct grilling

**PREP TIME** 20 minutes

**GRILLING TIME** 6 minutes

**GRILL/GEAR** Can be grilled over charcoal or gas but tastes best grilled over wood or a wood-enhanced fire. If you're enhancing a charcoal or gas fire, you'll also need hardwood chunks or chips (unsoaked), see page 8.

### INGREDIENTS

**FOR THE AVOCADOS**

Vegetable oil for oiling the grill grate

4 ripe but firm avocados

Extra virgin olive oil, for brushing

Coarse salt (sea or kosher) and freshly ground black pepper

**FOR THE SALBITXADA**

¼ cup Marcona almonds or blanched California almonds

2 large, luscious ripe tomatoes

1 jalapeño or serrano pepper, or a 3 × 2-inch piece of poblano pepper

3 cloves garlic, peeled and skewered on a toothpick (or 1 small shallot, peeled and cut in half)

3 tablespoons chopped fresh flat-leaf parsley leaves, plus 8 sprigs for serving

½ teaspoon freshly and finely grated lemon zest

1 tablespoon sherry vinegar, or to taste

3 tablespoons extra virgin olive oil

Coarse salt (sea or kosher) and freshly ground black pepper

1. Set up your grill for direct grilling and heat to high. If enhancing a charcoal fire, add the wood chunks or chips to the coals; if enhancing a gas fire, place the chunks or chips in your grill's smoker box or place chunks under the grate directly over one or more burners. Brush or scrape the grill grate clean and oil it well.

2. Meanwhile, halve and pit the avocados. Lightly brush the flesh of the avocados with olive oil and season with salt and pepper.

3. Arrange the avocados cut sides down on the grill, so each half runs on the diagonal to the bars of the grate. Grill until browned, 2 to 3 minutes. Transfer the avocados to a platter and cool to room temperature. Drizzle with a little more olive oil.

4. Meanwhile, make the salbitxada: Place a dry heavy skillet on the grill grate over the fire. Add the almonds and cook until roasted and fragrant, about 2 minutes, stirring frequently. Watch carefully. Transfer to a bowl and let cool.

5. If you don't feel like grilling the other ingredients for the salbitxada, char them in the dry skillet you used for the almonds, 1 to 2 minutes per side. Otherwise, arrange the tomatoes, jalapeño, and garlic on the grate. Grill until the tomato and jalapeño skins are blistered and the garlic is browned, about 1 minute per side, turning with tongs. Do not overcook the tomatoes—you want them to remain cool in the center. Transfer the vegetables to the cutting board and let cool. Peel the tomatoes if you feel like it (I usually don't bother). Cut in half widthwise and wring out and discard the seeds. Cut out and discard the stem ends. Cut the jalapeño in half and remove the seeds (or leave them in if you like your salbitxada spicy). Unskewer the garlic. Roughly chop the tomatoes, jalapeño, and garlic.

6. Coarsely grind the almonds in a food processor fitted with a metal chopping blade. Add the tomatoes, jalapeño, garlic, chopped parsley, and lemon zest and run the processor in short bursts to coarsely grind. I prefer a chunky salbitxada to a smooth one, but that's me; if you'd prefer a smoother sauce, pulse it more. Work in the sherry vinegar, olive oil, and salt and pepper to taste: The sauce should be a little tart and highly seasoned. You'll have about $1\frac{1}{2}$ cups. The avocados and salbitxada can be prepared to this stage several hours ahead. In fact, salbitxada tastes best if rested at room temperature a couple of hours before serving.

7. Just before serving, spoon the salbitxada into and over the avocados. Garnish each with a parsley sprig and serve at room temperature.

**WHAT ELSE** You'll want firm but ripe avocados for grilling—both Hass and Florida will work. Let them ripen at room temperature. For nuts, I've called for the aromatic round Spanish almonds known as Marconas (imagine the nuttiness of California almonds with the buttery richness of macadamias), but you can certainly use conventional almonds. If you don't have sherry vinegar, use red wine or rice vinegar, both enhanced with a few drops of sherry. Note: Tradition calls for blanching the tomatoes to peel them, but I prefer blistering them over a hot fire. This recipe calls for grilling both the avocados and the veggies for the salbitxada. You can grill the latter at a previous grill session.

# GRILLED AVOCADOS
# WITH PEPPADEW SALSA

You don't normally think of olives, currants, and pickled peppers in the same mouthful, but this sweet-salty-tart salsa works wonders on smoky grilled avocados. I first experienced it at the Malibu Beach Inn at Carbon Beach in Malibu, which serves this grilled avocado at its seaside restaurant. Peppadews are sweet pickled peppers from South Africa, today available online and in many supermarkets. If you can't find them, substitute pickled Spanish piquillo peppers or pickled cherry peppers.

## INGREDIENTS

½ cup drained Peppadew peppers (reserve the juices)

½ cup currants or raisins

½ cup pitted green olives, thinly sliced

½ cup extra virgin olive oil, plus extra for brushing

Coarse salt (sea or kosher) and freshly ground black pepper

Vegetable oil for oiling the grill grate

4 ripe avocados

½ cup chopped fresh cilantro or flat-leaf parsley leaves

¼ cup shelled pistachio nuts, toasted (see page 259)

**1.** Cut the Peppadews into ½-inch dice. Place in a mixing bowl with the currants, olives, and olive oil. Stir in a couple of tablespoons of the Peppadew juices (reserved from chopping and from the jar) and some salt and pepper to taste: The mixture should be highly seasoned. Let macerate at room temperature for 20 minutes.

**2.** Set up your grill for direct grilling and heat to high. If enhancing a charcoal fire, add the wood chunks or chips to the coals; if enhancing a gas fire, place the chunks or chips in your grill's smoker box or place chunks under the grate directly over one or more burners. Brush or scrape the grill grate clean and oil it well.

**3.** Meanwhile, halve and pit the avocados. Lightly brush the flesh of the avocados with olive oil and season with salt and pepper.

**4.** Arrange the avocados cut sides down on the grill, so each half runs on the diagonal to the bars of the grate. Grill until browned, 2 to 3 minutes. Transfer the avocados to a platter and cool to room temperature.

**5.** Just before serving, stir the cilantro into the Peppadew salsa. Spoon the salsa into and over the grilled avocados. Sprinkle with the pistachios and serve at room temperature.

# WOOD-GRILLED BRUSCHETTA
## WITH FIRE-BLISTERED TOMATOES AND RICOTTA

When Yotam Ottolenghi opened ROVI in London's Fitzrovia district, the Anglo-Israeli mega-chef made a massive wood-burning grill the focal point of his kitchen, and vegetables the stars of his menu. In short, just the sort of restaurant to which a grilled veggie fanatic will want to make a pilgrimage. When my wife and I last visited, we were rewarded with the likes of grilled celeriac shawarma and hasselback beets, not to mention the following wood-grilled tomato bruschetta—equally remarkable for the smoky, flame-blistered tomatoes as for the cool creamy ricotta and bread crustily toasted as it has been for millennia: over an open fire.

### INGREDIENTS

Vegetable oil for oiling the grill grate

1 pound cherry tomatoes, preferably a mix of red and yellow

1 tablespoon extra virgin olive oil, plus extra for drizzling

3 tablespoons chopped fresh chives and/or other fresh herbs, such as tarragon or basil leaves, for sprinkling

Coarse salt (sea or kosher) and freshly ground black pepper

4 slices of rustic country-style bread (each slice should be 6 to 8 inches long, 4 inches wide, and ¾ inch thick)

8 ounces fresh ricotta cheese

**YIELD** Makes 4 bruschetta and can be multiplied as desired

**METHOD** Direct grilling

**PREP TIME** 10 minutes

**GRILLING TIME** 6 to 7 minutes

**GRILL/GEAR** Can be grilled over charcoal or gas, but tastes best grilled over wood or a wood-enhanced fire. If you're enhancing a charcoal or gas fire, you'll also need hardwood chunks or chips (unsoaked), see page 8. You'll also need a vegetable grilling grid or basket.

**WHAT ELSE** You'll want a rustic white or wheat bread for this—a French boule or Italian pane Pugliese come to mind, but you could also use a crusty baguette sliced sharply on the diagonal.

**1.** Set up your grill for direct grilling. Have one hot zone, one medium-hot zone, and a fire-free safety zone in case the bread starts to burn. If enhancing a charcoal fire, add the wood chunks or chips to the coals; if enhancing a gas fire, place the chunks or chips in your grill's smoker box or place chunks under the grate directly over one or more burners. Brush or scrape the grill grate clean and oil it well. Note: If using a vegetable grilling grid, place it on the grill to preheat (no need to preheat a grill basket).

**2.** Place the cherry tomatoes in a bowl and toss with 1 tablespoon of olive oil. Stir in 1½ tablespoons chopped herbs and salt and pepper to taste. Tip the tomatoes into the heated vegetable grilling grid or a grilling basket.

**3.** Grill the tomatoes over the hot zone, stirring or shaking the basket occasionally, until the skins begin to blacken and split, about 5 minutes. Set aside.

**4.** Lightly brush the bread slices with the olive oil on both sides. Arrange the bread on the grate over the medium-hot zone and grill until toasted, 1 to 2 minutes per side. Watch carefully so it doesn't burn. If you're feeling fancy, give each slice a quarter turn on both sides halfway through to lay on a crosshatch of grill marks.

**5.** Remove the bread from the grill, and then, protecting your hand with a cloth napkin, spread one side of each slice with ricotta. Place the bruschetta on a platter and top with the grilled tomatoes. Drizzle with more olive oil, sprinkle with the remaining fresh herbs, and season with salt and pepper to taste.

## VARIATION

### GRILLED GRAPE, TOASTED PINE NUT, AND GOAT CHEESE BRUSCHETTA

Wood-grilling gives grapes an unexpected smoke flavor, not to mention an element of surprise (Americans don't normally eat grapes hot). Freshly grated lemon zest and balsamic vinegar syrup provide just the right note of acidity, counterpointed by tangy, creamy goat cheese and toasted pine nuts.

Substitute 1 pound of seedless purple grapes, stemmed, for the cherry tomatoes and 2 tablespoons of thinly slivered fresh sage (or other fresh herb) leaves and 1 teaspoon of freshly and finely grated lemon zest for the chives (though chives work nicely here, too). Grill the grapes as directed in Step 3 until blistered and smoky, 2 to 4 minutes, stirring gently. Oil and grill the bread as directed in Step 4. Substitute soft goat cheese, at room temperature, for the ricotta. Drizzle the assembled bruschetta with balsamic vinegar syrup and sprinkle with ¼ cup toasted pine nuts. Drizzle each bruschetta with a little more olive oil.

Grilled Grape, Toasted Pine Nut,
and Goat Cheese Bruschetta

# CRISPY GRILLED KALE CHIPS
## WITH POOR MAN'S PARMESAN

**YIELD** Serves 3 or 4

**METHOD** Direct grilling

**PREP TIME** 15 minutes

**GRILLING TIME** 10 minutes

**GRILL/GEAR** Can be grilled over charcoal, gas, or wood. You'll also need a 10-inch skillet.

**WHAT ELSE** You'll want a sturdy flat-leaf kale for this recipe: cavolo nero (black kale), aka dinosaur kale, aka Tuscan kale, aka lacinato, comes to mind. Kale is said to be sweeter after the first frost, so this is a great vegetable to grill in autumn and early winter.

Tired of kale Caesar salad? Kale soups, scrambles, and stir-fries? I guess we've overdone the kale thing, but if you'll stick with me for one more jolly green brassica, I think you'll find these crisp chips dusted with tangy poor man's Parmesan much to your liking. The secret is to direct grill the kale, which gives the leaves the crackling crunch of potato chips. So, what is poor man's Parmesan? Back in the day, when real Parmigiano-Reggiano cheese was too expensive for poor families in southern Italy, people made a tasty and umami-rich substitute by frying breadcrumbs, garlic, and anchovies in olive oil. Of course, if you don't like anchovies, you can dust the kale with plain toasted breadcrumbs and/or finely grated Parmigiano-Reggiano.

## INGREDIENTS

### FOR THE KALE

2 bunches black kale
(12 to 16 ounces total)

2 tablespoons extra virgin olive oil,
plus extra as needed

Coarse salt (sea or kosher) and
freshly ground black pepper

Vegetable oil for oiling the grill grate

### FOR THE POOR MAN'S PARMESAN

3 tablespoons extra virgin olive oil

1 clove garlic, peeled and gently
flattened with the side of a cleaver

1 or 2 oil-packed anchovies, blotted
dry and finely minced

½ cup plain breadcrumbs (toasted or
fresh—it doesn't matter)

**1.** Wash the kale and spin it dry in a salad spinner or shake it dry. Lay a leaf on a cutting board and use a sharp knife to make an elongated V-shaped cut around the thick part of the stem; remove it. (It's too tough for crisping on the grill.) You can leave the tender part of the stem near the top intact. Repeat with the remaining leaves— you may not need to stem the tender inner leaves of the bunch.

**2.** Lightly brush each kale leaf on both sides with the olive oil and season with salt and pepper.

**3.** Make the poor man's Parmesan: Place a 10-inch skillet over medium-high heat or on your grill's side burner. Add the olive oil, garlic, and anchovy, and fry until the garlic turns fragrant and golden and the anchovy melts, 1 to 2 minutes. Stir in the breadcrumbs and cook until toasted and browned, stirring with a wooden spoon, about 2 minutes. Discard the garlic. Set the breadcrumb mixture aside. The poor man's Parmesan can be prepared several hours ahead to this stage (let it cool to room temperature, then store in a covered container).

**4.** Set up your grill for direct grilling and heat to medium-high. (Note: If your grill burns hot, heat it to medium.) Brush or scrape the grill grate clean and oil it well.

**5.** Arrange the kale leaves in a single layer on the grate, working in batches as needed. Grill the kale until browned and crisp, 2 to 4 minutes per side, turning with tongs. Transfer the kale leaves to a platter, arranging in a single layer. Sprinkle the poor man's Parmesan over the kale. Fingers are the preferred utensil for eating.

# TOFU CHANNELING HAM

If tofu were pork, which it's not, and you cured and smoked it like ham, which you won't, you'd wind up with a plant food that delivers the same salty, smoky, umami ham-like flavors. And if you're fortunate enough to have eaten at Vedge restaurant in Philadelphia or Fancy Radish in Washington, DC, both run by the vegan husband-and-wife team of chef Rich Landau and chef Kate Jacoby, you already know what I'm talking about; smoked tofu (note we didn't say tofu ham) figures prominently on their stunning vegan charcuterie boards. I've grilled enough tofu to know that it doesn't behave like meat, but Landau and Jacoby have contrived an ingenious method for firming it up and loading it with smoke flavor. They cure it for 24 hours in a brine that contains a typical meat flavoring—Montreal steak seasoning. Then comes a double smoke: cold first, to infuse it with wood smoke, then hot, to lay on a smoky crust. But it's not until the tofu chills again for several hours that it firms up enough for slicing and serving. It sounds like a lot of work, but most of that time is waiting. Believe me, it's worth it. Serve it as part of your next appetizer or charcuterie spread and you'll see.

**YIELD** Serves 8 as an appetizer; 4 as a light entrée

**METHOD** Smoking followed by grilling

**PREP TIME** 20 minutes, plus 24 hours for marinating and 3 hours for resting

**GRILLING/SMOKING TIME** 15 minutes for cold-smoking, followed by 8 minutes for hot-smoking

**GRILL/GEAR** Best done on a charcoal grill or in a smoker plus a grill. You'll also need hardwood chunks or chips (unsoaked), see page 8; a wire rack set over a rimmed sheet pan; and an aluminum foil drip pan or metal baking pan filled with ice.

**WHAT ELSE** You want extra-firm tofu for this recipe. To cold-smoke tofu, heat your grill or smoker to 250°F. Arrange the tofu slices on a wire rack over a large baking pan of ice, and keep the smoking time brief.

## INGREDIENTS

1 cup tamari or soy sauce

½ cup Worcestershire sauce (regular or vegan)

1 tablespoon Montreal steak seasoning

1 teaspoon freshly ground black pepper

2 blocks (12 to 16 ounces each) extra-firm tofu, drained

2 cloves garlic, peeled and flattened with the side of a cleaver

2 bay leaves

Vegetable oil for oiling the grill grate

Your favorite deli-style mustard mixed with equal parts mayonnaise, for serving (optional)

**1.** Combine 2 cups of water with the tamari, Worcestershire sauce, Montreal steak seasoning, and pepper in a large deep bowl and whisk to mix. Add the tofu, garlic, and bay leaves. (The tofu should be completely submerged.) Cover, then brine the tofu in the refrigerator for 24 to 48 hours, turning the tofu blocks once or twice so they cure evenly. The longer, the better.

**2.** Remove the tofu from the brine and drain it on a wire rack until tacky, about 1 hour. Discard the brine.

**3.** Meanwhile, set up your smoker following the manufacturer's instructions, and heat to 250°F. If using a charcoal grill, use half as much charcoal as usual and heat to 250°F.

**4.** Place the tofu on the wire rack over a large pan of ice and transfer to the smoker or grill. Cold-smoke for 15 minutes.

**5.** Remove the tofu from the rack and transfer it to a plate. Let it rest at room temperature for 1 hour.

**6.** Increase your smoker temperature to high. If your smoker won't attain high temperatures, set up a charcoal grill for indirect grilling and heat to high. Again, add wood chunks or chips to the coals. Brush or scrape the grill grate clean and oil it well.

**7.** Place the tofu in the smoker or on the grill, close the lid, and hot-smoke until firm and bronzed with smoke, 6 to 8 minutes. Using a thin-bladed spatula (avoid touching the tofu with your fingers or you will disturb the smoky patina), transfer the tofu to a plate to cool to room temperature. Chill, covered, for at least 3 hours and up to 3 days. Cut into slices for serving and serve chilled or at room temperature with the mustard-mayo combo, if you like.

# CHAPTER 3

# DIPS & CHIPS

F rom Mexican guacamole to Middle Eastern baba ghanoush, dips do much for human happiness. And live fire is what takes the dips in this chapter over the top. Consider traditional Southern pimento cheese—here made with flame-roasted bell peppers. Or an Armenian vegetable dip (the secret is to ember-grill the eggplant)— fire endows the vegetables with an irresistible smoke flavor. And speaking of smoke, wood smoke transforms everyday hummus into a dip as delectable as it is otherworldly. From Caveman Caviar (made with vegetables grilled on embers) to a Greek feta cheese dip (electrified with flame-roasted jalapeños) to Middle Eastern muhammara (a grilled pepper and walnut spread sweetened with pomegranate molasses), this chapter will give you a whole new perspective on dips and spreads. And, yes, there will be grilled pita chips, pumpernickel, and tortilla chips for dipping.

# RECIPES

# SMOKED GUACAMOLE
## WITH GRILLED CHIA SEED TOTOPOS

**YIELD** Serves 4

**METHOD** Smoke-roasting (indirect grilling with wood smoke)

**PREP TIME** 10 minutes

**SMOKING TIME** 10 to 15 minutes

**GRILL/GEAR** Best smoked on charcoal or wood. If grilling, you can use a gas grill. You'll also need a wire rack set over an aluminum foil drip pan filled with ice; hardwood chunks or chips (unsoaked), see page 8; and a molcajete and tejolote (or mortar and pestle) or food processor.

**WHAT ELSE** You'll need ripe avocados for this recipe—preferably Hass (they're available year-round), or Florida avocados when in season. Ripen them at room temperature until gently yielding when squeezed between your thumb and forefinger. You have three options for adding wood smoke: traditional smoking, smoke-roasting, or grilling over a wood or wood-enhanced fire. For even more flavor, serve the guacamole in the smoky avocado skins.

Avocados may not be the first vegetable you think of for smoking or grilling. After all, as oceans of guacamole and acres of toast suggest, avocados are splendid raw. But wood smoke imparts haunting umami flavors that take guacamole from average to astonishing. To reinforce that smokiness, I like to add chipotles along with the customary jalapeños. For dipping, I propose Grilled Chia Seed Totopos (tortilla chips)—the recipe follows.

## INGREDIENTS

2 ripe avocados

3 tablespoons fresh lime juice (from 1 to 2 limes)

1 luscious ripe red tomato

1 jalapeño pepper

1 clove garlic, peeled (optional)

1 teaspoon minced canned chipotles in adobo

⅓ cup chopped fresh cilantro leaves

Coarse salt (sea or kosher) and freshly ground black pepper

Grilled Chia Seed Totopos (recipe follows) or other chips, for serving

**1.** Set up your grill for indirect grilling (or your smoker for smoking) and heat to medium-low. If enhancing a charcoal fire, add the wood chunks or chips to the coals; if enhancing a gas fire, place the chunks or chips in your grill's smoker box or place chunks under the grate directly over one or more burners.

**2.** Meanwhile, halve and pit the avocados, but leave the skin on. Rub the cut sides of the avocados with a bit of the fresh lime juice to keep them from discoloring; set the remaining juice aside. Cut the tomato in half widthwise. Cut the jalapeño in half lengthwise. Remove the seeds for milder guacamole; leave them in if you like more heat. Place the avocado, tomato, and jalapeño halves, cut sides up, on a wire rack over an aluminum foil pan filled with ice. (This keeps them cool during smoking.)

**3.** Place the ice-filled pan with the vegetables on the grate away from the heat. Place the garlic clove (if using) atop one of the tomato halves. Lower the lid and smoke-roast (indirect grill)

the vegetables until infused with wood smoke, 10 to 15 minutes. Don't overcook—you want the avocados and tomatoes to remain cool in the center.

**4.** Transfer the smoked vegetables to a cutting board and let cool. Scoop the avocado flesh out of the skins with a spoon (optional: save the skins for serving). Dice the tomato, discarding the stem end. Stem and mince the jalapeño and garlic (if using).

**5.** Traditionally, guacamole would be made and served in a pumice stone mortar called a molcajete. If you have one, add the jalapeño, garlic, and chipotle and grind to a paste with the stone pestle (the latter is called a tejolote). Work in the avocado, leaving it a little chunky. Work in the tomato, cilantro, lime juice, and salt and pepper to taste: The guacamole should be highly seasoned. Alternatively, chop the vegetables by hand and mash in the avocado with a fork. Or use a food processor: Combine the jalapeño, garlic, and chipotle in a food processor and finely chop, then add the avocado and pulse the processor in short bursts to coarsely chop. Work in the tomato, cilantro, lime juice, and salt and pepper—again, running the processor in short bursts: The guacamole should remain chunky.

**6.** Transfer the guacamole to a bowl (or serve directly in the molcajete or the smoked avocado skins). Serve with Grilled Chia Seed Totopos.

# VARIATION
## WOOD-GRILLED GUACAMOLE

You can also make guacamole with grilled avocados—preferably seared over wood or a wood-enhanced fire on a charcoal grill.

Set up your grill for direct grilling and heat to high. If using a wood-burning grill, start grilling while the fire is still smoky. If using a charcoal grill, add 1 to 2 hardwood chunks or 1½ cups wood chips (unsoaked), see page 8; to the coals. Brush or scrape the grill grate clean and oil it well. When the wood starts smoking, arrange the avocado halves and tomatoes (cut sides down) along with jalapeño and garlic on the grate. (Thread the jalapeño halves and garlic on a small bamboo skewer.) Grill just long enough to infuse the ingredients with wood smoke, but not long enough to cook them, 2 to 4 minutes. Transfer the ingredients to a cutting board to cool, then prepare the guacamole as described in the main recipe.

# GRILLED CHIA SEED TOTOPOS (TORTILLA CHIPS)

**YIELD** Serves 4

In some parts of Mexico, tortilla chips are called totopos. Grilled tortilla chips are more flavorful—and healthier—than the traditional fried variety. These have the added flavor of fire-toasted chia seeds.

## INGREDIENTS

Vegetable oil for oiling the grill grate

4 small (6-inch) flour or corn tortillas

Extra virgin olive oil or dark (toasted) sesame oil, for brushing

3 tablespoons chia or sesame seeds

Coarse salt (sea or kosher) and freshly ground black pepper (optional)

**1.** Set up your grill for direct grilling and heat to medium-high. Brush or scrape the grill grate clean and oil it well.

**2.** Lightly brush the tortillas on both sides with olive oil and sprinkle with chia seeds and salt and pepper (if using).

**3.** Arrange the tortillas on the grate and grill until lightly browned on both sides, 1 to 2 minutes per side. Do not let them burn.

**4.** Transfer the hot tortillas to a cutting board and immediately cut each into 6 wedges. Transfer the wedges to a wire rack—they'll crisp upon cooling. I eat them right away, but any stragglers can be stored at room temperature in a resealable plastic bag or airtight container for a day or so.

# FIRE-ROASTED PIMENTO CHEESE

**YIELD** Makes 2 cups, enough to serve 4 to 6

**METHOD** Ember-grilling (caveman grilling) or direct grilling

**PREP TIME** 15 minutes

**GRILLING TIME** 20 minutes

**GRILL /GEAR** Best grilled on charcoal.

**WHAT ELSE** There are two ways to roast the peppers: by ember-grilling (caveman grilling) or direct grilling. The former gives you a smokier char—that's my go-to method with peppers. (Note: The pepper can be roasted at a previous grill session. Keep it whole and refrigerated until using.)

Pimento cheese (or more accurately, cheese *spread*) is a staple of Southern cooking, traditionally made with jarred pimentos and cheddar cheese. You're going to up the ante by using fresh fire-roasted peppers and smoked cheddar. Serve with grilled bread or grilled pita (see pages 98 or 102). Slather it on sandwiches (see page 124). Serve it on grilled okra or asparagus. Stuff it in smoked eggs (see page 245). This recipe was inspired by Edna Lewis (1916–2006), chef, author, educator, and doyenne of Southern cooking.

## INGREDIENTS

1 red bell pepper

8 ounces smoked cheddar cheese or aged cheddar cheese, coarsely grated (2 cups)

4 ounces cream cheese, at room temperature

¼ cup mayonnaise, preferably Duke's, Hellmann's, or Best Foods

1 tablespoon Dijon mustard

1 teaspoon Tabasco sauce or other favorite hot sauce, or to taste

1 teaspoon smoked or sweet paprika

Freshly ground black pepper and coarse salt (sea or kosher), if needed

**1.** Set up your grill for ember-grilling or direct grilling and heat to high. Brush or scrape the grill grate clean (there's no need to oil it when you're grilling peppers).

**2.** Grill the pepper until the skin is charred on all sides, 2 to 3 minutes per side (8 to 12 minutes in all—if ember-grilling, a few minutes less). Don't forget to char the top and bottom. Transfer the pepper to a plate to cool.

**3.** Using a paring knife, scrape the burnt skin off the pepper. Cut the pepper in half, remove the stem, and scrape out and discard the seeds. Cut the pepper into ¼-inch dice.

**4.** Place the cheddar and cream cheese in a mixing bowl and stir with a wooden spoon to mix. Beat in the mayonnaise, mustard, hot sauce, paprika, and black pepper. Stir in the diced roasted bell pepper. (Alternatively, coarsely chop the ingredients together in a food processor.) Correct the seasoning, adding hot sauce and salt to taste: The pimento cheese should be highly seasoned. Serve now or store in a sealed container in the refrigerator (it will keep for at least 3 days), but let it warm to room temperature before serving.

# TYROKAFTERI
## (FETA DIP WITH FIRE-CHARRED CHILES)

Tex-Mex? How about Greek-Mex? How else do you describe a dip that starts with Greek feta cheese, which you electrify with flame-roasted poblanos and jalapeños? The first gives you that smoky fire-roasted chile flavor; the second cranks up the heat. Tip o' the hat to a Greek restaurant called Estia in Falmouth, Massachusetts, which serves this fiery dip with warm pita. You, my pyromaniacal friend, will grill the pita for dipping, and if it would occur to you to add a thoroughly un-Hellenic ingredient—fresh cilantro—well, great minds think alike.

### INGREDIENTS

2 poblano peppers

2 jalapeño peppers (optional)

8 ounces feta cheese in brine, drained and crumbled

3 to 5 tablespoons extra virgin olive oil, or as needed

3 tablespoons chopped fresh dill or cilantro leaves (optional)

Sesame Grilled Pita Chips (page 54) or Plancha Pita (page 102), for serving

**YIELD** Makes 1½ cups, enough to serve 4 to 6

**METHOD** Direct grilling or ember-grilling (caveman grilling)

**PREP TIME** 10 minutes

**GRILLING TIME** 6 to 12 minutes

**GRILL/GEAR** Can be grilled over charcoal, gas, or wood.

**WHAT ELSE** Tyrokafteri (also known as ktipiti) can be made with hot green or red peppers, and while jalapeños aren't native to Greece, many Greek restaurants in the United States add them for extra kick. For an interesting variation, substitute a soft goat cheese for the feta.

**1.** Set up your grill for direct grilling and heat to high. Brush or scrape the grill grate clean (there's no need to oil the grate when grilling peppers). Arrange the poblanos and jalapeños (if using) on the grate directly over the fire and grill until charred on all sides, 2 to 4 minutes per side, 6 to 12 minutes in all. Alternatively, set up your grill for ember-grilling and lay the peppers directly on the embers. Grill until charred on all sides, about 1 minute per side, 3 to 5 minutes in all.

**2.** Transfer the peppers to a cutting board (if ember-grilling the peppers, transfer to a rimmed sheet pan). Let cool to room temperature, then scrape off the charred skins. Cut the peppers in half lengthwise, remove the stems, and scrape out and discard the seeds. Cut the peppers into 1-inch pieces.

**3.** Place the peppers in a food processor fitted with a metal blade and coarsely chop. Add the crumbled feta and coarsely puree. Work in 3 tablespoons of the olive oil. If the mixture is too thick, add 1 to 2 tablespoons more olive oil. But don't overprocess: I like the mixture a little chunky. Work in the cilantro (if using). Transfer to a serving bowl.

Grilled Red Bell Pepper and
Feta Dip with Plancha Pita

**4.** Serve the Tyrokafteri with the grilled pita chips or wedges of pita bread for dipping.

# VARIATION

## GRILLED RED BELL PEPPER AND FETA DIP

Swap the poblanos and jalapeños for fire-roasted red bell peppers and you get another terrific Greek dip. The smoked pimentón (Spanish smoked paprika) isn't traditional, but I like the way it reinforces the smoke flavor.

### INGREDIENTS

2 red bell peppers

1 clove garlic, peeled and minced

1 teaspoon pimentón (Spanish smoked paprika) or sweet or hot paprika

8 ounces feta cheese in brine, drained and crumbled

2 tablespoons extra virgin olive oil, or as needed

1 teaspoon hot red pepper flakes, plus extra for sprinkling (optional)

**1.** Follow the preceding recipe through Step 2, substituting red bell peppers for the poblanos and jalapeños (note that the bell peppers will take a bit longer to char).

**2.** Place the bell peppers, garlic, and pimentón in a food processor and coarsely chop. Add the crumbled feta and coarsely puree. Work in the olive oil. For a spicy dip, work in the hot red pepper flakes. If the mixture is too thick, add an additional tablespoon or so of olive oil. But don't overprocess: I like the mixture a little chunky. Transfer to a serving bowl and sprinkle with hot red pepper flakes (if using).

# CHARRED WINTER SQUASH TZATZIKI

**YIELD** Makes 4 cups

**METHOD** Direct grilling

**PREP TIME** 10 minutes

**GRILLING TIME** About 12 minutes

**GRILL/GEAR** Can be grilled over charcoal or gas, but for the most flavor, grill over wood. You'll also need a rimmed sheet pan.

**WHAT ELSE** There are two ways to approach grilling the squash. The quickest is to cut it into wedges (the way kabocha squash is usually sold anyway) and direct grill it over a hot fire. You can also roast the whole squash caveman-style in the embers—a method particularly well suited to smallish pumpkins. Note: For an even smokier flavor, smoke the yogurt following the instructions on page 298.

Here's a charred squash tzatziki that's Israeli-inspired, although it may never have actually been served in Israel. Cardamom and cinnamon add sweet notes to counterpoint the smokiness of the charred squash. Serve with fresh pita (like the Plancha Pita on page 102) or the Sesame Grilled Pita Chips on page 54.

## INGREDIENTS

Vegetable oil for oiling the grill grate

12 ounces pumpkin, kabocha, or other firm orange winter squash, peeled and cut into 1-inch-wide wedges (discard the seeds or save them for roasting)

Extra virgin olive oil

Coarse salt (sea or kosher) and freshly ground black pepper

1 large shallot, unpeeled

2 cups Greek-style yogurt (choose the fat content you want)

½ teaspoon ground coriander

½ teaspoon ground cardamom

½ teaspoon ground cinnamon, plus extra for garnish

1 to 2 tablespoons brown sugar or pure maple syrup, or to taste

**1.** Set up your grill for direct grilling and heat to high. Brush or scrape the grill grate clean and oil it well.

**2.** Lightly brush the squash wedges with olive oil on all sides and season well with salt and pepper. Grill the squash until darkly browned, almost charred, on all sides, and tender when pierced with a skewer, 3 to 6 minutes per side, 6 to 12 minutes or so in all. Grill the shallot in its skin until charred on the outside and tender, 3 to 5 minutes per side.

**3.** Transfer the squash and shallot to a rimmed sheet pan to cool to room temperature. Using a paring knife, scrape off any burnt skin from the squash and shallot. Place them in a mixing bowl and mash with a fork, or place in a food processor and puree.

**4.** Stir or pulse in the yogurt, coriander, cardamom, cinnamon, 2 tablespoons olive oil, salt, pepper, and brown sugar to taste: The dip should be highly seasoned. Dust the top with cinnamon.

# SMOKED HUMMUS
## WITH SESAME GRILLED PITA CHIPS

It's hard to imagine how to improve the Middle Eastern chickpea dip known as hummus. But if you want to try, start with wood smoke. At the very least, smoke the chickpeas. Smoke the garlic if you're feeling ambitious (see page 299). You could even smoke the olive oil and tahini in foil pans next to the chickpeas. I've tried all three options, and you get the biggest bang for your buck from smoking the chickpeas (especially if you do so on a charcoal grill). In a world awash with hummus, this is one that will definitely make you sit up and take notice.

**YIELD** Makes about 2 cups, enough to serve 4

**METHOD** Smoke-roasting (indirect grilling with wood smoke)

**PREP TIME** 10 minutes

**GRILLING/SMOKING TIME** 10 to 15 minutes

**GRILL/GEAR** Can be smoked over charcoal, wood, or gas, but tastes best smoked over charcoal or wood. You'll also need hardwood chunks or chips (unsoaked), see page 8; an aluminum foil drip pan; and a food processor.

**WHAT ELSE** The purist will wish to start with dry chickpeas (garbanzo beans). Soak them in enough water to cover by 3 inches in the refrigerator overnight, then drain. Again, cover the chickpeas with enough water to cover by 3 inches and boil them until soft, 1 to 1½ hours. For the rest of us, cooked chickpeas in a can or jar (preferably organic or imported from Italy or Spain) will work just fine. Note: Tahini is sesame seed paste—available in most supermarkets and online. (One popular brand is Joyva.) If you can't find tahini, you'll need to add more water or olive oil to achieve the proper creamy texture.

## INGREDIENTS

2 cans (15.5 ounces each) chickpeas, preferably organic

2 cloves garlic, peeled (for an even smokier flavor, use smoked garlic; see page 299)

5 to 8 tablespoons extra virgin olive oil

½ cup tahini

½ teaspoon ground cumin

½ teaspoon freshly and finely grated lemon zest

3 to 5 tablespoons fresh lemon juice

Coarse salt (sea or kosher) and freshly ground black pepper

Sesame Grilled Pita Chips (recipe follows) or pita bread (see Plancha Pita, page 102), for serving

**1.** Set up your grill for indirect grilling and heat to medium-high.

**2.** Meanwhile, drain the chickpeas in a colander. Arrange them on an aluminum foil drip pan spread with clean kitchen towels. Blot dry with more towels. Remove the towels and add the garlic and 1 tablespoon olive oil. Mix well.

**3.** Place the chickpeas in their drip pan on the grate away from the heat.

If enhancing a charcoal fire, place the hardwood chunks or chips on the coals; if enhancing a gas fire, place the chunks or chips in your grill's smoker box or place chunks under the grate directly over one or more burners.

**4.** Close the lid and indirect grill until the chickpeas are smoky, 10 to 15 minutes, stirring once or twice so they smoke evenly.

**5.** Place the chickpeas and garlic in a food processor fitted with a metal blade and finely chop. Add the tahini, cumin, lemon zest, and lemon juice, and puree until smooth. Work in 3 tablespoons olive oil, 3 tablespoons water, and pepper to taste. You're looking for a creamy consistency. If the hummus is too thick, add more water or olive oil, a tablespoon or two at a time. Correct the seasoning, adding salt or more lemon juice to taste: The hummus should be highly seasoned.

Spoon the hummus into a serving bowl. Just before serving, drizzle 1 to 2 tablespoons olive oil on top.

**6.** Serve the hummus with Sesame Grilled Pita Chips or wedges of grilled pita chips or wedges of pita bread. Store any excess in a sealed container in the refrigerator: It will keep for at least 3 days. Let warm to room temperature before serving.

# SESAME GRILLED PITA CHIPS

**YIELD** Serves 4

### INGREDIENTS

Vegetable oil for oiling the grill grate

4 pita breads

3 tablespoons extra virgin olive oil, or as needed

3 tablespoons sesame seeds, or as needed

**1.** Set up your grill for direct grilling and heat to medium-high. Brush or scrape the grill grate clean and oil it well.

**2.** Meanwhile, lightly brush the pita breads on both sides with the olive oil and sprinkle both sides with the sesame seeds.

**3.** Grill the pita breads until lightly toasted, 1 to 2 minutes per side. Transfer to a cutting board and cut each into 6 wedges. The chips will crisp on cooling. Once cooled to room temperature, you can store the chips in a sealed container at room temperature: They'll keep for at least 24 hours. Not that they ever last that long.

# NOT YOUR USUAL BABA GHANOUSH

Baba ghanoush is the quintessential Middle Eastern dip, combining the region's love of creamy purees (to be scooped up and eaten with pita) with our primordial love of smoke flavor. It starts with that self-contained plant-based smoking system known as eggplant. All you need to do is char the skin—which you can accomplish over a hot fire on the grill, directly in the embers, or even on a stovetop burner (gas or electric). As the skin burns, the smoke is driven deep into the vegetable's flesh. It's a simple procedure practiced throughout the Middle East and the Mediterranean, which explains the proliferation of baba ghanoush–like dips around that region and in this book. So what makes this one not your usual baba ghanoush? For starters, it contains the tart Middle Eastern spice called sumac and such nontraditional ingredients as fresh basil and mint. And the garlic is fire-roasted, not added raw as custom dictates. Then there's the color—ash gray with black specks—achieved by the addition of some of the burnt eggplant skin. Finally, a scorching drizzle of chili oil by way of a finish. For dipping I suggest fresh pita, like the Plancha Pita (page 102) or pita chips (try the Sesame Grilled Pita Chips on the facing page).

**YIELD** Makes 2 cups, enough to serve 4 to 6

**METHOD** Direct grilling or ember-grilling (caveman grilling)

**PREP TIME** 10 minutes

**GRILLING TIME** 8 to 12 minutes, or as needed

**GRILL/GEAR** Can be grilled over charcoal, wood, or gas. You'll also need a rimmed sheet pan and a food processor.

**WHAT ELSE** Like all vegetable dips, this one lives and dies by the quality of the ingredients—in this case, eggplants. Choose small slender Italian or Japanese eggplants from your farmers' market (or better yet, from your garden) and the flavor will be rich and smoky. Avoid those giant bulbous eggplants often sold at the supermarket—size is no substitute for flavor. Tahini is sesame paste—available in cans at Middle Eastern markets and most supermarkets. Chili oil is a Chinese condiment—it's available in the international foods section of most supermarkets. Note the technique of larding the eggplant with garlic so you can roast both vegetables at the same time.

## INGREDIENTS

2 pounds small slender eggplants

2 cloves garlic, peeled and cut lengthwise into ¼-inch slivers

¼ cup tahini

½ teaspoon sumac powder

½ teaspoon freshly and finely grated lemon zest

2 to 3 tablespoons fresh lemon juice, or to taste

2 tablespoons extra virgin olive oil

Coarse salt (sea or kosher) and freshly ground black pepper

3 tablespoons thinly slivered fresh basil leaves

3 tablespoons thinly slivered fresh mint leaves

Chili oil or more olive oil, for drizzling

Fresh pita bread or pita chips, for serving

**1.** Using the tip of a paring knife, make a series of slits in the eggplants at 2-inch intervals. Insert a garlic sliver in each slit.

**2.** Set up your grill for direct grilling or ember-grilling (caveman grilling) and heat to high. Brush or scrape your grill grate clean (if using); there's no need to oil it when you're grilling eggplant.

**3.** Grill the eggplants, turning with tongs as needed, until the skin is charred black and the flesh is very tender (a skewer should pierce the eggplants easily), 2 to 3 minutes per side, 8 to 12 minutes in all.

**4.** Transfer the eggplants to a rimmed sheet pan and let cool. Using a paring knife, scrape most of the burnt skin off the eggplants and discard it. (Leave a little burnt skin—it adds color and flavor.) Remove the stems and cut the eggplants into 2-inch pieces.

**5.** Place the eggplants (with their garlic slivers), tahini, and sumac in a food processor and puree to a smooth paste. Work in the lemon zest and juice, olive oil, and salt and pepper to taste: The mixture should be highly seasoned. If too thick, add a little more olive oil.

**6.** Add the basil and mint. Pulse the processor just to mix. (Don't overprocess or the herbs will turn the dip green.) The baba ghanoush can be prepared several hours ahead to this stage, covered, and refrigerated.

**7.** Transfer the dip to a serving bowl. Drizzle with chili oil or olive oil. Serve with fresh pita or pita chips for scooping.

# ARMENIAN CHARRED EGGPLANT DIP
## WITH TOMATOES AND ONIONS

When it comes to fire-charred vegetable dips, baba ghanoush (see page 55) grabs the spotlight, but interesting variations exist throughout the Mediterranean, the Middle East, and the Caucasus region. The Armenian version ups the usual eggplant ante with two ingredients you probably have in your kitchen—tomatoes and onions. Their addition gives you a totally different texture and flavor. Serve with grilled lavash or pita.

**YIELD** Makes about 2 cups, enough to serve 4 to 6

**METHOD** Ember-grilling (caveman grilling) or direct grilling

**PREP TIME** 10 minutes

**GRILLING TIME** 6 to 10 minutes

**GRILL/GEAR** Charcoal, gas, or wood (the traditional Armenian method calls for charcoal). You'll also need a wire rack set over a rimmed sheet pan and a food processor.

**WHAT ELSE** As with many of the dips in this book, there are two ways to grill the veggies—charring directly on the embers (caveman grilling) or direct grilling over a hot fire. The former gives you a smokier flavor; the latter works for people who grill over propane.

### INGREDIENTS

- 2 small or 1 medium eggplant (preferably Italian—about 1 pound)
- 2 large ripe plum (Roma) tomatoes
- 1 small or ½ large sweet onion (unpeeled)
- 1 large clove garlic, peeled, loosely wrapped in aluminum foil
- ½ teaspoon freshly and finely grated lemon zest
- 2 tablespoons fresh lemon juice, or to taste
- 2 to 3 tablespoons extra virgin olive oil
- 2 tablespoons chopped fresh dill or flat-leaf parsley leaves
- Coarse salt (sea or kosher) and freshly ground black pepper
- Plancha Pita (page 102) or Sesame Grilled Pita Chips (page 54)

**1.** Set up your grill for ember-grilling. Rake out the coals in an even layer and fan off any loose ash. Alternatively, set up your grill for direct grilling and heat to high.

**2.** Lay the eggplants, tomatoes, onion, and foil-wrapped garlic on the coals, or place them on the grate, and grill until the skins are charred and the flesh is soft (it will be easy to pierce with a skewer), turning often with tongs. You'll need about 2 minutes in all for the garlic, about 4 minutes for the tomatoes, and 6 to 10 minutes for the eggplants and onions.

**3.** Transfer the veggies to a wire rack over a rimmed sheet pan to cool. Scrape off the eggplant, tomato, and onion skins, discarding any really burnt parts. Don't worry about getting it all: A little black skin adds color and flavor. Cut the eggplants, tomatoes, and onion into 1-inch pieces. Unwrap and roughly chop the garlic.

**4.** Place the veggies in a food processor and grind to a coarse puree, running the machine in short bursts. Work in the lemon zest and juice and enough olive oil to obtain a loose puree. Pulse in the dill, salt, and pepper to taste, and more lemon juice if needed: The dip should be highly flavorful.

**5.** Serve with the Plancha Pita or Sesame Grilled Pita Chips for scooping.

Grilling vegetables on the embers for Caveman Caviar

# CAVEMAN CAVIAR
# WITH GRILLED PUMPERNICKEL

Vegetable caviar is a popular Russian zakuska (hors d'oeuvre). This one won't fool anyone into thinking they're eating beluga, but it does have the soft, crunchy-gooey texture one associates with caviar and a robust flavor that would do any Russian appetizer spread proud. Ember-grilling imparts an irresistible smoke flavor, and, like all caveman grilling, looks cool as all get-out when you make it. Yes, the veggies can be roasted at a previous grill session. In addition to a dip, Caveman Caviar makes a great spread for sandwiches.

**YIELD** Makes 3 cups, enough to serve 6 to 8

**METHOD** Ember-grilling (caveman grilling)

**PREP TIME** 15 minutes

**GRILLING TIME** 20 minutes

**GRILL/GEAR** Best done on a charcoal grill, but can also be direct grilled on a wood-burning or gas grill (see What Else). You'll also need a rimmed sheet pan.

**WHAT ELSE** To ember-grill vegetables, you need embers—ideally in a charcoal or wood-burning grill. You can also direct grill the vegetables over a wood fire (resulting in a great smoke flavor) or over high heat on a gas grill. What's important is to char the vegetable skins, which will smoke the vegetable from the outside in.

## INGREDIENTS

1 medium onion (unpeeled)

1 medium Italian or Japanese eggplant (about 12 ounces)

1 green bell pepper

1 red bell pepper

1 medium carrot, trimmed and scrubbed

3 cloves garlic, peeled, loosely wrapped together in aluminum foil

1 luscious ripe red tomato or 2 ripe plum (Roma) tomatoes

2 ribs celery

1 jalapeño pepper

3 tablespoons chopped fresh dill

½ teaspoon freshly and finely grated lemon zest

2 tablespoons fresh lemon juice, or to taste

3 tablespoons extra virgin olive oil

Coarse salt (sea or kosher) and freshly ground black pepper

Grilled Pumpernickel (recipe follows), for serving

**1.** Set up your grill for ember-grilling, raking the embers into an even layer. Arrange the veggies on the coals and grill until tender and charred on all sides. This will take about 2 minutes for the celery and jalapeño, about 3 minutes for the tomato, about 4 minutes for the carrot and foil-wrapped garlic, 6 to 8 minutes for the bell peppers, 8 to 12 minutes for the eggplant, and 10 to 15 minutes for the onion. (Times are approximate, depending on your fire.) Use long-handled tongs to turn the vegetables so they char evenly (don't forget the ends) and a metal skewer to test for doneness—it should pierce the onion and eggplant easily. Transfer the veggies as they're done to a rimmed sheet pan to cool.

**2.** Once cooled, scrape the burnt skin off the veggies (you don't need to remove every last bit—a few black specks add color and flavor). Cut the veggies into 1-inch chunks, discarding any stems or seeds from the peppers.

**3.** Place the roasted vegetables in a food processor and process to a coarse puree, running the machine in short

bursts. Work in the dill, lemon zest, lemon juice, olive oil, and salt and pepper: The caviar should be highly seasoned.

**4.** Serve cold or at room temperature with the Grilled Pumpernickel. Store in a sealed container in the refrigerator; the caviar will keep for at least 3 days.

# GRILLED PUMPERNICKEL

**YIELD** Serves 6 to 8

## INGREDIENTS

Vegetable oil for oiling the grill grate

1 package (12 ounces) thin-sliced cocktail-style pumpernickel bread (it comes in long slender loaves)

5 tablespoons melted butter or extra virgin olive oil, or as needed

**1.** Set up your grill for direct grilling and heat to medium-high. Brush or scrape the grill grate clean and oil it well.

**2.** Lightly brush each pumpernickel slice on both sides with the melted butter. Arrange the pumpernickel on

the grill grate and grill until toasted, 1 to 2 minutes per side. Transfer to a wire rack over a rimmed sheet pan to cool. I serve them right away. If you wish to make them ahead, let cool to room temperature, then store in a sealed container at room temperature. Tastes best served within 24 hours.

# MUHAMMARA

**YIELD** Makes 2 cups, enough to serve 4 to 6

**METHOD** Direct grilling

**PREP TIME** 20 minutes

**GRILLING TIME** 10 to 15 minutes

**GRILL/GEAR** Can be grilled over charcoal, wood, or gas. The traditional Armenian way is to grill over charcoal. You'll also need a rimmed sheet pan and a food processor.

**WHAT ELSE** You'll need a couple of ingredients that may be unfamiliar. Pomegranate molasses is a sweet-tart syrup made from reduced pomegranate juice. There's really no substitute, but honey, balsamic syrup, or grape must (reduced grape juice) will get you close. Aleppo pepper is made from Syrian dried hot red peppers. Hot paprika or hot red pepper flakes work just fine. Look for both at Armenian and Middle Eastern markets or order them online. The easiest way to make pomegranate juice is to cut the fruit in half and juice it on a juicer. Or buy bottled pomegranate juice.

I first tasted muhammara at an Armenian restaurant back in my restaurant critic days for *Boston* magazine. (The Boston suburb of Watertown is home to a large Armenian community.) The mash-up of flavors remains indelibly vivid: from the tartness of pomegranate to the nuttiness of ground walnuts, from aromatic cinnamon and cumin to the pungent cilantro and garlic. And underlying them all: the smoky sweetness of fire-charred red bell peppers. It mesmerized me then, as it does today—especially when served with homemade pita chips. It's a little fussier to make than, say, hummus or baba ghanoush, but the result is eminently worth it.

## INGREDIENTS

2 red bell peppers

2 cloves garlic, peeled and skewered on a wooden toothpick

1 cup walnut pieces, plus 2 tablespoons for garnish

2 teaspoons Aleppo pepper or hot red pepper flakes, or to taste

1 teaspoon ground cumin

½ teaspoon ground cinnamon

1 teaspoon freshly and finely grated lemon zest

2 tablespoons fresh lemon juice, or to taste

¼ cup pomegranate juice

1 tablespoon pomegranate molasses or balsamic syrup

2 to 3 tablespoons extra virgin olive oil, or as needed

¼ cup chopped fresh cilantro leaves, plus 1 tablespoon for garnish

Coarse salt (sea or kosher) and freshly ground black pepper

Sesame Grilled Pita Chips (page 54) or Plancha Pita (page 102), for serving

**1.** Set up your grill for direct grilling and heat to high. Brush or scrape the grill grate clean (there's no need to oil it when grilling peppers). Place the peppers on the grate and grill until charred all over, turning with tongs. This will take 8 to 12 minutes. Alternatively, you can char the peppers directly on the embers, caveman-style (see page 9). While you're at it, grill the garlic until browned, about 2 minutes per side. Transfer the peppers and garlic to a rimmed sheet pan to cool. Using a paring knife, scrape the burnt skin off the peppers (you don't need to remove every last bit—a few black specks add color and flavor), then cut in half and remove the stem and seeds. Cut the peppers into 2-inch pieces. Unskewer the garlic.

**2.** Toast the walnuts in a dry cast-iron skillet on your grill grate or over medium heat on the stove until fragrant. This will take 2 to 3 minutes. Let cool. Reserve 2 tablespoons for a garnish. Transfer the remainder to the bowl of a food processor fitted with a chopping blade.

**3.** Running the food processor in short bursts, coarsely grind the walnuts. Add the bell peppers, garlic, Aleppo pepper, cumin, cinnamon, and lemon zest and grind to a coarse puree. Work in the lemon juice, pomegranate juice, pomegranate molasses, and enough olive oil to obtain a loose puree. Work in the cilantro and salt and pepper to taste: The muhammara should be highly seasoned.

**4.** Transfer the muhammara to a serving bowl and sprinkle with the remaining cilantro and the reserved walnuts. Serve with the Sesame Grilled Pita Chips or Plancha Pita.

Muhammara with ember-roasted peppers and pita bread for dipping

# CHAPTER 4
# SALADS, SLAWS & A SINGULAR SOUP

**A**t most barbecues, salads and slaws are dishes you serve on the side. In this chapter, they become the barbecue itself—from a classic wedge salad, the lettuce smartly branded with grill marks, to a leaf lettuce salad smoked with hay (really!) and drizzled with a delicate lemon herb dressing. Smoke adds an unexpected depth of flavor to a beet and goat cheese salad with a smoked raisin vinaigrette. To turn up the heat, try the Basque-inspired piperade salad, Armenian roasted eggplant salad, and pepper and onion salad—all grilled caveman-style, directly on blazing coals. No barbecue is complete without coleslaw, and in the following pages, you'll find versions made with grilled and ember-charred cabbage. Finally, if gazpacho has been called salad in soup form, meet gazpacho's smoky cousin—a fire-charred chilled tomato soup called salmorejo. You'll never think of soup—or salad—the same way.

# RECIPES

# SMOKED BEET SALAD
## WITH SMOKY RAISIN VINAIGRETTE

You've probably seen Steve Nestor even if you've never met him. He's the fire wrangler on my *Project Fire* TV show. He's the guy who assembles and fires up all our grills, and when I suddenly need an extra chimney starter or some burning logs during the shoot, Steve always seems to have them ready. He's also a physical therapist (with a practice in the Boston area—check him out) and an excellent cook. Steve's contribution to this book is a twist on the ubiquitous beet and goat cheese salad. He smoke-roasts the beets. He smoke-roasts the raisins, shallot, and garlic for the dressing. (He'd probably smoke the goat cheese if we'd let him.) The resulting salad plays pinball on your taste buds: sweet beets, smoky raisins, tart cranberries, tangy goat cheese, with nutty earthy walnuts for crunch.

## INGREDIENTS

### FOR SMOKING

3 to 4 red beets (2 inches in diameter), trimmed and peeled

3 to 4 yellow beets (2 inches in diameter), trimmed and peeled

1 large shallot, peeled and cut in half

2 cloves garlic, peeled and skewered on a toothpick

Extra virgin olive oil, for brushing

Coarse salt (sea or kosher) and freshly ground black pepper

½ cup golden or dark raisins

### FOR FINISHING THE SALAD

2 strips pancetta or bacon, cut crosswise into ¼-inch slivers (optional)

3 tablespoons Champagne vinegar or rice vinegar

2 tablespoons warm water, or as needed

½ cup extra virgin olive oil

1 large bunch arugula, washed and spun dry (optional)

¾ cup dried cranberries

¾ cup roughly chopped walnuts, toasted (see Note, page 84)

6 ounces crumbled fresh goat cheese

**YIELD** Serves 6

**METHOD** Smoke-roasting (indirect grilling with wood smoke)

**PREP TIME** 20 minutes

**GRILLING TIME** 1 hour

**GRILL/GEAR** Charcoal grill or smoker. You'll also need hardwood chunks or chips (soaked), see page 8; a vegetable grid or aluminum foil pan; a wooden toothpick; and a rimmed sheet pan.

**WHAT ELSE** This salad calls for a technique I call smoke-roasting (see page 9). You indirect grill the beets and other flavorings, adding hardwood to the fire, so the veggies cook and smoke at the same time. That goes for the raisins and shallot for the dressing, too. There are many options for beets—red, yellow, candy-striped; feast your eyes and use a mix. Here we finish the salad with pancetta bits (you could certainly use bacon or the shiitake bacon on page 26). I've made it optional in case you don't eat meat, but I love how the salty tang rounds out the flavors. Note: The easiest way to peel beets is with a sharp paring knife. Wear latex gloves to keep from staining your hands.

**1.** Set up your grill for indirect grilling and heat to medium-high.

**2.** Meanwhile, lightly brush the beets, shallot, and garlic with olive oil and season with salt and pepper. Place on the grilling grid or on an aluminum foil pan in the center of the grill over the drip pan. If enhancing a charcoal fire, add the wood chunks or chips to the coals; if enhancing a gas fire, place the chunks or chips in your grill's smoker box or place chunks under the grate directly over one or more burners. Close the grill lid.

**3.** Indirect grill the beets, shallot, and garlic for 10 minutes, then scatter the raisins on top. Continue indirect grilling until smoky and tender, about 20 minutes for the shallot and garlic, 45 to 60 minutes for the beets. Test for doneness with a slender skewer—it should pierce the flesh easily. Transfer the veggies as they cook to a rimmed sheet pan to cool. Unskewer the garlic.

**4.** Meanwhile, if using the pancetta, brown and crisp it in a skillet over medium-high heat (or direct grill it), 2 to 4 minutes per side. Drain in a strainer or on paper towels.

**5.** Make the vinaigrette: Combine the shallot, garlic, and raisins in a food processor and coarsely chop. The mixture should remain chunky. Running the processor in short bursts, work in the Champagne vinegar, water, and olive oil, plus salt and pepper to taste. The vinaigrette should be highly seasoned. If too intense, add a little more water.

**6.** Assemble the salad: Cut the beets crosswise into ¼-inch slices. Place in a salad bowl and stir in about one third of the vinaigrette. The warm beets will absorb the vinaigrette as they cool.

**7.** When the beets are cool, add the arugula (if using), cranberries, walnuts, goat cheese, and pancetta (if using). Add half the remaining vinaigrette and gently toss to mix. Serve the remaining vinaigrette on the side.

# GRILLED CORN SALAD
## WITH POMEGRANATE AND MINT

This colorful corn and pomegranate salad—supremely refreshing for summer—comes from an unlikely source, a haute French restaurant called La Petite Maison in my hometown, Miami (with branches in London, Dubai, Abu Dhabi, and Hong Kong). Nigerian engineer turned chef patron Raphael Duntoye had the genial idea to pair sweet, smoky, charcoal-grilled corn with tart juicy pomegranate seeds, with plenty of fresh cilantro and mint to keep the buzz going.

### INGREDIENTS

Vegetable oil for oiling the grill grate

4 ears fresh sweet corn, husked

Extra virgin olive oil, for brushing

Coarse salt (sea or kosher) and freshly ground black pepper

1 ripe pomegranate
(or 1 cup pomegranate seeds)

2 tablespoons chopped fresh mint leaves

2 tablespoons chopped fresh cilantro leaves (or more mint)

2 tablespoons chopped fresh chives

1½ tablespoons Champagne vinegar or rice vinegar, or to taste

**1.** Set up your grill for direct grilling and heat to high. Brush or scrape the grate clean and oil it well. If enhancing a charcoal fire, add the wood chunks or chips to the coals; if enhancing a gas fire, place the chunks or chips in your grill's smoker box or place chunks under the grate directly over one or more burners.

**2.** Brush the corn with olive oil and season with salt and pepper on all sides. Grill until the kernels are darkly browned in patches, 2 to 3 minutes per side, 8 to 12 minutes in all.

**3.** Let the corn cool. Cut the kernels off the cobs using broad strokes of a sharp chef's knife. (The easiest way to do this is to lay the corn flat on a cutting board.)

**YIELD** Serves 4

**METHOD** Direct grilling

**PREP TIME** 20 minutes

**GRILLING TIME** 8 to 12 minutes

**GRILL/GEAR** Can be grilled over charcoal or gas, but for the best results, grill over wood or a wood-enhanced fire. If you're enhancing a charcoal or gas fire, you'll also need hardwood chunks or chips (unsoaked), see page 8.

**WHAT ELSE** This salad owes its succulent crunch and musky sweet-tart flavor to fresh pomegranate seeds. The pomegranate (from the Latin for "many-seeded apple") is a red orb whose leathery skin harbors a multitude of ruby berries, called arils, the size and shape of corn kernels (how convenient!). Many supermarkets sell small containers of pomegranate seeds—look for them in the refrigerated produce section— and this is definitely the easiest way to make the salad. Alternatively, follow the seeding instructions in Step 4.

**4.** If using a whole pomegranate, cut a slice off the top: It should be ½ to ¾ inch thick—just enough to expose the lines of white pith. (The lines will radiate from the center like the spokes of a wheel.) Following these lines, score the outside of the pomegranate from top to bottom. (Your cuts should be about ¼ inch deep.) Working over a large mixing bowl, gently break the pomegranate into sections. Pull the seeds from each section and return them to the bowl (discard the peel and pith). Breathe a sigh of relief—the hard part is over.

**5.** Stir the corn kernels into the pomegranate seeds. The salad can be prepared several hours ahead to this stage. Store in a sealed container in the refrigerator, but let warm to room temperature before serving.

**6.** Just before serving, stir the mint, cilantro, chives, and 1½ tablespoons of the vinegar into the salad. Stir in 2 to 3 tablespoons of olive oil and toss to mix. Correct the seasoning, adding vinegar or salt to taste: The salad should be highly seasoned.

# ESQUITES

**YIELD** Serves 4

**METHOD** Direct grilling

**PREP TIME** 10 minutes

**GRILLING TIME** 8 to 12 minutes

**GRILL/GEAR** Can be grilled over charcoal or gas, but for the best results, grill over wood or a wood-enhanced fire. If you're enhancing a charcoal or gas fire, you'll also need hardwood chunks or chips (unsoaked), see page 8.

It's hard to believe that in the time since I wrote about elote more than twenty years ago, it has become an international phenom. Today, you can find this Oaxacan grilled street corn across the United States, not to mention as far afield as Montreal, London, and Tokyo. You probably know how it's made: Slather smokily grilled corn with mayonnaise and dust it with crumbled Cotija cheese, chili powder, and lime juice. Esquites (from íquitl, the Nahuatl word for "roasted corn") is a Mexican corn salad that features similar ingredients—except the corn is cut off the cob and everything is tossed together (in many parts of Mexico, it's served as a street food in a cup). My take on the dish acquires additional fire power from chipotles and grilled poblano peppers.

## INGREDIENTS

4 ears sweet corn, husked

1½ tablespoons extra virgin olive oil or melted butter, for brushing

Coarse salt (sea or kosher) and freshly ground black pepper

1 large poblano pepper

2 to 3 ounces Cotija, queso fresco, feta, Pecorino Romano, or other piquant cheese, crumbled

1 teaspoon minced canned chipotles in adobo

1 to 2 jalapeño peppers, stemmed and sliced paper-thin

2 tablespoons mayonnaise, preferably Hellmann's or Best Foods, or to taste

2 tablespoons crema (Mexican sour cream) or sour cream (or more mayonnaise)

½ teaspoon freshly and finely grated lime zest

2 tablespoons fresh lime juice, or to taste

⅓ cup chopped fresh cilantro leaves, plus 1 sprig for garnish

**WHAT ELSE** Cotija is a Mexican cow's milk cheese with a crumbly texture and a sharp tang that will remind you of feta. Look for it at Mexican markets and most supermarkets. Queso blanco (another crumbly Mexican cheese), feta, or even Pecorino Romano make good substitutes. Note: Use this recipe as a guideline rather than a blueprint. Summer tomatoes warm off the vine? Dice and add them for sure. Epazote or fresh mint? They're pungent alternatives to cilantro. All taste great.

**1.** Set up your grill for direct grilling and heat to high. If enhancing a charcoal fire, add the wood chunks or chips to the coals; if enhancing a gas fire, place the chunks or chips in your grill's smoker box or place chunks under the grate directly over one or more burners. Brush or scrape the grill grate clean (there's no need to oil it).

**2.** Brush the corn with the olive oil and season with salt and pepper. Grill the corn until darkly browned in patches, 2 to 3 minutes per side, 8 to 12 minutes in all. While you're at it, grill the poblano until charred on all sides, 2 to 3 minutes per side.

**3.** Cut the kernels off the corn as described in Step 3 on page 69. Scrape any burnt skin off the poblano. Cut the poblano into ½-inch dice, discarding the stem, seeds, and veins. Place the corn and poblano in a large mixing bowl.

**4.** Add the crumbled cheese, chipotle, jalapeños, mayonnaise, crema, lime zest, lime juice, and cilantro leaves and stir to mix. Add salt and pepper and additional lime juice as needed to taste: The esquites should be highly seasoned. Transfer to a serving bowl and garnish with the cilantro sprig.

# HAY-SMOKED LETTUCE SALAD
## WITH LEMON HERB VINAIGRETTE

**YIELD** Serves 2 and can be multiplied as desired

**METHOD** Hay-smoking

**PREP TIME** 10 minutes

**SMOKING TIME** 3 to 5 minutes

**GRILL/GEAR** Can be grilled over charcoal or gas. You'll also need a wire rack or cake pan; an aluminum foil drip pan filled with ice; and 2 quarts hay.

**WHAT ELSE** You want to use a delicate leaf lettuce for this recipe. Several varieties come to mind, including Boston, Bibb, and Little Gem. For smoking, you can use either hay or straw—available at garden shops, pet stores, and online. In case you're wondering, hay is a grass; straw is a stalk—typically from wheat. Note: The lettuce can be smoked several hours ahead and refrigerated.

Whuen it comes to smoking and barbecue, most Americans think wood. But Italians devised an ingenious method for smoking delicate and melt-prone foods, like mozzarella, with smoldering hay. To that list you can now add lettuce. The process takes all of 3 minutes, so your greens remain cool and crisp. The resulting salad tastes both familiar and otherworldly—and unlike any salad you've ever experienced. I've kept the dressing simple—an herb vinaigrette—to keep the focus on the smoked lettuce.

### INGREDIENTS

1 large or 2 small heads green leaf lettuce (like Little Gem, Boston, or Bibb)

2 tablespoons mayonnaise, preferably Hellmann's or Best Foods

1 tablespoon Dijon mustard

1 tablespoon tarragon vinegar or red wine vinegar

2 tablespoons vegetable oil

2 tablespoons extra virgin olive oil (or more vegetable oil)

½ teaspoon freshly and finely grated lemon zest

1½ tablespoons fresh lemon juice

2 tablespoons chopped fresh tarragon leaves or dill

2 tablespoons thinly sliced fresh chives or scallion greens

Coarse salt (sea or kosher) and freshly ground black pepper

**1.** Break the lettuce into leaves and wash and spin dry in a salad spinner. Alternatively, cut the lettuces in quarters through the stem, wash, and spin dry. Pile the lettuce on a wire rack or in a cake pan. Keep refrigerated until it's time to smoke it.

**2.** Make the dressing: Place the mayonnaise in a mixing bowl and whisk in the mustard and tarragon vinegar. Gradually whisk in the oils in a thin stream: The sauce should thicken. Whisk in the lemon zest and juice, tarragon, 1 tablespoon of the

Smoke the lettuce next to, not directly over, the smoldering hay.

chives, and salt and pepper to taste: The dressing should be highly seasoned. The dressing can be made several hours ahead and stored in the refrigerator, but stir in the tarragon and chives not more than 15 minutes before serving.

**3.** Set up your grill for hay-smoking in the following manner: Heat one side to medium and leave one side flame-free.

**4.** Place the hay on the grate over the lit side of the grill. When it starts to smoke and catch fire (you may need to help it ignite with a match), turn off the burner if using a gas grill (if using charcoal, leave as is). Set the lettuce (still on its wire rack or cake pan) atop a drip pan of ice on the opposite side of the grill away from the hay and heat. Close the lid and smoke the lettuce until the hay burns out, 3 to 5 minutes.

**5.** Return the lettuce to the refrigerator until serving. Serve it within 2 hours of smoking.

**6.** To serve, spoon the dressing over the hay-smoked lettuce. Sprinkle the remaining 1 tablespoon chives on top.

# GRILLED CAESAR #5
## RECONSTRUCTED AS AN OPEN-FACE SANDWICH

**YIELD** Serves 4

**METHOD** Direct grilling

**PREP TIME** 20 minutes

**GRILLING TIME** 2 to 4 minutes

**GRILL/GEAR** Can be grilled over charcoal or gas, but for the best results grill over wood. If you're enhancing a charcoal or gas fire, you'll need hardwood chunks or chips (unsoaked), see page 8. You'll also need a blender or food processor.

I've been making Caesar salad since I was ten (it was the first dish in my repertory)—and grilling it since I wrote *BBQ USA* in 2003. There's something about the flavor dynamic (briny anchovies, tangy lemon, sharp Pecorino Romano cheese, fruity olive oil) and the play of textures (crisp romaine lettuce, crunchy croutons, creamy egg) that has captured our culinary zeitgeist. The combination only gets better when you harness the flavor-boosting power of live fire. In this iteration, the salad gets reconstructed as a sort of crostini, with the croutons becoming slabs of grilled bread crowned with smoked eggs, grilled lettuce, and shaved Pecorino. Now *that's* what I call a grilled Caesar!

## INGREDIENTS

### FOR THE DRESSING

1 oil-cured anchovy fillet, drained and roughly chopped

1 clove garlic, peeled and roughly chopped

¼ cup coarsely grated Pecorino Romano cheese

2 tablespoons mayonnaise, preferably Hellmann's or Best Foods

2 tablespoons extra virgin olive oil

2 tablespoons fresh lemon juice, or to taste

1 tablespoon Worcestershire sauce

2 teaspoons Dijon mustard

Coarse salt (sea or kosher) and freshly ground black pepper

### FOR FINISHING THE SALAD

Vegetable oil for oiling the grill grate

2 hearts romaine lettuce, sliced in half lengthwise, washed, and spun dry

Extra virgin olive oil, for brushing

4 slices country-style white bread (each slice should be ½ inch thick)

1 clove garlic, peeled, cut in half widthwise

2 smoked eggs (see page 245) or hard-cooked eggs, peeled and quartered

2 ounces Pecorino Romano cheese

4 oil-cured anchovy fillets

1 tablespoon chopped fresh chives

**WHAT ELSE** The traditional cheese for Caesar is Pecorino Romano (an aged, tangy sheep's milk cheese), not the now ubiquitous Parmesan. The anchovies should be oil-cured, not salt-cured or vinegary Spanish boquerones. For a meatless version, replace the anchovy in the dressing with 2 teaspoons white miso and omit the anchovy garnish.

**1.** Make the dressing: Place the anchovy, garlic, cheese, mayonnaise, olive oil, lemon juice, Worcestershire sauce, and mustard in a blender or food processor and blend or process to a creamy dressing. (If too thick, add a tablespoon of water.) Add salt, pepper, and lemon juice to taste: The dressing should be highly seasoned.

**2.** Just before serving, set up your grill for direct grilling and heat to high. If enhancing a charcoal fire, add the wood chunks or chips to the coals; if enhancing a gas fire, place the chunks or chips in your grill's smoker box or place chunks under the grate directly over one or more burners. Brush or scrape the grill grate clean and oil it well. If enhancing a charcoal fire, place the hardwood chunks or chips on the coals; if enhancing a gas fire, place the chunks or chips in your grill's smoker box or place chunks under the grate directly over one or more burners.

**3.** Lightly brush the romaine halves on all sides with olive oil. Lightly brush

the bread slices on both sides with olive oil.

**4.** Grill the bread until toasted on both sides, 1 to 2 minutes per side. Transfer to a wire rack and rub the top of each slice with the cut garlic.

**5.** Grill the cut sides of the romaine until lightly singed, 1 to 2 minutes, giving each a quarter turn halfway

through to lay on a crosshatch of grill marks. Do not overcook—the romaine should remain crisp.

**6.** Place the bread slices on a platter. Top with the romaine hearts, cut sides up. Drizzle the dressing over the lettuce. Arrange the eggs on top. Shave the cheese over the salad. Top with anchovies and chives.

# GRILLED WEDGE SALAD
## WITH SMOKY RANCH DRESSING

Here's a live-fire twist on America's classic wedge salad: You sear the lettuce wedges over a hot smoky fire. The key is to work quickly so you char the outside, but leave the lettuce in the center cool and crisp. (Hmm—sweet-scented burning leaves—remind you of another plant we light and smoke?) To reinforce the smoke flavor, the ranch dressing gets fortified with chipotles and chopped smoked almonds on top for crunch.

**YIELD** Serves 4

**METHOD** Direct grilling

**PREP TIME** 15 minutes

**GRILLING TIME** 3 to 4 minutes

**GRILL/GEAR** Can be grilled over charcoal or gas, but ideally, you'll grill over a wood or wood-enhanced fire. If you're enhancing a charcoal or gas fire, you'll need hardwood chunks or chips (unsoaked), see page 8.

**WHAT ELSE** I call for iceberg lettuce for this salad (preferably organic) in true wedge salad fashion, but you could also use romaine. For the best flavor, work over a wood or wood-enhanced fire so some smoke works its way between the leaves.

### INGREDIENTS

⅓ cup mayonnaise, preferably Hellmann's or Best Foods

⅓ cup buttermilk

1 tablespoon rice vinegar, or to taste

1 teaspoon minced canned chipotles in adobo

½ teaspoon freshly and finely grated lime zest

1 tablespoon fresh lime juice

Coarse salt (sea or kosher) and freshly ground black pepper

3 tablespoons chopped fresh cilantro leaves or dill

Vegetable oil for oiling the grill grate

1 head iceberg lettuce, cut into quarters through the core

Extra virgin olive oil, for brushing

¼ cup chopped smoked almonds

1. Make the dressing: Place the mayonnaise in a mixing bowl and whisk in the buttermilk, vinegar, chipotle, and lime zest and juice. Add salt and pepper to taste: The dressing should be highly seasoned. (Note: The dressing can be made several hours ahead to this stage and refrigerated.) Stir in the cilantro just before dressing the salad.

2. Just before serving, set up your grill for direct grilling and heat to high. If enhancing a charcoal fire, add the wood chunks or chips to the coals; if enhancing a gas fire, place the chunks or chips in your grill's smoker box or place chunks under the grate directly over one or more burners. Brush or scrape the grill grate clean and oil it well.

3. Lightly brush the cut sides of the lettuce with olive oil. Arrange the wedges on the grill grate, cut sides down, running on a diagonal to the bars of the grate. Grill until lightly singed, 1 to 2 minutes, giving each wedge a quarter turn after 30 to 60 seconds to lay on a crosshatch of grill marks. Grill the other cut side the same way. Work quickly so the lettuce remains raw and crunchy in the center.

4. Transfer the lettuce wedges to a platter or plates. Spoon the dressing over them and sprinkle with the chopped almonds. If you like a hot-cold salad, serve at once. Otherwise, dress and serve within 2 hours of grilling the lettuce. (If grilling ahead, cover and chill the lettuce until serving.)

# PIPERADE SALAD

**YIELD** Serves 4 to 6

**METHOD** Ember-grilling (caveman grilling) or direct grilling

**PREP TIME** 10 minutes

**GRILLING TIME** 15 to 20 minutes

**GRILL/GEAR** If ember-grilling the peppers, use charcoal. If direct grilling, use wood or gas. You'll also need a rimmed sheet pan.

Visit the Basque country (straddling the borders of France and Spain) and you're sure to be served piperade—an exuberant sauté of bell peppers, tomatoes, onion, and garlic, often scrambled with eggs and always fired up with local Espelette pepper. (Coincidentally, red, yellow, and green are the colors of the Basque flag.) In other words, just the sort of dish that's been waiting to be transformed by smoke and fire. I've reimagined it as a salad—made smoky by ember-grilling the peppers and onions, with crisp grilled jamón Serrano and crusty grilled croutons added to punch up the excitement. And now that it's a salad, this is one piperade you can prepare ahead of time.

## INGREDIENTS

1 red bell pepper

1 yellow bell pepper

1 green bell pepper

2 ripe plum (Roma) tomatoes

1 medium sweet onion,
    unpeeled, halved through
    the stem end

2 cloves garlic, peeled and
    loosely wrapped together
    in aluminum foil

Vegetable oil for oiling the grill grate

3 ounces thinly sliced jamón Serrano
    or Bayonne ham (optional)

Extra virgin olive oil

2 slices country-style bread or
    baguette (each slice should be
    ½ inch thick; if using a baguette,
    slice it sharply on the diagonal
    for maximum surface area to
    expose to the fire)

2 tablespoons sherry vinegar or
    red wine vinegar

1 teaspoon pimentón
    (Spanish smoked paprika)

½ to 1 teaspoon Espelette pepper or
    hot paprika

Coarse salt (sea or kosher) and freshly
    ground black pepper

¼ cup coarsely chopped fresh
    flat-leaf parsley leaves

**WHAT ELSE** To be strictly
authentic, you'd use Espelette
pepper—a spicy powder made
from a fiery pepper from the
French Basque country. In the
absence of that, a combination
of paprika and cayenne, or
hot paprika, make reasonable
substitutes. To make a main-
course salad, grill-fry a few
eggs, such as Wood Fire Eggs
on page 242 and slide them
on top of the salad. Note: As
always, you'll get the richest
flavor by ember-grilling
(caveman grilling), but direct
grilling (see Variation, page 80)
produces a fine piperade, too.

**1.** Set up your grill for ember-grilling. Rake out the coals in an even layer and fan off any loose ash.

**2.** Lay the peppers, tomatoes, onion, and garlic on the embers. Grill until charred on all sides, 1 to 3 minutes per side, turning with tongs. Grill the garlic until soft, 1 to 2 minutes per side. Transfer the veggies to a rimmed sheet pan to cool.

**3.** Place the grate on the grill. Brush or scrape it clean and oil it well.

**4.** Lightly brush the ham slices (if using) on both sides with olive oil. Arrange on the grate. Grill until sizzling and lightly browned, 1 to 2 minutes per side. Transfer to a wire rack: The ham will crisp as it cools. Note: This step should be done not more than 1 hour before serving the salad.

**5.** Lightly brush the bread slices on both sides with olive oil. Grill until toasted, 1 to 2 minutes per side. Transfer to the wire rack to cool.

**6.** Using a paring knife, scrape any burnt skin off the peppers, tomatoes, and onion. You don't need to remove every last bit—a few specks of black add color and flavor. Transfer the peppers to a cutting board and cut in half lengthwise. Remove the stems and scrape out and discard the veins and seeds. Cut the peppers and onion into 1-inch pieces. Thinly slice the tomatoes crosswise. Unwrap and mince the garlic. Place the vegetables and garlic in a mixing bowl.

**7.** Stir in 2 tablespoons olive oil, the vinegar, pimentón, and Espelette pepper. Add salt and pepper to taste: The salad should be highly seasoned. The salad can be prepared up to 48 hours ahead to this stage. Store, covered, in the refrigerator, but let it warm to room temperature before serving.

**8.** Right before serving, break the crispy ham (if using) and grilled bread into 1-inch pieces over the salad. Add the parsley and stir just to mix. Wow!

## VARIATION

### DIRECT GRILLING

Set up your grill for direct grilling and heat as hot as it will go. Grill the peppers, tomatoes, onion, and garlic until charred, or at least dark brown, on all sides. (You may not actually be able to char the peppers black on a gas grill.) Charring may take a little longer on the grill grate than in the embers. Prepare and serve the salad as described previously.

# GRILLED PANZANELLA
## (TUSCAN BREAD AND TOMATO SALAD)

**YIELD** Serves 4 to 6

**METHOD** Direct grilling

**PREP TIME** 20 minutes

**GRILLING TIME** 10 minutes

**GRILL/GEAR** Can be grilled over charcoal or gas, but for the best flavor, grill over wood or a wood-enhanced fire. If you're enhancing a charcoal or gas fire, you'll need hardwood chunks or chips (unsoaked), see page 8. You'll also need wooden toothpicks and a wire rack.

Italians call it panzanella; Lebanese call it fattoush. It's one of the most refreshing salads you can make in summer, not to mention a great way to resuscitate less than fresh bread. Traditional Italian panzanella is not grilled, so it lacks the charred smoky flavors that keep us pyromaniacs wed to our grills. What makes this version truly extraordinary is the contrast of grilled and raw ingredients—crisp toast and fire-charred onions, crunchy cucumbers and juicy tomatoes. Serve as a substantial salad or a light summer meal. Note: I write this recipe in broad strokes, not precise lines. Substitute other vegetables depending on what's freshest and best.

## INGREDIENTS

Vegetable oil for oiling the grill grate

4 thick slices country-style bread (each slice should be 1 inch thick and, ideally, the bread will be slightly stale)

Extra virgin olive oil

1 large red onion, peeled and cut into 6 wedges

2 large luscious ripe red tomatoes

Coarse salt (sea or kosher) and freshly ground black pepper

1 cucumber, peeled and cut into 1-inch dice (seeded or not—your choice)

2 ribs celery, thinly sliced on the diagonal

½ cup kalamata or other brined or cured black olives

1 tablespoon drained brined capers

8 basil leaves, rolled up and thinly slivered, plus a sprig for garnish

1 to 2 tablespoons red wine vinegar, or to taste

3 ounces ricotta salata cheese (optional)

**1.** Set up your grill for direct grilling and heat to high. If enhancing a charcoal fire, add the wood chunks or chips to the coals; if enhancing a gas fire, place the chunks or chips in your grill's smoker box or place chunks under the grate directly over one or more burners. Brush or scrape your grill grate clean and oil it well.

**2.** Lightly brush the bread slices on both sides with olive oil. Pin the onion wedges crosswise with toothpicks (this helps them hold together). Lightly brush the onion wedges and whole tomatoes with olive oil and season with salt and pepper.

**3.** Grill the bread slices until darkly toasted, 1 to 2 minutes per side. Grill the onion wedges until browned, 1 to 2 minutes per side. Grill the tomatoes until blistered and browned all over, but still raw in the center,

4 to 6 minutes total. Transfer the bread, onion, and tomatoes to a wire rack and let cool.

**4.** Break the grilled bread into 1-inch pieces into a mixing bowl. Remove the toothpicks from the onion wedges and thinly slice the onions crosswise. Add it to the bread in the bowl. Cut the tomatoes into 1-inch chunks (remove and discard any stems), and add them with their juices to the bread. Add the cucumber, celery, olives, capers, slivered basil, vinegar, and 5 tablespoons of olive oil (or to taste). Toss well and let stand so the tomato juices soften the bread, about 5 minutes. Correct the seasoning, adding salt, pepper, or vinegar to taste: The salad should be highly seasoned. Shave, slice, or crumble the ricotta salata (if using) over the salad and garnish with the basil sprig.

**WHAT ELSE** You'll want to use a rich-flavored country-style bread from an artisanal bakery for this salad: Italian pane Pugliese or French boule come to mind, but any rustic bread will do. The tomatoes should be vine-ripened and farmstead (if not from your garden) and should never have seen the inside of a refrigerator. Ricotta salata is a firm salty cheese made from pressed ricotta— it's great for shaving, slicing, or crumbling over the salad.

# A SIMPLE SALAD OF EMBER-GRILLED PEPPERS AND ONIONS

**YIELD** Serves 4 to 6

**METHOD** Ember-grilling (caveman grilling) or direct grilling

**PREP TIME** 10 minutes

**GRILLING TIME** 15 to 20 minutes

**GRILL/GEAR** Charcoal or wood (if you're ember-grilling); can also be grilled over gas. You'll also need a rimmed sheet pan.

**WHAT ELSE** In a perfect world, you'd ember-grill the peppers and onions on charcoal, but gas grillers can achieve a similar effect by cranking up the heat as hot as the grill will go. I like the sharpness of red wine vinegar, but you could also go for an Asian-inspired flavor with rice vinegar, Spanish-inspired with sherry vinegar, or Italian-inspired with balsamic. Likewise, you can vary the toasted nuts, from almonds or pine nuts to pistachios or macadamias.

Of all the vegetables you can "caveman" (grill on the embers), none delivers the payoff of bell peppers. The charred skins impart an inimitable smoke flavor and simultaneously intensify the peppers' natural sweetness. Combine them with ember-grilled onions (another source of sweetness) and enough wine vinegar to counterpoint the plant sugars, and you have a salad that's simple, unpretentious, and explosively flavorful. Alternatively, it makes a great topping for bruschetta (see page 35), a foil for fresh or grilled cheese, and a terrific relish for grilled seafood or meat.

## INGREDIENTS

2 red bell peppers

2 yellow bell peppers

2 green bell peppers

1 large sweet onion, unpeeled

½ cup pine nuts, shelled pistachios, or slivered almonds

2 tablespoons red wine vinegar, or to taste

2 tablespoons extra virgin olive oil

Coarse salt (sea or kosher) and freshly ground black pepper

⅓ cup chopped fresh flat-leaf parsley leaves, and/or other fresh herb, such as cilantro leaves or dill

**1.** Set up your grill for ember-grilling (caveman grilling). Rake out the coals in an even layer and fan off any loose ash. Alternatively, set up your grill for direct grilling and heat to high.

**2.** Lay the peppers and onion on the embers. Grill until the peppers are charred black on all sides, 2 to 3 minutes per side, turning with tongs. If using a gas grill, brush or scrape the grill grate clean (there's no need to oil it) and direct grill the peppers until charred. Transfer the peppers to a rimmed sheet pan to cool.

**3.** Grill the onion on the embers or on a gas grill until charred black on all sides and soft in the center, 15 to 20 minutes, turning with tongs. (When ready, a metal skewer will pierce it easily.) Transfer the onion to the sheet pan to cool.

**4.** Meanwhile, place the pine nuts in a dry cast-iron skillet on the hot grill or your stovetop burner. Toast until browned and fragrant, 1 to 2 minutes. Transfer the nuts to a bowl to cool. Note: The nuts can be toasted ahead of time.

**5.** Using a paring knife, scrape the burnt skin off the peppers and onion. Transfer the peppers to a cutting board and cut in half. Remove and discard the stems and scrape out and discard the veins and seeds. Cut the peppers into finger-width strips, or as thick or thin as you desire. Cut the onion in half from root to tip, then cut each half lengthwise into pieces the size of the peppers. Place the vegetables in a mixing bowl with any juices that have accumulated on the sheet pan or cutting board.

**6.** Stir in the vinegar, olive oil, and salt and pepper to taste: The salad should be highly seasoned. The salad can be made several hours ahead to this stage and stored in a sealed container in the refrigerator. Let warm to room temperature before serving.

**7.** Right before serving, stir in the parsley and pine nuts.

## VARIATION

To give this salad a Sicilian touch, add currants and drained, brined capers. Crumbled goat cheese or shaved ricotta salata makes a welcome embellishment, too.

# CHARRED EGGPLANT SALAD
## WITH TAHINI, WALNUTS, POMEGRANATE, AND FRIED MINT

Kashk bademjan is one of the half dozen salads and dips served at the start of an Armenian meal, and few restaurants make it better than Nersses Vanak in Glendale, California. (Glendale has one of the world's largest expat Armenian communities.) Picture sweet, smokily charred eggplants topped with buttery whey and a fragrant slick of mint oil. You probably won't find whey (the liquid that's left when you separate the curds from milk) at your local market, but tahini (sesame paste) mixed with yogurt makes a culturally appropriate substitute. The mint oil adds fragrance and richness, and for crunch, there are pomegranate seeds and toasted walnuts. Best of all, you can make the salad ahead, charring the eggplant at a previous grill session.

**YIELD** Serves 4

**METHOD** Ember-grilling (caveman grilling) or direct grilling

**PREP TIME** 15 minutes

**GRILLING TIME** 10 minutes

**GRILL/GEAR** Charcoal (if you're ember-grilling); can also be grilled over wood or gas. You'll also need a wire rack set over a rimmed sheet pan.

**WHAT ELSE** A dish this simple lives and dies by the quality of its ingredients. Try to buy your eggplants at your local farmers' market or from a Middle Eastern grocer. Use fresh mint, of course, and walnuts from an Armenian or Middle Eastern market. Pomegranate molasses is a sweet-sour condiment made from reduced pomegranate juice. Balsamic vinegar glaze, which you can buy at many supermarkets (find it by the vinegars) or online, makes a workable substitute.

## INGREDIENTS

1½ pounds eggplant (3 or 4 small eggplants)

¼ cup tahini

¼ cup plain Greek yogurt

1 to 2 tablespoons fresh lemon juice

¼ cup extra virgin olive oil

½ cup packed fresh mint leaves or 3 tablespoons dried mint

½ cup walnut halves, toasted and roughly chopped (see Note)

½ cup fresh pomegranate seeds and/ or 1 tablespoon pomegranate molasses, for garnish (optional)

**1.** Set up your grill for ember-grilling (caveman grilling. Rake out the coals in an even layer and fan off any loose ash. Alternatively, set up your grill for direct grilling and heat to high. If using a grate, brush or scrape it clean (there's no need to oil it).

**2.** Lay the eggplants on the coals or place them on the grate, and grill until the skins are charred and the flesh is very soft (it will be easy to pierce with a skewer), turning with tongs. This will take 6 to 8 minutes for small eggplants; a bit longer for large. Transfer the eggplants to a wire rack set over a rimmed sheet pan to cool.

**3.** Using a paring knife, scrape off any really burnt parts—don't worry about getting it all: A little black skin adds color and flavor. Transfer the cooled eggplants to a platter, remove and discard the stem(s), and roughly chop them with a knife and fork.

**4.** Meanwhile, make the tahini sauce: Combine the tahini and yogurt in a small mixing bowl and whisk until smooth. Whisk in the lemon juice and enough water to obtain a thick but pourable sauce.

**5.** Make the mint oil: Heat the olive oil in a small skillet over medium heat. When the oil shimmers (it will be 350°F on a frying thermometer), add the mint leaves and fry until crisp, 1 to 2 minutes. Transfer with a slotted spoon to a paper towel–lined plate to drain and cool. Reserve the oil.

**6.** Drizzle the tahini sauce over the eggplant on the platter. Spoon the mint oil on top in small puddles. Sprinkle the salad with the fried mint, toasted walnuts, and pomegranate seeds (if using). Or drizzle with pomegranate molasses (if using). That's all there is to it.

**NOTE:** To toast walnuts, place them in a dry skillet over medium-high heat. Cook until fragrant and toasted, stirring or shaking the pan, about 2 minutes. Transfer to a bowl and let cool.

# GRILLED LEEKS
## WITH ASH VINAIGRETTE

It may seem odd to look to the godfather of molecular cuisine for a dish involving the world's most ancient cooking method: grilling. But when Spanish uber-chef José Andrés put grilled leeks with leek ash vinaigrette on the menu at Little Spain, his Spanish food court in Manhattan, he took his inspiration from modernist culinary visionary and his mentor Ferran Adrià. That recipe involved charring (make that incinerating) leek greens, then blending the resulting ash with sherry vinegar and olive oil into a vinaigrette. As for the leeks themselves, they're slow-roasted by indirect grilling—a process that makes the vegetable as meltingly tender as marmalade, and almost as sweet. Tip o' the hat to my stepson, chef Jake Klein, who figured out how to transform burnt leek greens into one of the most striking sauces on Planet Barbecue.

**YIELD** Serves 4 to 6

**METHOD** Indirect grilling/ direct grilling

**PREP TIME** 15 minutes

**GRILLING TIME** 40 minutes

**GRILL/GEAR** Can be cooked on a gas or charcoal grill. You'll also need a rimmed sheet pan.

**WHAT ELSE** This salad involves a two-step grilling process. You indirect grill the white part of the leeks to make them sweet and tender. Then you char the leek greens directly over the fire until coal-black and use them to color and flavor the sauce. This isn't quite as complicated as it sounds, but it does take a little time. Happily, you serve the leeks chilled or at room temperature, so you can grill them ahead of time.

## INGREDIENTS

2 pounds leeks (each ideally ¾ inch in diameter)

Vegetable oil for oiling the grill grate

3 tablespoons sherry vinegar

1 tablespoon fresh lemon juice

¼ cup extra virgin olive oil

3 tablespoons vegetable oil

2 teaspoons sugar, or to taste

Coarse salt (sea or kosher) and freshly ground black pepper

**1.** Trim the top 2 inches off the green part of the leeks and discard. Cut what remains of the leeks crosswise in half to separate the white part from the remaining green part. Leave the furry roots on the white part of the leeks for now—they'll help hold it together during grilling.

**2.** Set up your grill for indirect grilling and heat to medium-high. Brush or scrape the grill grate clean and oil it well.

**3.** Indirect grill the white part of the leeks until the outsides are browned and the insides are very tender, 30 to

40 minutes, or as needed. Check for doneness by squeezing or by inserting a slender skewer—it should pierce the flesh easily. Transfer the leek whites to a rimmed sheet pan to cool.

**4.** Now set up your grill for direct grilling and heat to high. (The grill should be screaming hot—"the sort of heat that singes the hair on your forearms," Jake says.) Place the greens from two of the leeks on the grate and char until coal-black, about 5 minutes per side, or as needed, turning with tongs. Transfer the charred leek greens to the sheet pan and let cool, then crumble to make leek ash. The ash can be prepared ahead to this stage and stored in a sealed jar in the refrigerator for several weeks. (Note: You'll have more leek greens than you need for this recipe. I like to char them all and save the extra leek ash for other recipes. It makes an interesting addition to sauces.)

**5.** Trim the roots off the roasted leek whites and remove and discard the outer layer. (It will be leathery and stringy.) Set aside half of one leek white for the sauce. Arrange the remaining soft leek centers on a platter like logs. Or cut them crosswise into ½-inch-thick coins and arrange on the platter.

**6.** Make the leek ash vinaigrette: Place the reserved leek white in a blender. Add ¼ cup of the leek ash, the vinegar, lemon juice, oils, sugar, and ½ cup of water. Blend until smooth. Add salt and pepper to taste.

**7.** Let the vinaigrette sit for 20 minutes in the blender; it will thicken. If too thick (it should be pourable), add a little more water as needed. Correct the seasoning, adding salt or vinegar to taste: The vinaigrette should be highly seasoned. This makes about 1 cup.

**8.** Spoon the vinaigrette over the tender leek centers and serve.

**NOTE:** If the leeks are sandy or gritty, wash them: Make a lengthwise cut from the green end halfway toward the root end. Roll the leek 90 degrees and make a second lengthwise cut halfway toward the root end. (Leave the furry root end intact for the moment.) Plunge the leek, cut end down, in a pitcher or deep bowl of cold water, moving it up and down as you would a plumber's plunger, to wash out any grit. Change the water and repeat as needed until the leeks are clean. Drain the leeks well and blot dry with paper towels. For really gritty leeks, cut the green part and white part in half lengthwise. Wash under cold running water, separating the layers with your fingers so you can wash out the grit.

# SMOKE-ROASTED GERMAN-STYLE POTATO SALAD

**YIELD** Serves 4 to 6

**METHOD** Indirect grilling/ ember-grilling (caveman grilling)

**PREP TIME** 10 minutes

**GRILLING TIME** 30 to 45 minutes

**GRILL/GEAR** Can be grilled over charcoal or gas, but tastes best grilled over wood. You'll also need a disposable aluminum foil drip pan and, if using a charcoal or gas grill, hardwood chunks or chips (soaked), see page 8.

**WHAT ELSE** I like to make this salad with white or yellow fingerling potatoes. Three incredibly flavorful varieties are Ratte and Bintje, now available in some US markets, and Baby Dutch Yellow (distributed by Melissa's). Alternatively, use Yukon Golds.

When it comes to potato salad, there are two basic schools: German-style (flavored with vinegar and bacon) and American-style (mayonnaise- and mustard-based). Both get a Raichlen makeover by, you guessed it, smoke-roasting the spuds instead of boiling them. Here's the German version—sweet with sugar, tart with vinegar, and smoky with bacon. If meat isn't your thing, you could substitute the shiitake bacon on page 26 (or leave it out). A more familiar American mayonnaise- and mustard-based potato salad follows.

## INGREDIENTS

**FOR THE POTATO SALAD**

2 pounds fingerling potatoes or Yukon Gold potatoes

1 medium onion, peeled and quartered

1½ tablespoons extra virgin olive oil, plus extra as needed to finish the salad

Coarse salt (sea or kosher) and freshly ground black pepper, plus extra for the dressing

**FOR THE DRESSING**

4 strips thick-cut bacon (about 6 ounces), cut crosswise into ¼-inch slivers

¼ cup white wine vinegar or distilled white vinegar

2 to 3 tablespoons sugar

1 tablespoon Düsseldorf-style or Dijon mustard, or to taste

1 tablespoon prepared horseradish

**1.** Smoke-roast the potatoes: Scrub the spuds under running water with a stiff vegetable brush. (There is no need to peel them.) Blot dry with paper towels. Cut any large potatoes in quarters or halves so that all are the same size (about 1 inch).

**2.** Set up your grill for indirect grilling and heat to medium-high.

**3.** Arrange the potatoes and onion in a disposable aluminum foil pan.

Toss with the olive oil and season generously with salt and pepper.

**4.** Place the foil pan with the potatoes and onion on the grill grate away from the heat. If enhancing a charcoal fire, add the wood chunks or chips to the coals; if enhancing a gas fire, place the chunks or chips in your grill's smoker box or place chunks under the grate directly over one or more burners. Close the grill lid.

**5.** Smoke-roast the potatoes and onion until just tender, 30 to 40 minutes, or as needed. Stir a few times so they cook evenly.

**6.** Move the pan directly over the fire and direct grill the vegetables until browned and crusty, about another 3 minutes, stirring often. Transfer the potatoes to a large heatproof mixing bowl and cover with aluminum foil to keep warm. Dice the onion and add it to the potatoes; re-cover the bowl.

**7.** Meanwhile, make the dressing: Place the bacon in a large skillet. Cook over medium-high heat on your grill's side burner (or on the stovetop) until browned and crisp, 3 to 4 minutes, stirring while it cooks. (You'll get less sticking and better crisping if you start with a cool pan.) Using a slotted spoon, transfer the bacon to the bowl with the potatoes (leave the bacon fat in the pan) and keep warm.

**8.** Add the vinegar and sugar to taste to the bacon fat in the pan and bring to a boil, whisking to dissolve the sugar. Remove the pan from the heat and stir in the mustard, horseradish, and salt and pepper to taste.

**9.** Pour the hot dressing over the still warm potatoes and onion and toss to mix. Add salt, pepper, olive oil, or more vinegar to taste: The salad should be highly seasoned. The salad should also be moist—add olive oil as needed. Transfer the salad to a serving bowl. Serve warm or at room temperature.

# VARIATION

## SMOKE-ROASTED CREAMY POTATO SALAD WITH OLIVES, CAPERS, AND PICKLES

Here's a tangy mayonnaise- and mustard-based American-style potato salad, once again transformed by the mythical power of wood smoke.

### INGREDIENTS

#### FOR THE DRESSING

¼ cup mayonnaise, preferably Hellmann's or Best Foods

2 tablespoons Dijon mustard

1 tablespoon red wine vinegar

2 tablespoons chopped pimento-stuffed olives

2 tablespoons drained brined capers

2 tablespoons chopped dill pickle

1 scallion, trimmed, white and green parts thinly sliced

Prepare the potato salad recipe on the facing page through Step 6. Omit the bacon. Let the potatoes and onions cool to room temperature. Meanwhile, make the dressing: Combine the mayonnaise, mustard, vinegar, olives, capers, dill pickle, and scallion in a large mixing bowl and whisk to combine. Stir the potatoes and onion into the dressing, tossing to coat well. Add salt, pepper, and vinegar as needed: The salad should be highly seasoned. Transfer to a serving bowl and keep refrigerated until serving (it will keep for at least 48 hours).

# GRILLED NAPA SLAW
## WITH GINGER, PEANUTS, AND ASIAN PEAR

**YIELD** Serves 6

**METHOD** Direct grilling

**PREP TIME** 15 minutes

**GRILLING TIME** 15 to 20 minutes

**GRILL/GEAR** Can be grilled over charcoal, gas, or wood. You'll also need a rimmed sheet pan.

**WHAT ELSE** Native to China and available at Asian markets and most supermarkets, napa is an elongated cabbage that looks like romaine lettuce on steroids. There are several options for chili paste here, including Indonesian sambal oelek, Korean gochujang, or even California-made Thai sriracha.

Coleslaw (from the Dutch term *koolsla*, meaning "cabbage salad") is as popular in the East as in the West. Think Thai som tum or Sichuan cabbage salad. This one combines a passion for spice with an obsession with smoke. The secret? You char the cabbage over a hot fire, driving vegetable smoke between the leaves, infusing the resulting slaw with an unexpected barbecue flavor. Napa (Chinese cabbage) is great for grilling for at least two reasons: Its elongated shape provides a greater surface area to char—and thus smoke—over a hot fire than conventional cabbage. And its crenellated leaves are less densely packed, allowing for a deep penetration of the smoke. This slaw explodes with the Asian flavors of sesame oil, ginger, and chili paste, with roasted peanuts for crunch.

## INGREDIENTS

### FOR THE SALAD

Vegetable oil for oiling the grill grate

1 head napa cabbage (about 2 pounds)

1 Asian pear

2 scallions

1½ tablespoons dark (toasted) sesame oil for brushing

Coarse salt (sea or kosher) and freshly ground black pepper

1 red bell pepper

2 jalapeño peppers

### FOR THE DRESSING

2 tablespoons granulated sugar, plus extra to taste

1 tablespoon minced peeled fresh ginger

1 clove garlic, peeled and minced

2 tablespoons rice vinegar, plus extra to taste

3 tablespoons dark (toasted) sesame oil

2 teaspoons of your favorite Asian chili paste or hot sauce, or to taste

½ cup chopped fresh cilantro leaves (optional)

¼ cup chopped roasted peanuts or black or toasted sesame seeds

**1.** Set up your grill for direct grilling and heat to high. Brush or scrape the grill grate clean and oil it well.

**2.** Meanwhile, use a chef's knife to cut the napa cabbage lengthwise into quarters through the core. Cut the pear in half lengthwise, remove the stem, and scoop out the core. Lightly brush the cabbage, pear, and scallions all over with the sesame oil and season with salt and pepper.

**3.** Grill the cabbage until darkly charred on all sides, 2 to 3 minutes per side. The inside should remain cool, firm, and crisp. Transfer to a rimmed sheet pan to cool.

**4.** Grill the cut sides of the pear until grill-marked, 2 to 3 minutes. Grill the scallions, bell pepper, and jalapeños until browned and grill-marked, turning halfway through, about 4 minutes. Transfer to the sheet pan. Let the pear and vegetables cool to room temperature.

**5.** Make the dressing: In a large bowl, mash together the sugar, ginger, and garlic with ½ teaspoon each salt and pepper. Add the rice vinegar and whisk until the salt and sugar are dissolved. Whisk in the sesame oil and the chili paste.

**6.** Place the cabbage on a cutting board. Remove and discard any really charred leaves. Use a sharp knife to cut away and discard the tough core of each quarter, then thinly slice the cabbage crosswise. Add it to the dressing. Cut the pear, bell pepper, and jalapeños into matchsticks and add them to the slaw, discarding the seeds and ribs from the bell pepper and jalapeños. Thinly slice the scallions crosswise, discarding the root ends, and add them as well. Stir in the cilantro (if using).

**7.** Taste the slaw for seasoning, adding more vinegar, sugar, and salt to taste. Cover and refrigerate until serving. The slaw is best when served within a couple of hours of mixing. Sprinkle with the toasted peanuts or sesame seeds and serve.

# EMBER-CHARRED CABBAGE
## WITH CARAWAY AND MINT

**YIELD** Serves 6

**METHOD** Ember-grilling (caveman grilling)

**PREP TIME** 15 minutes

**GRILLING TIME** 6 minutes

**GRILL/GEAR** Must be cooked on a charcoal or wood-burning grill. You'll also need a rimmed sheet pan.

**WHAT ELSE** My cabbage of choice for this slaw is savoy, a pale green vegetable with crinkled leaves and a mild sweet flavor. The leaves are less tightly packed than regular green cabbage, so the smoke flavor circulates more freely. Note: For a richer, nuttier flavor, use hazelnut oil in place of the vegetable oil.

Inspired by what is undoubtedly the world's most ancient method of cooking, ember-grilled cabbage seems to be turning up everywhere, from the charred cabbage with muhammara and hazelnuts at Safta restaurant in Denver (for my version of muhammara, see page 62) to the cabbage roasted in embers and served with yogurt, sumac, and lemon zest at Charcoal Venice in Los Angeles. I call the technique "cavemanning" (caveman grilling), and it imparts a decisive smoke flavor that turbocharges conventional slaw. The sweet-sour, Düsseldorf-style mustard and caraway-inflected dressing pays homage to German coleslaw, with mint leaves stirred in at the end for freshness.

## INGREDIENTS

3 tablespoons apple cider vinegar, plus extra to taste

3 tablespoons granulated sugar, plus extra to taste

3 tablespoons vegetable oil or hazelnut oil

1 tablespoon Düsseldorf-style or Dijon mustard

½ teaspoon caraway seeds (1 teaspoon if you really like caraway)

Coarse salt (sea or kosher) and freshly ground black pepper

1 large head savoy cabbage (about 2 pounds), quartered lengthwise through the core

¼ cup thinly sliced fresh mint leaves

**1.** Light a charcoal or wood-burning grill and let the coals burn down to glowing embers. Rake out the coals in an even layer and fan off any loose ash.

**2.** Meanwhile, make the dressing: Combine the vinegar and sugar in a large bowl and whisk together until the sugar dissolves. Whisk in the oil, followed by the mustard and caraway seeds. Season to taste with salt and pepper.

**3.** Lay the cabbage quarters directly on the coals and grill until all sides are charred, turning with tongs, about 2 minutes per side, 6 minutes in all. Transfer the charred cabbage to a rimmed sheet pan and let cool.

**4.** Place the cabbage on a cutting board. Remove any really charred leaves. Use a chef's knife to cut away and discard the tough core of the cabbage, then thinly slice the cabbage crosswise. Add the sliced cabbage to the dressing and toss to coat. Season with salt, sugar, and vinegar to taste. You can serve the slaw right away or rest it in the refrigerator for a couple of hours to meld the flavors. Just before serving, stir in the mint.

# NANCY'S SALMOREJO
# (SPANISH SMOKED CHILLED TOMATO SOUP)

Think of salmorejo as gazpacho's minimalist cousin. My assistant, Nancy Loseke, first tasted this chilled tomato soup in Córdoba, Andalusia, on one of her olive oil scouting trips. (Nancy was one of the founders of the Fresh-Pressed Olive Oil Club, my personal source for premium EVOO.) Salmorejo acquires its velvety texture from the emulsification of bread and olive oil. Add more bread and you get a great dip for grilled bread and vegetables. Add more water and you have an intensely flavorful sauce for grilled poultry or seafood. Garnish with diced jamón Serrano and chopped or quartered hard-cooked eggs (for smoked eggs, see page 245) and you could serve the soup as a light entrée.

**YIELD** Serves 4

**METHOD** Smoke-roasting (indirect grilling with wood smoke)/smoking/direct grilling

**PREP TIME** 15 minutes plus 2 hours to chill

**GRILLING/SMOKING TIME** 15 to 20 minutes (40 minutes if using a smoker)

**GRILL/GEAR** Best made on a charcoal grill, wood-burning grill, or smoker (if using the latter, you'll need a grill for the ham). You'll also need hardwood chunks or chips (unsoaked), see page 8; a disposable aluminum foil drip pan; and a wire rack.

## INGREDIENTS

2½ pounds ripe red tomatoes, stem ends removed, halved lengthwise

2 cloves garlic, peeled

2 ounces thinly sliced jamón Serrano or prosciutto (optional)

½ to ¾ cup extra virgin olive oil, preferably Spanish, plus extra for brushing and drizzling

¼ cup cold water, plus extra as needed

1 to 2 tablespoons sherry vinegar, plus extra to taste

Coarse salt (sea or kosher) and freshly ground black pepper

4 thick slices country-style bread (each slice should be about ¾ inch thick and 4 inches wide), crusts removed, torn into several pieces

2 smoked or hard-cooked eggs, peeled and roughly chopped or quartered (optional)

1 tablespoon minced fresh chives

**1.** Set up your grill for indirect grilling and heat to medium-low. Alternatively, set up your smoker to 250°F.

**2.** Place the tomatoes, cut sides up, and garlic in an aluminum foil drip pan on the grill grate away from the heat. If enhancing a charcoal fire, add the wood chunks or chips to the coals; if enhancing a gas fire, place the chunks or chips in your grill's smoker box or place chunks under the grate directly over one or more burners. Close the lid and cook until the tomatoes are bronzed with smoke, but still raw in the center, 15 to 20 minutes. If using a smoker, smoke the tomatoes and garlic low and slow, 30 to 40 minutes. Transfer the tomatoes and garlic to a wire rack to cool.

**3.** Meanwhile, lightly brush the jamón Serrano (if using) with olive oil. Place it in a single layer directly over the fire and grill until the jamón Serrano is sizzling and browned, 1 to 2 minutes per side. Transfer to the wire rack. The jamón Serrano will crisp as it cools. Set aside. If you don't use it right away, store in a sealed plastic bag in the refrigerator, but let it warm to room temperature before serving.

**4.** Cut the tomatoes into 1-inch chunks and roughly chop the garlic. Place in a blender jar with the water, vinegar, salt, and pepper. Puree on high speed until the mixture is smooth. Add the bread to the tomato puree and use a wooden spoon to submerge it. Let it soften for a few minutes, then blend until smooth. With the blender running on medium speed, slowly add the olive oil, starting with ½ cup, until the mixture is the consistency of thin mayonnaise. Correct the seasoning, adding vinegar or salt to taste: The soup should be highly seasoned. If the soup is too thick, add a tablespoon or two of cold water.

**5.** Chill the soup, covered, for at least two hours, or as long as overnight.

**6.** Ladle or pour the salmorejo into four shallow soup bowls. Drizzle with olive oil. Serve with the grilled jamón Serrano (if using) or crumble it over each serving and sprinkle with the smoked or hard-cooked eggs (if using) and chives.

**NOTE:** For the smoothest texture, you could strain the soup through a chinois or run it through a food mill, discarding any tomato seeds or skin before you chill it. I never bother with this.

# CHAPTER 5
# BREADS, PIZZAS, QUESADILLAS & SANDWICHES

Long before there were ovens, our forebears baked bread on heated stones next to the fire—or directly in the fire itself. And long before there were toasters or toaster ovens, people toasted bread on the grill. Which brings us to one of my favorite chapters in this book. We start with grilled bread and simple flatbreads, such as made-from-scratch pita you grill dramatically in the embers. From pita, it's a short etymological leap to pizza, which we cook on the grill with toppings ranging from a not-so-traditional margherita to an avocado pizza with jalapeños. Next come grilled quesadillas followed by sandwiches—like a grilled pimento cheese and a "cheesesteak" sandwich made with mushrooms and seitan. Talk about staff of life!

# RECIPES

# YOUR BASIC GRILLED BREAD

**YIELD** Serves 4 to 8

**METHOD** Direct grilling

**PREP TIME** 10 minutes

**GRILLING TIME** 2 to 8 minutes

**GRILL/GEAR** Can be grilled over charcoal or gas, but tastes best grilled over a wood or wood-enhanced fire. If you're enhancing a charcoal or gas fire with wood (optional), you'll need hardwood chunks or chips (unsoaked), see page 8. You'll also need a pastry brush.

**WHAT ELSE** You can grill any type of bread: French baguettes for dipping, brioche or pullman for sandwiches, broad slices of country-style bread, or saltless Tuscan bread for bruschetta. The recipe that follows is for baguettes, but other breads would be grilled the same way.

Readers of my books know my enthusiasm for grilled bread. Grilled and smoked dips (see Chapter 3), grilled cheese, and even grilled soups would be impoverished without it. Here's the basic procedure (with two basic shapes—slices and sticks), which you, intrepid griller, will customize with an almost limitless range of flavors. Rub the grilled bread with cut garlic to make Tuscan bruschetta, for example, or with a luscious ripe red tomato to make Catalan *pa amb tomàquet* (tomato bread). Grill it with anchovy butter (mash 2 anchovy fillets, then work in a few tablespoons of softened butter). Sprinkle the bread with grated Parmigiano-Reggiano or slather it with room-temperature Gorgonzola. The possibilities are endless!

## INGREDIENTS

1 baguette (15 inches long)

6 tablespoons butter (unsalted or salted—your call), extra virgin olive oil, brisket or duck fat, or other flavorful fat

**ANY OR ALL OF THE FOLLOWING FLAVORINGS**

1 clove garlic, peeled and minced; or 1 shallot, peeled and minced; or 1 scallion, trimmed and finely chopped

3 tablespoons minced fresh flat-leaf parsley leaves, cilantro leaves, or chives, or a mix

½ teaspoon freshly and finely grated lemon zest

½ cup freshly and finely grated Parmigiano-Reggiano (optional)

Vegetable oil for oiling the grill grate

**1.** To make grilled bread slices, use a serrated knife to cut the baguette on a sharp diagonal into ½-inch slices, working from the top of the loaf to the bottom. Why on a diagonal? To maximize the surface area of bread exposed to the fire. (I call these "rabbit ears" on account of their elongated shape.) To make grilled bread "sticks," cut the baguette in half crosswise. Slice each half lengthwise into quarters or sixths (depending on the diameter of your baguette).

**2.** Melt the butter or other fat in a small saucepan over medium heat. Add the garlic, herbs, and lemon zest and cook, stirring, until the garlic is sizzling and translucent, about 2 minutes. Do not let the butter brown or scorch. Remove from the heat.

**3.** Lightly and evenly brush the cut bread on all sides with the butter mixture. If using the cheese, sprinkle it on now. The bread can be buttered up to an hour ahead and covered with plastic wrap.

**4.** Meanwhile, set up your grill for direct grilling and heat it to medium-high. Have a fire-free safety zone where you can move the bread if it starts to burn. If enhancing a charcoal fire, add the wood chunks or chips to the coals; if enhancing a gas fire, place the chunks or chips in your grill's smoker box or place chunks under the grate directly over one or more burners. Brush or scrape the grill grate clean and oil it well.

**5.** Arrange the bread slices/sticks on the grill and grill until toasted and browned, 1 to 2 minutes per side, turning with tongs. Watch carefully, as bread can burn in seconds. Serve immediately: Grilled bread waits for no one.

# EMBER FLATBREAD

I've always been fascinated by the notion of grilling bread—from India's buttery naan (cooked in a charcoal-fired clay barbecue pit known as a tandoor) to the grilled pizza pioneered in the 1980s by Al Forno restaurant in Rhode Island and today served around the world. This recipe takes you back even further—indeed, to the very dawn of bread-making, when flatbread dough was cooked on fire-heated stones around a campfire, or even directly on the embers. The latter produces a unique char, crust, and smoke flavor, and you certainly can't beat the process for theatrics. The trick is to grill the breads long enough to make them puff and brown, but not so long that they burn—an interval measured in seconds, not minutes. I give you the granddaddy of all flatbreads and pizzas. Serve it brushed with melted butter or dipped in the Ember-Grilled Salsa on page 288.

**YIELD** Makes 12 flatbreads (6 inches each)

**METHOD** Ember-grilling (caveman grilling)

**PREP TIME** 20 minutes to make the dough, plus about 1½ hours for rising, or as needed, and 10 minutes for rolling out the flatbreads

**GRILLING TIME** 1 to 2 minutes per flatbread

**GRILL/GEAR** Must be cooked on a charcoal or wood-burning grill. You'll also need a rimmed sheet pan.

**WHAT ELSE** This recipe calls for ember-grilling, and the resulting char and smoke flavor produce a flatbread unlike any you've ever tasted. However, you can make a pretty awesome flatbread on a gas grill. Set it up for direct grilling and work over high heat. Note: I've given you three options for making the dough: You'll find the food processor method in the recipe, and the stand mixer and hand methods in the variations that follow.

## INGREDIENTS

2 packages (5 teaspoons) active dry yeast

1 tablespoon granulated sugar

1¼ cups warm water

About 4 cups all-purpose flour, plus extra for rolling out the flatbreads

2 teaspoons coarse salt (sea or kosher)

⅔ cup plain yogurt

1 tablespoon extra virgin olive oil, plus extra for oiling the bowl and sheet pan

4 tablespoons (½ stick) melted unsalted butter or extra virgin olive oil

Coarse salt (sea or kosher) and/or toasted sesame seeds, for serving (optional)

**1.** Place the yeast, sugar, and water in a measuring cup and mix well with a fork. Let stand until bubbly, about 10 minutes.

**2.** Place 3½ cups flour and the salt in a food processor fitted with a dough blade and process to mix. Add the yeast mixture, yogurt, and oil and process, running the machine in short bursts, to obtain a smooth dough, 30 seconds to 1 minute. The dough should be soft and moist, but not downright sticky—if too wet, add a little more flour.

**3.** Place the dough in an oiled bowl, turning to coat all sides. Cover the bowl with plastic wrap. Place in a warm spot and let it rise until doubled in bulk, 1 to 1½ hours. Punch the dough down and let it rise until doubled in bulk again, about 30 minutes. You can do this a couple of hours before grilling or you can make the dough the night before and let it rise overnight in the refrigerator.

**4.** Punch the dough down and cut it into 12 equal pieces. Working on a floured surface, roll the dough pieces into balls with your hands, then, using a rolling pin, roll each one into a flat 6-inch circle. Make sure each dough circle is well floured on both sides: The flour will prevent it from sticking to the embers.

**5.** Meanwhile, set up your grill for ember-grilling. That is, light your charcoal in a chimney starter. When glowing red, pour the embers over the bottom grate of your grill and rake them out into an even layer. Fan off any loose ash.

**6.** Lay 2 or 3 dough circles (you don't want to crowd them) directly on the embers. Grill until browned and blistered on the bottom and puffed on the top, 30 to 60 seconds. Turn the breads with long-handled tongs and grill the other side the same way.

**7.** Transfer the breads to a rimmed sheet pan. Brush off any ash or cinders with a pastry brush. Brush the top of each flatbread with the melted butter. Sprinkle with coarse salt and/or sesame seeds. Serve at once.

**8.** Finish the remaining dough circles as directed in Steps 6 and 7.

## VARIATIONS

### STAND MIXER DOUGH

Fit a stand mixer with a dough hook. Place the yeast, sugar, and water in the mixer bowl. Mix well and let it stand for 10 minutes. Add the yogurt, salt, butter, and 3½ cups flour. Mix at low speed to form a smooth dough, 3 to 5 minutes. The dough should be soft and moist, but not downright sticky—if too wet, add a little more flour. Continue with Step 3.

### HAND-KNEADED DOUGH

Place the yeast, sugar, and water in a measuring cup and mix well with a fork. Let stand for about 10 minutes. Mound 3½ cups flour on your work surface and make a well in the center. Place the yeast mixture, yogurt, salt, and butter in the well. Start mixing the dough with your fingertips, working from the center outward, gradually incorporating the flour. Work the dough into a ball, then knead until smooth, about 5 minutes. Add flour as needed. Continue with Step 3.

# PLANCHA PITA

**YIELD** Makes 8 pita breads (6 inches each)

**METHOD** Indirect grilling

**PREP TIME** 10 minutes for the dough, plus 1 to 1½ hours for rising, plus 5 minutes for rolling the breads

**GRILLING TIME** 3 to 5 minutes per batch

Long before there were baguettes or brioche, before pullman loaves and focaccia, there was pita. This puffy flatbread from the Middle East may well be the world's most ancient bread. You don't even need an oven to bake it. Originally, it was probably cooked on hot flat stones next to the fire. Even today, in small villages, pita is cooked on a metal sheet over a campfire. So why bother to make it from scratch when you can buy pita in any supermarket? Well, first of all, watching pita puff when it hits the hot stone or metal is nothing short of miraculous. And when you do it on a grill or over a campfire, you introduce the soulful scent of wood smoke. Finally, this is one of the few breads you can grill, not bake, and when it comes off the fire, singed on the outside, puffy and steamy inside, you'll feel like you're eating pita—real pita—for the first time.

## INGREDIENTS

### FOR THE DOUGH

1 cup warm water

1 package (2½ teaspoons) active
   dry yeast

1 tablespoon honey or sugar

2 cups all-purpose flour, plus extra
   for sprinkling

1¼ teaspoons coarse salt
   (sea or kosher)

2 tablespoons extra virgin olive oil,
   plus extra for oiling the bowl and
   sheet pan

½ cup whole wheat flour
   (or more all-purpose flour)

### FOR FINISHING THE BREADS
### (OPTIONAL)

3 tablespoons melted unsalted butter
   or olive oil

3 tablespoons toasted sesame seeds
   or za'atar

**GRILL/GEAR** Can be grilled over charcoal, gas, or wood. You'll also need a food processor or stand mixer (optional), rimmed sheet pans, and a plancha (see page 7) or pizza stone. If enhancing a charcoal fire or gas grill (optional), you'll also need hardwood chunks or chips (unsoaked), see page 8.

**WHAT ELSE** There are several ways to cook pita over a live fire. The first is on a plancha (or on its ceramic analogues, a pizza stone or the floor of a pizza oven). The second is directly on the grate, which darkens the outside of the pita more than you may be accustomed to, but delivers a flavor dividend far beyond what you expect of normal pita. I've given you three options for making the dough: You'll find the food processor method in the recipe, and the mixer and hand methods in the variations that follow.

**1.** Place the warm water in a large measuring cup. Stir in the yeast and honey. Stir in ¾ cup all-purpose flour to make a thick paste. Let it stand, uncovered, until the mixture is bubbly, about 20 minutes.

**2.** Transfer this mixture to the bowl of a food processor fitted with a dough blade or chopping blade. Add the salt, olive oil, whole wheat flour, and remaining 1¼ cups all-purpose flour. Pulse the processor in short bursts to bring the ingredients together into a smooth ball. It should be soft and moist, but not downright sticky—if too wet, add a little more flour.

**3.** Place the dough in an oiled bowl, turning to coat all sides. Cover the bowl with plastic wrap. Place in a warm place and let the dough rise until it's doubled in size, 1 hour to 1½ hours, or as needed. You can do this a couple of hours before cooking or you can make the dough the night before and let it rise slowly overnight in the refrigerator.

**4.** Punch down the dough and cut it into 8 equal pieces. Roll into balls and arrange on an oiled rimmed sheet pan. Cover with a clean dish towel. Let rise until soft and puffy, about 20 minutes.

**5.** Using a lightly floured rolling pin and working on a lightly floured work surface, roll each ball into a flat 6-inch circle. (Don't over-flour or the pita will be heavy.) Let the rolled pita rest at room temperature for 5 minutes.

**6.** Meanwhile, set up your grill for indirect grilling. Place a plancha or pizza stone on the grate, away from direct heat. Heat the grill and plancha or stone to high. Optional: If enhancing a charcoal fire, add the wood chunks

Ember flatbread piled up and ready for serving

or chips to the coals; if enhancing a gas fire, place the chunks or chips in your grill's smoker box or place chunks under the grate directly over one or more burners.

**7.** Place a few pita breads on the plancha, leaving 1 inch between them. After 2 to 3 minutes, the pita breads should puff dramatically. Turn them over with tongs and cook until the bottoms are lightly browned, another 1 to 2 minutes. As the pita breads are cooked, transfer them to a rimmed sheet pan. Brush with the melted butter (if using), and sprinkle with the sesame seeds. Or just serve them plain: They'll still be plenty delicious. If not serving hot off the fire, place the breads in a cloth-lined basket and cover with the cloth to keep warm.

# VARIATIONS

### STAND MIXER DOUGH

Fit a stand mixer with a dough hook. Place the warm water in the mixer bowl. Mix in the yeast and honey, then add ¾ cup all-purpose flour. Mix to make a thick paste. Let it stand, uncovered, until the mixture is bubbly, 20 minutes.

Work in the salt and olive oil, followed by the whole wheat flour and remaining 1¼ cups all-purpose flour. Mix at low speed to form a smooth, pliable dough, 3 to 5 minutes. The dough should be soft and moist, but not downright sticky—if it's too wet, add a little more flour. Continue with Step 3.

### HAND-KNEADED DOUGH

Place the warm water in a large measuring cup. Stir in the yeast and honey. Stir in ¾ cup all-purpose flour to make a thick paste. Let it stand, uncovered, until the mixture is bubbly, 20 minutes. Mound the remaining flour on your work surface and make a well in the center. Place the yeast mixture, salt, and oil in the well. Start mixing the dough with your fingertips, working from the center outward, gradually incorporating the flour. Work the dough into a ball, then knead until smooth, about 5 minutes. Add flour as needed. Continue with Step 3.

### DIRECT GRILLED PITA

Direct grilling gives you less puff, but more crust. It's a great alternative for cooking pita, no matter which method you use to make the dough.

**1.** Prepare the recipe through Step 5.

**2.** Set up your grill for direct grilling and heat to medium-high. Brush or scrape the grill grate clean and oil it well with vegetable oil. Lightly brush each pita on both sides with the melted butter.

**3.** Arrange the pita breads on the grate and grill until the bottoms are browned and the tops puffed, 1 to 2 minutes. Turn them over and grill the other side the same way, 1 minute more. Work in batches so as not to overcrowd the grill.

# GRILLED PIZZA DOUGH

The American grill scene has changed a lot since Al Forno restaurant in Providence, Rhode Island, pioneered grilling pizza dough directly over a hot fire. (Notice that I said directly over fire, not on a hot pizza stone.) To judge from the number of grill-top and portable pizza ovens and other accessories available, grilled pizza is very nearly as popular as the pie you get at your local pizza parlor. Direct grilling gives you a dramatically different texture and flavor than using a pizza stone, and both produce a different pizza than the one you cook in the oven. If you like your pizza crust simultaneously softly chewy and crackling crisp, this is the dough for you. Note: The recipe was inspired by Nancy Silverton of Pizzeria Mozza in Los Angeles.

**YIELD** Makes 4 pizzas (9 × 14 inches each if rectangular; 12 inches each if round)

**METHOD** Direct grilling or pizza stone (variation follows)

**PREP TIME** 15 minutes for the dough, plus 2 hours for rising the levain and 1½ to 2 hours for rising the dough

**GRILLING TIME** 6 to 8 minutes if direct grilled; 8 to 12 minutes if grilled on a pizza stone

**GRILL/GEAR** Can be grilled over charcoal, gas, or wood (but if using a wood-burning grill, don't cover it). You'll also need a food processor fitted with a dough blade or a stand mixer fitted with a dough hook (optional) and a rimmed sheet pan. For the pizza stone method, you will need a pizza stone and a pizza peel or rimless baking sheet (you can use the back of a sheet pan if need be).

## INGREDIENTS

**FOR THE LEVAIN (SPONGE STARTER)**

1¼ cups warm water

1 package (2½ teaspoons) active dry yeast

1½ cups bread flour

¼ cup whole wheat flour (or extra bread flour)

**TO FINISH THE DOUGH**

1 cup warm water

2½ to 2¾ cups bread flour, plus extra for the work surface

1 tablespoon malt (powder or syrup) or honey

2 teaspoons coarse salt (sea or kosher)

Extra virgin olive oil for the bowl and for stretching the dough

Vegetable oil for oiling the grill grate

**1.** Make the levain (sponge starter): Place 1¼ cups water in a mixing bowl. Sprinkle the yeast over the water and let it dissolve for 2 minutes. Stir in the 1½ cups bread flour and the ¼ cup whole wheat flour with a wooden spoon. The mixture should resemble a loose paste. Tightly cover with plastic wrap and let stand at room temperature until lightly bubbly, 2 hours.

Being a do-it-yourself kind of guy, when I grill pizza, I make the dough from scratch. This allows for the addition of interesting flours (like rye and whole wheat) and lets me take the time to make a levain (sponge starter), which gives a better rise and richer flavor than a simple yeast dough. (I've given you three options for making the dough: You'll find the food processor method in the recipe, and the stand mixer and hand methods in the variations that follow.) But I appreciate the convenience of using ready-made dough, so no judgment passed if you do. Grilling still delivers an amazing pizza. Note: Malt powder is available at most supermarkets (and online, of course); it improves the texture and browning of the crust.

**2.** Finish the dough: Fit a food processor with a dough blade. Place the sponge in the food processor and add the 1 cup warm water and the 2½ cups bread flour, malt, and salt. Run the processor in short bursts until a soft, pliable dough forms—it should pull away from the sides of the bowl, but just barely—3 to 5 minutes. If too sticky, work in a little more flour.

**3.** The first rise: Turn the dough out onto a lightly floured work surface and knead by hand for 1 to 2 minutes to give it a human touch. Gather it into a ball and place in a lightly oiled bowl; turn it over to coat with the olive oil. Tightly cover the bowl with plastic wrap, then a clean dish towel. Let rise in a warm place until doubled in bulk, 1 to 1½ hours.

**4.** The second rise: Turn the dough out onto a lightly floured surface and knead gently. Cut in quarters. Form each quarter into a ball with your hands, kneading until it is smooth and firm. Place the dough balls on a lightly floured, rimmed sheet pan. Cover each with plastic wrap and a dish towel and let rise until doubled in bulk, 30 minutes.

The pizza dough is ready for stretching and grilling. Alternatively, wrap the dough balls tightly in plastic wrap and refrigerate for up to 24 hours or freeze for up to 2 weeks. (If freezing, let the dough thaw overnight in the refrigerator.) If the dough has been chilled, let it rest at room temperature for 20 minutes before forming the pizza crust. This makes it easier to shape.

**5.** Form the crust: Generously oil a rimmed sheet pan with olive oil. Put one of the dough balls on the pan (turn it a couple of times to oil all sides). Oil your hands and stretch the dough into a rectangle about 9 × 14 inches.

**6.** Heat one side of your grill to medium-high. The other side should be low or off. Brush or scrape the grill grate clean and oil it well.

**7.** Grill the crust: Carefully lift the pizza off the sheet pan by one side (I start with the short side) and drape it onto the grate over the hot part of the grill. Grill until the bottom of the crust is browned and blistered and the top starts to bubble, 2 to 4 minutes.

**8.** Top the pizza: Using tongs and a spatula, turn the crust over, moving it to the cooler part of the grill. Arrange any toppings on the crust. Slide the pizza back over the hot part of the grill. Lower the grill lid to hold in the heat. Continue grilling the pizza until the toppings are cooked (any cheese in the topping will be melted), 2 to 4 minutes more. Serve hot off the grill. Cut the pizza into wedges or squares.

# VARIATIONS

### STAND MIXER DOUGH

Make the levain as described in Step 1. Fit the mixer with a dough hook. Place the bowl on the mixer and add the remaining 1 cup water, 2½ cups bread flour, malt, and salt. Mix at low speed until the dough is soft and pliable and pulls away from the sides of the bowl, but just barely, 3 to 5 minutes. If too sticky, work in a little more flour. Continue with Step 3.

### HAND-KNEADED DOUGH

Make the levain as described in Step 1. Mound the remaining 2½ cups bread flour on your work surface and make a well in the center. Place the 1 cup warm water, the malt, and salt in the center and mix with your fingertips to dissolve the salt. Add the levain and start mixing the dough with your fingertips, working from the center outward, gradually incorporating the flour. Work the dough into a ball, then knead until smooth, about 5 minutes. If it's too sticky, add flour as needed. Continue with Step 3.

### PIZZA STONE METHOD

**1.** If cooking on a rectangular pizza stone, make a rectangular crust; if cooking on a round stone, make a round crust. Dust a pizza peel or rimless baking sheet with cornmeal or semolina flour and pull the pizza dough onto it (or slide the peel or pan under the dough—whichever method works best). It's easier to top the pizza with the dough already on the peel. Add your desired toppings and follow the instructions for grilling in Step 7.

**2.** Set up your grill for indirect grilling. Place a pizza stone in the center and heat the grill and stone to high. (Use a point-and-shoot laser thermometer to check the stone's surface temperature; it should be 500°F.)

**3.** Optional: To add more smoke flavor, add wood. If enhancing a charcoal fire, add the wood chunks or chips to the coals; if enhancing a gas fire, place the chunks or chips in your grill's smoker box or place chunks under the grate directly over one or more burners.

**4.** Slide the pizza with its toppings from the pizza peel onto the stone. Close the lid and indirect grill the pizza until the bottom is blistered and browned and the toppings are sizzling, 8 to 12 minutes.

**5.** Transfer the pizza to a cutting board and cut into wedges or squares.

**GRILLING HACK:** Cool trick: DC Pie in Miami, Florida, sprinkles the serving tray for hot pizza with panko (Japanese breadcrumbs) before sliding the pizza on top. This creates air pockets that keep the bottom of the crust from getting soggy.

# THE RAICHLEN MARGHERITA

This is it—the primal pizza, named for Queen Margherita of Savoy in honor of her visit to Naples in 1889, or so the legend goes. The three colors—red tomato sauce, white mozzarella, and green basil—mirror the colors of the flag of the newly unified Italy. It's hard to improve on a traditional margherita, but I'm going to try by using smoked tomato sauce and that cream-rich sibling of mozzarella: burrata. And, of course, by grilling the pizza dough. Mission accomplished!

## INGREDIENTS

Vegetable oil for oiling the grill grate

½ batch Grilled Pizza Dough (page 105) or 7 ounces of your favorite premade dough

Extra virgin olive oil for oiling and drizzling

3 cups Smoked Tomato Sauce (page 290) or Grilled Tomato Sauce (page 291)

8 ounces burrata cheese, cut into ½-inch slices (slice at the last minute so you can capture the cream that comes out of it)

Dried oregano flakes

Hot red pepper flakes

1 small bunch fresh basil, stemmed, smaller leaves left whole, larger leaves torn

**1.** Set up your grill for direct grilling. One side should be medium-hot; the other side low or fire-free. Brush or scrape the grill grate clean and oil it well.

**2.** Stretch out half the pizza dough on a well-oiled rimless baking sheet into a rectangle about 9 × 15 inches or a 12-inch circle. Use plenty of olive oil when stretching.

**3.** Bring the baking sheet to the edge of your grill. Carefully lift up the dough by one side and drape it onto the grill. Grill until the bottom is blistered and browned and the top starts to bubble, 2 to 4 minutes.

**4.** Using tongs and a spatula, turn the crust over, moving it to the cooler part of the grill. Ladle half the tomato sauce onto the crust. I like it in patches, rather than spread from edge to edge, but that's just me. Dot the top with half the sliced burrata—again, I like it in patches, not all over. Spoon the burrata cream over the cheese. I like

**YIELD** Makes 2 pizzas (9 × 15 inches each if rectangular; 12 inches each if round)

**METHOD** Direct grilling

**PREP TIME** 10 minutes, plus the time for making the dough and the Smoked Tomato Sauce (if using)

**GRILLING TIME** 8 to 12 minutes

**GRILL/GEAR** Can be grilled over charcoal, gas, or wood. You will also need a rimless baking sheet (you can use the back of a sheet pan if need be).

**WHAT ELSE** For the full effect of this pizza, you'll want to use the smoked or grilled tomato sauce. If you don't have time to make that, use your favorite commercial tomato sauce. Or for a simple sauce, puree fire-roasted canned tomatoes with their juices (one good brand is Muir Glen) in a food processor.

The Raichlen Margherita—yes that's burrata, not mozzarella.

to leave some bare crust so people can enjoy that, too. Drizzle the top of the pizza with olive oil and sprinkle with oregano and hot red pepper flakes.

**5.** Slide the pizza back over to the hot part of the grill. Lower the lid. Continue grilling until the toppings are hot and the cheese is melted, 2 to 4 minutes more.

**6.** Transfer the pizza to a cutting board and sprinkle some fresh basil leaves on top. Make the other pizza the same way. Cut into wedges or squares for serving.

# VARIATIONS

### PIZZA STONE METHOD

**1.** Set up your grill for indirect grilling. Place the pizza stone on the grate away from the heat and heat both the grill and the stone to high (use a point-and-shoot thermometer to check the temperature; it should be about 500°F).

**2.** Meanwhile, stretch half the dough into a thin 12-inch circle (if using a round pizza stone) or 9 × 15-inch rectangle (if using a rectangular pizza stone) on a pizza peel or rimless baking sheet sprinkled with cornmeal or semolina flour. Ladle the tomato sauce onto the crust. Arrange the burrata slices on top. Drizzle the top of the pizza with olive oil and sprinkle with oregano and hot red pepper flakes.

**3.** Slide the pizza onto the hot pizza stone. Close the grill lid and grill until the top is bubbling and the bottom is crisp and brown, 5 to 8 minutes.

**4.** Transfer the pizza to a cutting board and sprinkle some fresh basil leaves on top. Make the other pizza the same way. Cut into wedges or squares.

### PIZZA PUTTANESCA

YIELD Makes 2 pizzas (9 × 15 inches each if rectangular; 12 inches each if round)

Puttanesca is that infamously named Roman tomato sauce tarted up with capers, olives, anchovies, and hot peppers. Traditionally served on spaghetti, the sauce makes an invigorating topping for pizza. Jalapeños aren't traditional, but they certainly provoke.

Prepare the pizzas through Step 3 as described on page 109. In Step 4, spread the top of the pizza with the Smoked Tomato Sauce or 3 cups of your favorite sauce. Top with ⅓ cup kalamata or other flavorful black olives; ¼ cup drained capers; 2 jalapeños or serranos, thinly sliced, or 2 teaspoons hot red pepper flakes; 8 oil-packed anchovies, drained and cut crosswise into 1-inch pieces; and 2 teaspoons dried oregano flakes on top. Shave or grate 3 ounces of Pecorino Romano cheese (optional) on top and drizzle with olive oil. Continue grilling the pizza as described in Step 5.

# AVOCADO PIZZA

Uber-chef Jean-Georges Vongerichten serves this singular pie—think of it as pizza channeling avocado toast—at his Matador Room restaurant in Miami Beach. It's the perfect way to show off your grilled pizza crust, and the contrast of hot, crisp grilled dough and creamy, cool avocado and jalapeño is as unexpected as it is thrilling.

**YIELD** Makes 2 pizzas (9 × 15 inches each if rectangular; 12 inches each if round)

**METHOD** Direct grilling

**PREP TIME** 15 minutes, plus the time for making the dough

**GRILLING TIME** 6 to 8 minutes

**GRILL/GEAR** Can be grilled over charcoal, gas, or wood.

**WHAT ELSE** Have the avocados cut and shingled on a cutting board before you start grilling the dough so they're ready to top the pizzas as soon as they come off the heat.

## INGREDIENTS

6 ripe avocados

Fresh lime juice

3 to 4 jalapeño or serrano peppers (preferably red), or to taste, stemmed

Vegetable oil for oiling the grill grate

½ batch Grilled Pizza Dough (page 105) or your favorite premade dough

Extra virgin olive oil

Maldon salt or coarse salt (sea or kosher) and freshly ground black pepper

½ cup stemmed cilantro leaves

⅓ cup crumbled Cotija cheese (optional)

**1.** Halve, pit, and peel an avocado. Place the avocado halves facedown on a cutting board. Thinly slice each half crosswise from the narrow end to the fat end. Now, push the slices from the narrow end to the fat end to flatten and shingle them out. Brush or squeeze lime juice over them to keep them from discoloring. Repeat with the remaining avocados.

**2.** Slice the jalapeños crosswise paper-thin (this is most easily done on a mandoline).

**3.** Direct grill the pizza dough as described in Steps 3 to 5 on pages 109–110 (skip the topping of the pizzas—you'll do that later). Both sides should be crisp and browned. Transfer the crusts to a wire rack. Brush the tops with olive oil.

**4.** Arrange the shingled avocado slices on the grilled pizza crusts (slide a metal palette knife or thin-bladed spatula under them to move them). Sprinkle the tops with jalapeño slices. Squeeze on more fresh lime juice and drizzle with more olive oil. Season generously with salt and pepper. Sprinkle the cilantro leaves and crumbled Cotija cheese (if using) over the pizzas. Work quickly, so the crusts stay hot, or slide the pizzas back on the grill for a minute or two to reheat the crusts. (Do not cook the avocado.) Cut into wedges or squares and serve at once.

# ADJARIAN KHACHAPURI
## (GEORGIAN EGG AND CHEESE PIZZA)

**YIELD** Makes 2 pizzas

**METHOD** Indirect grilling

**PREP TIME** 15 minutes, plus 2 to 2½ hours for rising the dough

**GRILLING TIME** 8 to 12 minutes

**GRILL/GEAR** Can be cooked on a charcoal or gas grill. You'll also need a pizza stone or plancha; hardwood chunks or chips (unsoaked), see page 8; a rimmed sheet pan; a pizza peel or rimless baking sheet (you can use the back of a sheet pan if need be); and a point-and-shoot thermometer.

**WHAT ELSE** I like to cook these pizzas on a charcoal grill, adding wood chunks or chips to the fire to simulate the smoke of a wood-burning oven.

Adjarian khachapuri may not be a household food name in America—not yet—but if you frequent restaurants featuring foods of the Caucasus region, you've surely seen this Georgian pizza, boat-shaped with tapered ends, formed from a soft, puffy, milk-enriched yeast dough, topped with tangy cheese, and a pair of eggs cooked right into the top. It looks cool (the two eggs sort of stare at you); it tastes even cooler; and it will definitely set you apart from the now-ubiquitous grilled-pizza crowd.

## INGREDIENTS

**FOR THE DOUGH**

⅓ cup warm water

1 packet (2½ teaspoons) dry active yeast

2 teaspoons granulated sugar

1⅔ cups all-purpose flour, plus additional flour for your work surface

1 scant teaspoon coarse salt (sea or kosher)

⅓ cup warm milk (about 90°F)

1 tablespoon extra virgin olive oil, plus extra for oiling the bowl and rimmed sheet pan

Fine cornmeal or semolina flour for the pizza peel

**FOR THE TOPPING**

8 ounces melting cheese, such as Gouda or Monterey Jack (ideally, 4 ounces of each), coarsely grated

4 ounces feta cheese, crumbled or coarsely grated

2 teaspoons dried oregano flakes

4 large eggs, preferably organic

2 tablespoons minced fresh chives

**1.** Proof the yeast: Place the warm water, yeast, and sugar in a small bowl and stir to mix. Let stand until the yeast is foamy, about 10 minutes.

**2.** Make the dough: Place the flour and salt in a food processor (ideally, one fitted with a dough blade, although a metal blade will work, too). Add the yeast mixture, milk, and olive oil. Process in short bursts until the mixture comes together in a smooth ball. Knead for 2 minutes in the processor. Transfer the dough ball to a lightly floured work surface and knead with your hands until smooth, 1 to 2 minutes. (I always like to add a human touch to dough—even when kneading it in a processor.)

**3.** Transfer the dough to a large, lightly oiled bowl, turning it to coat all sides. Cover with plastic wrap and a dish towel and place in a warm spot in your kitchen. Let the dough rise until doubled in bulk, 1 to 1½ hours. Punch the dough down, cut it in half, re-form into two balls, and let the dough rise on an oiled rimmed sheet pan covered with plastic wrap and a dish towel until doubled in bulk again, 30 to 60 minutes.

**4.** Meanwhile, set up your grill for indirect grilling. Place a pizza stone or plancha on the grate between the fires. Heat your grill and the stone or plancha to high (use a point-and-shoot thermometer to check the temperature; it should be about 500°F).

**5.** Lightly flour your work surface. Punch down each dough ball and, using a lightly floured rolling pin, roll it into an oval 9 to 10 inches long. Pinch the short ends together to form slender points. Pinch and build up the sides of each oval to make a ½-inch lip. Viewed from the top, what results will look like a canoe with a pointy bow and stern. Sprinkle a pizza peel or the rimless baking sheet with cornmeal and arrange the pizza crusts on top.

**6.** Sprinkle the top of each pizza with the cheeses, covering the flat part. Sprinkle with the oregano. Using the pizza peel or baking sheet, slide the pizzas onto the hot pizza stone. If enhancing a charcoal fire, add the wood chunks or chips to the coals; if enhancing a gas fire, place the chunks or chips in your grill's smoker box or place chunks under the grate directly over one or more burners. Close the lid and cook for about 4 minutes.

**7.** Crack 2 eggs onto each pizza, one toward each end. Continue cooking until the dough browns, the cheese melts, and the eggs are just set, another 4 minutes or so, 8 to 12 minutes in all.

**8.** Transfer the pizzas to a platter or plates, sprinkle with the chopped chives, and serve at once. Note: To eat, tear off one of the pointy ends and use it to break the yolk and mix it with the cheese, then tear off sections and eat. It's also acceptable to use a knife and fork.

# QUESADILLAS
## WITH GRILLED PEPPERS AND NORDIC SHRIMP

**YIELD** Makes 4

**METHOD** Ember-grilling (caveman grilling)/direct grilling

**PREP TIME** 15 minutes

**GRILLING TIME** 20 minutes

**GRILL/GEAR** Can be grilled over charcoal, gas, or wood. You'll also need a pizza peel or rimless baking sheet (you can use the back of a sheet pan if need be).

**WHAT ELSE** Nordic shrimp are tiny, supernaturally sweet-briny shrimp from the far North Atlantic. They're widely available fresh and frozen in Canada and frozen in the United States. Alternatively, use your favorite local shrimp: Key West pinks in Florida, spot prawns on the West Coast, white shrimp from the Carolinas, or sweet Maine shrimp.

I created these quesadillas for the Festi-GrÎles barbecue festival in Sept-Îles, Quebec, on the far north shore of the St. Lawrence River. My goal was to play the smoky sweetness of charred poblanos and scallions against the briny sweetness of a local seafood specialty: Nordic shrimp. And to bring a little Tex-Mex heat to the icy North. For the smokiest flavor, grill the peppers and scallions directly on the embers, caveman-style. On a gas grill, direct grill over high heat. Use this as a general guide rather than a recipe to be followed slavishly to the teaspoon. Don't have shrimp? Substitute diced cooked lobster or crab (ideally fresh, but thawed if frozen). Poblanos too hot for you? Try charred yellow or red bell peppers. Grilled corn kernels or fire-blistered tomatoes would be welcome, too.

### INGREDIENTS

Vegetable oil for oiling the grill grate

1 large poblano or yellow or red bell pepper

1 to 2 large jalapeño peppers

1 bunch scallions, trimmed

8 large (8-inch) flour tortillas

3 tablespoons butter, melted

12 ounces (about 3 cups) white cheddar cheese, coarsely grated

1½ cups (about 12 ounces) small Nordic shrimp

½ cup fresh cilantro leaves

Coarse salt (sea or kosher) and freshly ground black pepper

**1.** Set up your grill for ember-grilling (caveman grilling). Rake out the coals in an even layer and fan off any loose ash. Alternatively, set up your grill for direct grilling and heat to high; brush or scrape the grill grate clean and oil it well.

**2.** Arrange the poblano, jalapeños, and scallions on the embers. Grill until charred on all sides, 1 to 2 minutes for the jalapeños and scallions, 2 to 3 minutes per side for the poblano, turning with tongs. Transfer to a rimless baking sheet to cool.

Alternatively, direct grill the poblano, jalapeños, and scallions until darkly browned over a hot fire—the cooking times may be a little longer.

**3.** Scrape any really burnt skin off the poblano and jalapeños and remove the stems. Cut the poblano in half lengthwise, scrape out and discard the veins and seeds, and cut into ¼-inch dice. Thinly slice the jalapeños crosswise (for milder quesadillas, discard the seeds). Scrape off and discard any really burnt portions on the scallions. Thinly slice the remaining scallions crosswise.

**4.** Brush one side of 4 tortillas with melted butter and lay on a pizza peel or rimless baking sheet, buttered sides down. Top the tortillas with the cheese,

shrimp, poblanos, jalapeños, scallions, and cilantro. Season with salt and pepper. Top each quesadilla with a second tortilla and brush the tops with the remaining butter.

**5.** Set up your grill for direct grilling and heat to medium-high. Brush or scrape the grill grate clean and oil it well.

**6.** Carefully slide each quesadilla onto the grill grate and grill until nicely browned on both sides and the cheese is melted and bubbling, 1 to 2 minutes per side. (Use the peel or a wide-bladed spatula to rotate the quesadillas so they cook evenly and to turn them.) Transfer to a cutting board. Cut each into wedges for serving.

# THE RAICHLEN LUNCH QUESADILLA

The quesadilla was the first Mexican dish I learned to prepare, and it remains a go-to lunch in our house. It's infinitely customizable: You can stuff it with whatever you have on hand. As long as you have cheese (queso) to hold it together and chiles to kick up the heat, you're in business.

## INGREDIENTS

2 large (8- to 10-inch) or 4 small (6-inch) flour or corn tortillas

1½ tablespoons melted butter or extra virgin olive oil

¼ cup sour cream (optional)

4 ounces cheddar or pepper Jack cheese or any melting cheese, thinly sliced or coarsely grated

1 scallion, trimmed, white and green parts thinly sliced

1 to 2 jalapeño peppers, stemmed and thinly sliced crosswise (for milder quesadillas, remove the seeds)

½ cup chopped fresh cilantro leaves

½ cup diced tomato or avocado (optional)

Vegetable oil for oiling the grill grate

**YIELD** Serves 2 and can be multiplied as desired

**METHOD** Direct grilling

**PREP TIME** 10 minutes

**GRILLING TIME** 6 to 8 minutes

**GRILL/GEAR** Can be grilled over charcoal, gas, or wood. You'll also need a rimless baking sheet (you can use the back of a sheet pan if need be).

**WHAT ELSE** If you have large tortillas (8 inches or more), fold them to make half moon–shaped quesadillas. With smaller tortillas, use 2 per quesadilla (4 total) and stack them as you would to make a sandwich.

**1.** Lightly brush one side of the tortillas with melted butter and place each, buttered side down, on a rimless baking sheet. Spread the top of one half with the sour cream (if using). Arrange the cheese on top, followed by the scallion, jalapeño, cilantro, and tomato or avocado (if using). Fold the tortilla in half to make a half moon–shaped quesadilla. Make the other quesadilla the same way.

**2.** Meanwhile, set up your grill for direct grilling and heat to medium-high. Brush or scrape the grill grate clean and oil it well.

**3.** Carefully slide the quesadillas onto the grate and grill until the bottom is browned and the cheese starts to melt, 1 to 2 minutes. Using a wide spatula,

carefully turn the quesadillas and grill the other sides the same way. Cut each into wedges for serving.

## VARIATION

### QUESADILLAS RANCHEROS

Feeling hungry? Turn these quesadillas into huevos rancheros. Grill the quesadillas (use 2 small flour tortillas for each serving, not 1 large one folded over) as described in Step 1. When each quesadilla comes off the grill, top it with warmed refried beans, then your favorite salsa Meanwhile, fry a couple of eggs in a hot oiled skillet and slide them on top. Thanks to Josiah Citrin, chef-owner of Charcoal Venice in Los Angeles, for the idea!

# ELOTE QUESADILLAS
## WITH GRILLED CORN, POBLANOS, AND PEPPER JACK CHEESE

**YIELD** Makes 4

**METHOD** Direct grilling

**PREP TIME** 20 minutes

**GRILLING TIME** 16 minutes

**GRILL/GEAR** Can be grilled over charcoal, gas, or wood. You'll also need a pizza peel or rimless baking sheet (you can use the back of a sheet pan if need be).

**WHAT ELSE** In my house, quesadillas are fast food—often concocted from leftovers. So I'm not about to suggest you grill corn from scratch solely to make this recipe. (If you like grilled corn as much as I do, you'll probably have some extra ears in your refrigerator from a previous grill session.) For that matter, the next time you ember-grill, roast some extra poblano peppers and keep them in the refrigerator or freezer. Their sweet, smoky heat always comes in handy.

"How did Americans live without elote (Mexican grilled street corn slathered with chili powder and lime juice)?" If you've read my previous books, you know how to make it, and if you haven't, I wager there's a restaurant in your neighborhood that will be happy to enlighten you. I'm more interested in the flavor dynamic of the dish: the sweet corn, the piquant mayo, the sharp salty cheese—brought together by the vivifying embrace of fire. That dynamic reappears here in the form of a quesadilla. Note: Tasty as Cotija cheese is, it isn't a great melter. I've replaced a portion of it with pepper Jack cheese, which does melt well enough to hold the quesadillas together.

### INGREDIENTS

Vegetable oil for oiling the grill grate

3 ears of sweet corn, husked

4 tablespoons (½ stick) butter, melted, salted or unsalted

Coarse salt (sea or kosher) and freshly ground black pepper

1 large poblano pepper

Eight 8-inch flour tortillas

4 tablespoons mayonnaise, preferably Hellmann's or Best Foods

8 ounces coarsely grated pepper Jack cheese

4 ounces grated or crumbled Cotija cheese (or more pepper Jack)

1 cup fresh cilantro leaves

2 serrano or jalapeño peppers, stemmed and thinly sliced crosswise (optional; for milder quesadillas, remove the seeds)

**1.** Set up your grill for direct grilling and heat to high. Brush or scrape the grill grate clean and oil it well.

**2.** Lightly brush the corn with the melted butter (you'll need about 1 tablespoon for this) and season it well with salt and pepper. Arrange the corn on the grill grate. Grill until darkly browned on all sides, 2 to 3 minutes per side, turning with tongs as needed. While you're at it, grill the poblano until charred on all sides, 3 to 4 minutes per side.

**3.** Transfer the corn and poblano to a cutting board to cool. Cut the kernels off the cobs. (The easiest way to do this is to lay the corn flat on the cutting board and make broad lengthwise strokes with a chef's knife.) Using a paring knife, scrape any really burnt skin off the poblano. Cut it in half lengthwise, and scrape out and discard the veins, seeds, and the stem. Cut the poblano into ¼-inch strips. The corn and poblano can be prepared up to 24 hours ahead and refrigerated.

**4.** When you're ready to cook the quesadillas, set up your grill for direct grilling (if it isn't already) and heat to medium-high. Brush one side of 4 tortillas with melted butter and lay them on a pizza peel or rimless baking sheet, buttered sides down. Spread the other sides (the ones facing up) with the mayonnaise and sprinkle with the cheeses. Top with the grilled corn, poblano strips, cilantro, and serranos. (Why both poblano and serrano peppers? One is grilled and soft; the other raw and crisp, each with a different sort of heat.) Top each quesadilla with a second tortilla and brush the tops with melted butter.

**5.** Carefully slide each quesadilla onto the grill grate and grill until nicely browned on both sides and the cheese is melted and bubbling, 1 to 2 minutes per side. (Use the pizza peel or a wide-bladed spatula to rotate the quesadillas so they cook evenly and to turn them.) Transfer to a cutting board. Cut each into wedges for serving.

# THE PORTOBELLO CHIVITO

The chivito is Uruguay's epic steak sandwich. So what's it doing in a vegetable-forward grill book? The truth is that by the time you load the bun with grilled peppers and onions, hard-cooked eggs (the smoked eggs on page 245 would be amazing), melted cheese, lettuce, tomato, and mayonnaise, you could easily slip in grilled portobellos in place of steak, and few people would be the wiser. I like to think of this as the ultimate vegetable Dagwood.

**YIELD** Serves 2 and can be multiplied as desired

**METHOD** Direct grilling

**PREP TIME** 20 minutes

**GRILLING TIME** 20 minutes

**GRILL/GEAR** Can be grilled over charcoal, gas, or wood. You'll also need a rimmed sheet pan and wooden toothpicks.

## INGREDIENTS

2 large portobello mushrooms

1 small onion, peeled

Extra virgin olive oil

Coarse salt (sea or kosher) and freshly
ground black pepper

Dried oregano flakes

Hot red pepper flakes (optional)

Vegetable oil for oiling the grill grate

1 large red bell pepper

4 strips thin-cut bacon or pancetta
(optional)

2 slices (2 ounces) Monterey Jack
or provolone cheese, or a vegan
cheese such as Chao or Daiya

2 kaiser rolls, cut in half through
the side

3 tablespoons mayonnaise, preferably
Hellmann's or Best Foods, or vegan
mayonnaise

2 Boston lettuce leaves

2 smoked eggs (see page 245) or
hard-cooked eggs, peeled and
cut crosswise into ¼-inch slices

1 luscious ripe red tomato, thinly sliced

**1.** Wipe the portobello caps clean with
a moist paper towel and remove and
discard the stems. Place the caps on a
rimmed sheet pan.

**2.** Cut the onion crosswise into
½-inch-thick slices. Run a toothpick
or bamboo skewer through the side
of each slice to the center to keep the
slices from falling apart. Place the
onion slices on the sheet pan.

**3.** Brush the portobellos and onion
slices on both sides with olive oil and
season generously with salt, pepper,
oregano, and hot red pepper flakes
(if using).

**4.** Set up your grill for direct grilling
and heat to medium-high. Brush or
scrape the grill grate clean and oil
it well.

**5.** Arrange the red bell pepper on the
grate and grill until darkly browned
on all sides and soft, 3 to 4 minutes
per side, turning with tongs. Transfer
to a cutting board and let cool. Cut
lengthwise in quarters, removing and
discarding the stem, veins, and seeds.

**6.** Grill the bacon strips (if using) until
sizzling and browned, 2 to 4 minutes
per side, turning with tongs. Keep the
bacon moving to dodge any flare-ups.
Drain the bacon on paper towels.

**WHAT ELSE** Uruguayans
debate the proper ingredients
for a chivito the way Kansas
Citians argue what should go in
a proper barbecue sauce. Some
people use fried eggs instead of
hard-cooked. Others add grilled
onion in place of or in addition
to the peppers. Tradition calls
for bacon or ham on a chivito,
and tradition is always welcome
at my house. If you prefer to
go meatless, use the shiitake
bacon on page 26, or omit it
entirely—you'll still have plenty
of flavor. Note: If you have a
large grill, you can grill the
peppers, bacon, portobellos,
and onions at the same time.

**7.** Arrange the portobellos (gill sides down) and onion slices on the grate and grill until sizzling and darkly browned, 3 to 4 minutes per side. Invert the portobellos and lay the cheese slices on top. Close the lid and continue grilling until the cheese melts and the bottoms of the portobellos are sizzling and browned, 3 to 4 minutes more.

**8.** At the last minute, grill the rolls, cut sides down, until lightly browned, 1 to 2 minutes.

**9.** Spread the cut sides of the rolls with mayonnaise. Line the bottom half of each with a lettuce leaf. Place a grilled portobello on top of each and top with 2 grilled bell pepper quarters, onion, egg slices, tomato slices, and bacon (if using). Sprinkle a little more salt, pepper, oregano, and hot pepper flakes (if using) on top.

**10.** Close the sandwiches, cut in half for serving, and get ready for sandwich nirvana.

# SPICY BARBECUED TOFU SANDWICH
## WITH SRIRACHA MAYONNAISE

**YIELD** Serves 2 and can be multiplied as desired

**METHOD** Direct grilling (with smoke added)

**PREP TIME** 20 minutes for assembly, plus 24 hours for freezing and thawing the tofu (optional)

**GRILLING TIME** 6 to 10 minutes

I have a confession to make. Your grill guy—author of such staunchly carnivorous titles as *The Brisket Chronicles* and *Best Ribs Ever*—likes tofu. A lot. Enough to grill it at home once a week. And here's a trick that has revolutionized grilling tofu for me: Freeze it first, then squeeze out all the liquid. This gives you a firmer, drier texture than you get with fresh tofu (added advantage: You can always keep some on hand in your freezer). But if you don't have time for freezing, fresh tofu grills up great, too.

## INGREDIENTS

1 block (12 to 16 ounces) extra firm tofu, drained

2 tablespoons extra virgin olive or melted butter (or Ember Oil, page 300); plus 2 tablespoons for the onions and buns

2 tablespoons of your favorite barbecue rub (see page 301 or use a commercial rub, like my Project Smoke Carolina Pit Powder)

Vegetable oil for oiling the plancha

1 small sweet onion or spring onion, cut crosswise into ½-inch-thick slices

4 thin slices cheddar or provolone cheese or vegan cheese such as Chao or Daiya, trimmed to fit the sliced tofu

4 brioche buns or whole wheat hamburger rolls

### FOR THE TOPPINGS

4 to 6 tablespoons Sriracha Mayonnaise (see Note), or other favorite condiment, such as barbecue sauce or sriracha (optional)

4 lettuce leaves

1 luscious red ripe tomato, thinly sliced

8 sweet pickle slices

**GRILL/GEAR** Can be grilled over charcoal, gas, or wood; if using charcoal or gas, you'll also need hardwood chunks or chips (unsoaked), see page 8; and a plancha or cast-iron skillet for searing the tofu (optional).

**WHAT ELSE** Sure, you can grill extra firm tofu directly on the grate. But I prefer using a plancha (see page 7)—you get a better crust and the tofu is less likely to stick or fall apart. To turn your grilled tofu into barbecue, work on a charcoal grill and add wood chunks or chips (unsoaked) to the embers. Another way to add a smoke flavor is to grill the tofu over wood. Yet another, baste the tofu with Ember Oil (page 300).

**1.** Optional—freeze the drained tofu overnight.

**2.** The next day, thaw the tofu at room temperature (this will take 2 to 4 hours) and drain well.

**3.** Cut each tofu block widthwise into ½-inch-thick slices. Firmly press these between the palms of your hands to wring out as much liquid as possible. Or press the slices between 2 cutting boards for about 30 minutes with a 2-inch-tall object under one end of the cutting boards so they slope.

**4.** Blot each tofu slice dry on both sides, using paper towels. Brush all sides with the olive oil and season generously with the barbecue rub.

**5.** Meanwhile, set up your grill for direct grilling and heat to high. Place a plancha on the grill and heat it as well. Brush or scrape the plancha clean. Optional: If enhancing a charcoal fire, add the wood chunks or chips to the coals; if enhancing a gas fire, place the chunks or chips in your grill's smoker box or place chunks under the grate directly over one or more burners.

**6.** Oil the plancha and arrange the tofu pieces and onion slices on it. Close the lid to hold in the smoke. Grill until the tofu is browned and crisp on the bottom and the onions are browned on the bottom, 3 to 5 minutes. Turn the tofu and onions with a thin-bladed spatula. Arrange the cheese on top of the tofu. Continue grilling the tofu and onions until the cheese melts. Just before you take the tofu and onions off the grill, brush the cut sides of the buns with oil or butter and grill them on the plancha or directly on the grill grate until browned, 1 to 2 minutes.

**7.** To assemble the sandwiches, spread a little Sriracha Mayonnaise on the bottom buns. Top each with a lettuce leaf, then the tofu with its melted cheese, some grilled onions, a tomato slice, and pickles. Dollop a tablespoon or so of barbecue sauce on top and a squirt of sriracha if you like. Top with the other grilled bun half. Prepare to eat a grilled tofu sandwich that even an avowed carnivore would get in line for.

**NOTE:** To make Sriracha Mayonnaise, stir together equal parts sriracha and mayo (Hellmann's or Best Foods or vegan).

# GRILLED PIMENTO CHEESE SANDWICH

**YIELD** Serves 2 and can be multiplied as desired

**METHOD** Direct grilling/plancha grilling

**PREP TIME** 10 minutes (plus the time it takes to make the pimento cheese)

**GRILLING TIME** 10 minutes

**GRILL/GEAR** Can be grilled over charcoal, gas, or wood.

Call it comfort food. Call it a culinary oxymoron. For despite the name, the grilled cheese sandwich is almost always cooked in a skillet or on a griddle and almost never on the grill. You're about to change that, harnessing the flavor-enhancing powers of live fire in a sandwich with a gloriously buttery crisp crust and gooey cheesy filling. The former comes from buttered brioche, the latter from the richest gooiest cheese of them all, pimento, here made smoky by the addition of ember-grilled peppers. Did I mention two other essential Southern ingredients? Grilled green tomatoes and pickled peppers. And if you eat meat, take the sandwich over the top with grilled Benton's bacon or country ham. Kudos to Husk restaurant in Nashville for the inspiration.

This sandwich owes its tangy lusciousness to pimento cheese. In the best of all possible worlds, you'd make it from scratch using ember-grilled red bell peppers (see page 51) instead of the usual jarred pimentos. If bacon or ham are in your repertory, try to order them from the legendary Tennessee smokehouse, Benton's. Note: If green tomatoes are unavailable, use ripe red tomatoes, but don't grill them. And for even more flavor, grill these sandwiches over a wood or wood-enhanced fire (see page 8).

## INGREDIENTS

1 large green tomato, cored and cut crosswise into ½-inch slices

3 tablespoons extra virgin olive oil or melted butter

Coarse salt (sea or kosher) and freshly ground black pepper

2 thin slices country-style ham or 2 strips thick-cut bacon (optional)

Vegetable oil for oiling the grill grate

4 slices brioche bread or artisanal white bread

1½ cups pimento cheese, preferably homemade (see page 48), at room temperature

¼ cup pickled peppers (hot or sweet—your choice)

Pimentón (Spanish smoked paprika)

**1.** Set up your grill for direct grilling and heat it to medium-high. Have one zone medium and one zone fire-free as your safety zone.

**2.** Lightly brush the green tomato slices on both sides with the olive oil and season with salt and pepper. Lightly brush the ham (if using) on both sides with oil.

**3.** Brush or scrape your grill grate clean and oil it well. Grill the green tomato slices over the hotter section of the grill until browned and soft, 2 to 3 minutes per side. Grill the ham over the hotter side until browned, 2 to 3 minutes per side. Transfer the tomatoes and ham to a wire rack to cool—the latter will crisp on cooling.

**4.** Lightly brush the brioche slices on one side with olive oil. Place 2 slices, oiled sides down, on your work surface. Spread pimento cheese on top. Arrange the pickled peppers, grilled green tomatoes, and crisp ham (if using) on top of each. Sprinkle with pimentón. Place the remaining brioche slices, oiled sides up, on top.

**5.** Using a spatula, carefully slide the sandwiches onto the grill, running on the diagonal to the bars of the grate. Grill until the bread is browned on the bottom, 1 to 2 minutes. Using the spatula, carefully invert the sandwiches and grill until the other side is browned the same way. The pimento cheese should be melted and gooey. Serve hot off the grill—cut in half for easy eating.

# VEGAN "CHEESESTEAK"
## WITH RUTABAGA WIZ

I promised my publisher that this would not be a vegetarian or vegan cookbook. That I'd keep away from ersatz meat recipes, like faux bacon or un-chicken. Well, you don't get much meatier than a classic Philadelphia cheesesteak. (Never mind that the steak is often a cheap tough cut of industrial beef and that the "cheese" sometimes comes from a tub.) But when I tasted the "cheesesteak" created by Philadelphia vegan super-chef Rich Landau, I had to make an exception. Here was a sandwich that roared with flavor—earthy, luscious, and decidedly meaty—an effect achieved by combining seitan (wheat protein) with umami-rich mushrooms, Montreal steak seasoning, and tamari. The cheese spread was piquant, tangy, and all the more remarkable in that its primary ingredient was rutabaga. It was a great cheesesteak, a benchmark cheesesteak, the sort of cheesesteak worth making a special trip to Philly for—and so much the better that you can serve it to that vegan friend or family member.

**YIELD** Serves 8

**METHOD** Plancha grilling (with smoke added)

**PREP TIME** 20 minutes plus 30 minutes for boiling the rutabaga

**GRILLING TIME** 8 minutes

**GRILL/GEAR** Can be grilled over charcoal, gas, or wood. You'll also need a plancha or large cast-iron skillet and hardwood chunks or chips (unsoaked), see page 8.

### INGREDIENTS

1 pound seitan

1 pound mixed mushrooms (button mushrooms, oyster mushrooms, creminis, and so on), cleaned and trimmed

½ cup vegan or regular Worcestershire sauce

¼ cup safflower or other vegetable oil

2 tablespoons tamari

2 tablespoons Montreal steak seasoning

1 to 2 cloves garlic, peeled and minced

1 tablespoon freshly ground black pepper (or to taste)

1 tablespoon nutritional yeast

1 teaspoon dried crumbled sage

Vegetable oil for oiling the plancha

8 soft hoagie rolls, cut in half through the side

Rutabaga Wiz (recipe follows) or 8 slices American or provolone cheese or vegan cheese, such as Chao or Daiya

**WHAT ELSE** You'll need a few special ingredients, which, if you're not a vegan or vegetarian, may be unfamiliar or downright scary. Seitan is a firm, protein-rich food made from wheat gluten. (It looks a bit like tofu, but denser.) Buy it at Whole Foods or a natural foods store. Nutritional yeast is a deactivated yeast (you can't use it to brew beer or leaven bread) with a nutty, cheesy flavor that makes it popular with vegans and nonvegans alike. Look for it at the same stores that sell seitan. (One popular brand is Bragg.) Traditional Worcestershire sauce contains anchovies, so if you want to play this strictly meatless, use a vegetarian Worcestershire sauce like Annie's or Wizard's. Chef Rich Landau sears his cheesesteak mixture on a griddle. I use a plancha on the grill, adding hardwood to the fire to generate smoke.

**1.** Thinly slice the seitan and mushrooms. Place in a large mixing bowl. Stir in the Worcestershire sauce, oil, tamari, Montreal steak seasoning, garlic, pepper, nutritional yeast, and sage. Marinate the mixture in the refrigerator for at least 2 hours, or as long as overnight—the longer, the richer the flavor.

**2.** Set up your grill for direct grilling and heat to medium-high. Have a plancha on the grate and heat it as well. Scrape it clean and oil it well. Optional (for smoke flavor): If enhancing a charcoal fire, add the wood chunks or chips to the coals; if enhancing a gas fire, place the chunks or chips in your grill's smoker box or place chunks under the grate directly over one or more burners.

**3.** Arrange the seitan-mushroom mixture in a single layer on the plancha. Close the lid to hold in the smoke and cook for about 2 minutes. Uncover the grill and turn the mixture with a spatula. Cover again for about 2 minutes to hold in the smoke. Uncover and continue cooking the mixture until darkly browned, turning with the spatula, 6 to 8 minutes in all.

**4.** Spoon the browned seitan mixture onto the hoagie rolls. Top with the Rutabaga Wiz and dig in.

# RUTABAGA WIZ

**YIELD** Makes about 2½ cups

S o what do you serve on a vegan cheesesteak? An equally vegan "cheese" spread made from rutabaga, with mustard for bite, turmeric for color, and miso and nutritional yeast providing the cheesy funk of cheddar. Note: Rutabaga is a large member of the turnip family with a purplish top, cream-colored bottom, and yellowish flesh with a pungent earthy flavor that may make you think of cheese. Skeptical? I'd rather eat this than the "cheez" that comes in a tub or can.

## INGREDIENTS

1 pound rutabagas, peeled and cut into 1-inch chunks (about 3 cups)

1 clove garlic, peeled and minced

1 cup vegan mayonnaise, such as Nasoya or Earth Balance, or egg mayonnaise, such as Hellmann's or Best Foods

¼ cup white miso

¼ cup nutritional yeast

2 teaspoons Dijon mustard

1 teaspoon sherry vinegar, or to taste

1 teaspoon ground turmeric

1 teaspoon coarse salt (sea or kosher)

1 teaspoon white pepper

**1.** Place the rutabagas and garlic in a large pot with water to cover by 1 inch. Bring the rutabagas to a boil and cook until very tender (they will mash easily with a fork), about 30 minutes, or as needed. Drain the rutabagas in a strainer, collecting the cooking liquid in a bowl positioned beneath it. Reserve this liquid.

**2.** Place the hot rutabagas in a food processor. Add the mayonnaise, miso, nutritional yeast, mustard, vinegar, turmeric, salt, and pepper and puree until smooth, adding enough rutabaga cooking liquid little by little to obtain a spreadable paste. Correct the seasoning, adding vinegar or salt to taste: The mixture should be piquant and highly seasoned. Let the Wiz cool to room temperature, then cover and refrigerate until serving. Store it in a sealed container in the refrigerator; it will keep for at least 3 days.

**NOTE:** This will make more Wiz than you need for the sandwiches. Any excess goes great on grilled bread or potatoes.

# CHAPTER 6

# VEGETABLE SMALL PLATES

This chapter brings us to the heart of the book—grilled vegetables. In particular, to grilled vegetable dishes that are small enough to serve as starters or small plates—or that can be mixed and matched to make a meal. Some take the form of classic Spanish tapas, such as Sunchokes Bravas and Grilled Asparagus Bundles with Cabrales Cheese and Jamón Serrano. Others look to traditional street foods, like grilled corn and Broccolini in the Style of Thai Satay. Some will bolster your kebab repertory, from Armenian Potato Kebabs (they look *really* cool) to sweet-salty Brussels Sprout, Bacon, and Date Kebabs with Honey Sage Butter. Others will give you an entirely new perspective on grilled vegetables, such as Smoke-Roasted Parsnips with Crispy Capers. All serve as a welcome reminder that, while vegetables can be steamed, boiled, sautéed, or fried, they almost always taste best grilled.

# RECIPES

# GRILLED ARTICHOKES
## WITH HARISSA MAYONNAISE

**YIELD** Serves 4

**METHOD** Direct grilling

**PREP TIME** 10 minutes for trimming the artichokes, plus 10 to 15 minutes for boiling them

**GRILLING TIME** 6 to 8 minutes

**GRILL/GEAR** Can be grilled over charcoal, gas, or wood. You'll also need a wire rack set over a rimmed sheet pan and hardwood chunks or chips (unsoaked), see page 8.

**WHAT ELSE** I call for big fleshy artichokes, like the globe variety, but when in season, you can also grill baby artichokes. (Cut them in half lengthwise. There is no need to blanch.) For that matter, on page 214 you'll find instructions for direct grilling your artichokes without blanching. The process takes a bit longer, but the flavor is out of this world.

In traditional meat grilling—think ribs—we're taught never, *ever* to boil. Not so with artichokes, for which blanching (cooking briefly in boiling water) prior to grilling can dramatically improve the texture. Artichokes are intrinsically dense and dry, and blanching softens and moistens their tough plant fibers, making them all the more ready to absorb the smoke flavor that will come from your wood or wood-enhanced fire. Said smoke becomes trapped between the leaves, adding a barbecue flavor you don't normally associate with this edible overgrown thistle. By way of a dip, I suggest a spicy Harissa Mayonnaise, but the Ember Butter (page 301), Salsa Brava (page 292), or Smoked Allioli (page 296) make great alternatives.

## INGREDIENTS

1 lemon

4 artichokes, preferably large globe artichokes

Coarse salt (sea or kosher)

Vegetable oil for oiling the grill grate

½ cup extra virgin olive oil in a small bowl

1 clove garlic, peeled and minced

Freshly ground black pepper

Harissa Mayonnaise (recipe follows) plus 1 tablespoon harissa, for serving

1 tablespoon minced fresh chives (optional)

**1.** Finely grate the lemon zest and set it aside. Cut the lemon in half.

**2.** Using kitchen scissors, cut the prickly tips off the artichoke leaves. Trim ⅛ inch off the end of the artichoke stems. (The rest of the stem is edible.) Using a chef's knife, cut each artichoke in half lengthwise. Cut the top half inch off each artichoke half and discard. Using a melon baller or spoon, scrape out and discard the "choke" (the clump of fibers just above the heart). Rub the cut parts of the artichokes with the cut sides of the lemon to keep the artichokes from browning.

**3.** Bring 1 gallon of water with 4 teaspoons of salt to a boil in a large stockpot.

**4.** Place the artichokes in the boiling water and cook until just tender, 10 to 15 minutes, or as needed. Use a metal skewer to test for doneness: It should pierce the artichoke with just a little resistance. Do not overcook: The artichokes should remain firm. Drain the artichokes in a colander, running cold water over them until they are cool. Position the artichokes cut side down on a wire rack over a rimmed sheet pan and drain well. The artichokes can be cooked ahead to this stage and refrigerated for up to 24 hours.

**5.** Set up your grill for direct grilling and heat to high. If using a charcoal grill, place hardwood chunks or chips on the coals. If using a gas grill, place a few wood chunks in the smoker box or directly over the burners under the grate. If using a wood-burning grill, do nothing more than light it: Don't let the flames die down completely—flames mean smoke and smoke means flavor. Brush or scrape the grill grate clean and oil it well.

**6.** Stir the lemon zest and garlic into the olive oil. Brush the cut sides of the artichokes with the lemon-garlic oil and dab more oil between and over the leaves. Season with salt and pepper. Arrange the artichoke halves, cut sides down, on the grill, running diagonal to the bars of the grate. Grill for about 2 minutes or so, then give each artichoke a quarter turn to lay on a crosshatch of grill marks. Grill until the cut side is darkly browned, about 2 minutes more. Baste the tops of the artichokes with the oil, dabbing it under the leaves.

**7.** When the cut sides are nicely browned, turn the artichokes over and grill the leaf side, again basting with the lemon-garlic oil. The artichokes are ready when sizzling hot and browned on both sides and easy to pierce with a fork, another 2 to 4 minutes, 6 to 8 minutes in all. Transfer the artichokes to a platter or plates, cut sides up. Spoon some of the Harissa Mayonnaise into the hollow part of the artichokes. Spoon a dab of straight harissa in the center and sprinkle with the chives (if using). Serve the remaining Harissa Mayonnaise on the side.

# HARISSA MAYONNAISE

**YIELD** Makes a little more than 1 cup

Harissa is North African hot sauce made with garlic, spices, and roasted hot peppers to give it a richer flavor. Once found solely at specialty markets in the United States, this newly fashionable gullet scorcher is available today at many supermarkets and online. For an interesting variation, use a Southeast Asian chili paste in place of harissa. For an even more interesting dipping sauce, replace the lemon zest and lemon juice with 2 tablespoons minced preserved lemon. The latter is a pickled lemon originally from Morocco. Find it at gourmet stores or online. Two good brands are Mina and Casablanca Market.

## INGREDIENTS

1 cup mayonnaise, preferably Hellmann's or Best Foods

3 tablespoons harissa, or to taste

½ teaspoon freshly and finely grated lemon zest, plus 1 tablespoon fresh lemon juice (or 2 tablespoons minced preserved lemon)

Combine the mayonnaise, harissa, and lemon zest and lemon juice (or preserved lemon) in a mixing bowl and whisk to mix. Refrigerate in a covered container until using. It will keep for at least 3 days.

# GRILLED ASPARAGUS BUNDLES
## WITH CABRALES CHEESE AND JAMÓN SERRANO

**YIELD** Makes 8, enough to serve 4 to 8

**METHOD** Direct grilling

**PREP TIME** 15 minutes

**GRILLING TIME** 6 minutes

**GRILL/GEAR** Can be grilled on charcoal or gas. You'll also need butcher's string.

**WHAT ELSE** When buying asparagus, look for thick stalks. When in season (spring), you can use white asparagus. Jamón Serrano is Spanish cured ham—sweeter than prosciutto—and it comes in different grades. The best is Jabugo, followed by pata negra, but any jamón Serrano will work. (For that matter, bacon would make a pretty tasty variation, too.) Cabrales is a Spanish blue cheese made from cow, sheep, and goat milk and aged in caves, like French Roquefort. Note: For a meatless version, wrap the asparagus in grape leaves instead of ham.

Readers of my books know my enthusiasm for grilled asparagus. I love how the high dry heat of the fire crisps the stalks without softening them (as do boiling and steaming). I love how the fire brings out asparagus's sweetness, while imparting nutty, smoky flavors that weren't there before. Here, asparagus gets the Spanish treatment with tangy Cabrales blue cheese and a crusty wrapping of sweet-salty jamón Serrano.

### INGREDIENTS

24 thick stalks of asparagus (about 1½ pounds)

2 to 3 ounces Cabrales cheese, or Roquefort or Gorgonzola

8 paper-thin slices jamón Serrano (about 6 ounces)

Vegetable oil for oiling the grill grate

Extra virgin olive oil

Freshly ground black pepper

**1.** Break or cut off the tough fibrous ends off the asparagus stalks (you'll be discarding the bottom quarter of the stalk (see page 28). Alternatively, do as the French do, and peel the bottom quarter of the asparagus stalks with a vegetable peeler. Cut the cheese into 8 slender strips, each about 3 × ¼ × ¼ inches.

**2.** Lay a slice of jamón Serrano on your work surface. Arrange 2 asparagus stalks on the bottom of the slice running perpendicular to the long side of the ham. Place a sliver of cheese on top, followed by a third asparagus stalk. Starting at the bottom, tightly roll the asparagus and cheese in the jamón

Serrano and tie it in place with a piece of butcher's string. The idea is to create a neat bundle—viewed from the end, it will look like a pyramid. The bundles can be assembled several hours ahead to this stage. Store covered in the refrigerator.

**3.** Just before serving, set up your grill for direct grilling and heat to medium-high. Brush or scrape the grill grate clean and oil it well.

**4.** Lightly brush the asparagus bundles on all sides with olive oil. Season with pepper. (You likely won't need salt, as the jamón Serrano and cheese are salty already.) Arrange them on the grate, running diagonal to the bars. Grill until the jamòn Serrano is crisp, the asparagus stalks are browned, and the cheese is melted and bubbling, about 2 minutes per side, 6 minutes in all, turning with tongs. Transfer to a platter, snip off the strings, then serve.

# BROCCOLINI IN THE STYLE OF THAI SATAY

Broccolini is one of my favorite vegetables for grilling—especially when it is marinated, grilled, and sauced like Thai satay. The marinade plays the creaminess of coconut milk against the spice of curry and salty funk of fish sauce (a vegetarian could substitute soy sauce for the latter), while grilling lays a smoky crosshatch of grill marks. The sauce is a creamy Thai peanut sauce—here, enlivened with toasted peanuts and crispy shallots for crunch. Maybe you don't like broccolini or broccoli—or think you don't. This will make you a convert.

**YIELD** Serves 2 to 4

**METHOD** Direct grilling

**PREP TIME** About 10 minutes

**GRILLING TIME** 6 to 10 minutes

**GRILL/GEAR** Can be grilled over charcoal, gas, or wood. You'll also need an aluminum foil drip pan or baking dish and a rimmed sheet pan.

**WHAT ELSE** You have two options for curry here: Thai Massaman (Muslim) curry—a yellow paste sold in cans—or Indian/Madras-style curry powder. These and coconut milk are available in the international foods section of most supermarkets. Note: This preparation works well for asparagus, too.

## INGREDIENTS

**FOR THE BROCCOLINI AND SHALLOT OIL**

1 pound broccolini

¼ cup vegetable oil, plus extra for oiling the grate

2 large shallots, peeled and thinly sliced crosswise (½ cup)

**FOR THE PEANUT SAUCE**

2 cloves garlic, peeled and minced

1 tablespoon minced, peeled fresh ginger

½ cup chopped fresh cilantro leaves

2 to 3 tablespoons Thai Massaman (yellow) curry paste or 1 tablespoon curry powder, or to taste

1 cup unsweetened coconut milk (full-fat or low-fat—your choice)

1½ tablespoons Asian fish sauce or soy sauce, or to taste

½ teaspoon freshly and finely grated lime zest

1 tablespoon fresh lime juice, or to taste

1 tablespoon brown sugar, or to taste

Freshly ground black pepper

¼ cup creamy peanut butter

¼ to ½ cup vegetable or chicken stock or water

Coarse salt (sea or kosher)

¼ cup coarsely chopped toasted peanuts

**1.** Trim the ends off the broccolini and arrange in an aluminum foil drip pan or baking dish just large enough to hold it.

**2.** Make the shallot oil: Heat the oil in a saucepan over medium heat. Dip a shallot into the oil; when the temperature is right (350°F on a frying thermometer), bubbles will dance around it. Add the remaining shallots and fry until golden-brown and crisp, 2 to 3 minutes, stirring with a slotted spoon. Work in batches as needed so as not to crowd the pan. Transfer the fried shallots to a plate lined with paper towels to drain. Let the fried shallots cool to room temperature. Pour half the shallot oil into a small heatproof bowl and set it aside for basting the broccolini.

**3.** Make the peanut sauce: Add the garlic, ginger, and half the cilantro to the shallot oil remaining in the saucepan and fry until fragrant and golden, about 2 minutes. Stir in the curry paste and fry for 1 minute. Stir in the coconut milk, fish sauce, lime zest, lime juice, brown sugar, and pepper to taste. Gently simmer the mixture until richly flavored, about 2 minutes, whisking well to blend the ingredients. Whisk in the peanut butter and ¼ cup vegetable stock. Gently simmer the sauce until thick and richly flavored, about 3 minutes, whisking well. It should be thick, but pourable. If too thick, add more stock. Correct the seasoning, adding salt and pepper to taste. Keep the sauce warm while you grill the broccolini.

**4.** Meanwhile, set up your grill for direct grilling and heat to medium-high. Brush or scrape the grill grate clean and oil it well.

**5.** Brush the broccolini on all sides with the reserved shallot oil and season with salt and pepper. Arrange the broccolini on the grate and grill until browned and crisp on the outside and fork tender, 3 to 5 minutes per side, turning often with tongs. Baste the broccolini with shallot oil as it grills.

**6.** To serve, arrange the broccolini on a platter. Spoon the warm peanut sauce over it. Sprinkle the fried shallots, peanuts, and remaining cilantro on top. Yes, it's permissible—even advisable—to eat the broccolini with your fingers.

# BRUSSELS SPROUT, BACON, AND DATE KEBABS
## WITH HONEY SAGE BUTTER

Brussels sprouts. Bacon. Dates. Sage. Four bold-flavored ingredients you might not think of combining in a single dish. Yet the combination works and works big-time. You can cook the brussels sprouts from start to finish on the grill, but I find a quick blanch in boiling water makes them milder and sweeter—a perfect foil for the other ingredients. To round out the flavors and by way of a sauce, I recommend a fried-sage honey butter piqued with fiery Calabrian peppers.

**YIELD** Serves 4

**METHOD** Direct grilling

**PREP TIME** 15 minutes

**GRILLING TIME** 8 to 12 minutes

**GRILL/GEAR** Can be grilled over charcoal, gas, or wood. You'll also need bamboo or metal skewers.

**WHAT ELSE** Brussels sprouts are available pretty much year-round, but they taste sweetest after the first frost—especially baby brussels sprouts, which start turning up in markets in November. You'll want pitted dates for these kebabs—preferably, sweet Medjools. They're easier to slice if you stand them up. And thick-sliced artisanal bacon, like Nueske's. Calabrian peppers, available dried or in paste form, are smoky and fiery; hot red pepper flakes make a reasonable substitute.

## INGREDIENTS

1 pound brussels sprouts

1 bunch fresh sage leaves

8 ounces pitted Medjool dates, cut in half lengthwise

Coarse salt (sea or kosher)

4 to 5 strips thick-cut artisanal bacon, cut crosswise into 1-inch pieces

6 tablespoons unsalted butter

1 clove garlic, peeled and gently flattened with the side of a knife (optional)

½ to 1 teaspoon crumbled Calabrian peppers, Calabrian pepper paste, or hot red pepper flakes

Freshly ground black pepper

Vegetable oil for oiling the grill grate

2 tablespoons honey, or to taste

**1.** Cut any large brussels sprouts in half through the stem ends, trimming off any blemished leaves. If using small brussels sprouts, leave them whole. Press a sage leaf to the cut side of each of the date halves. (Set aside 8 leaves for the flavored butter.)

**2.** Bring 3 quarts of salted water to a rolling boil in a large saucepan.

Add the brussels sprouts and boil for 1 minute. Drain in a colander, rinse with cold water, and drain again. Blot the brussels sprouts dry with paper towels.

**3.** Thread the brussels sprouts onto skewers, alternating with sage-topped date halves and pieces of bacon.

**4.** Melt the butter in a small saucepan. Add the garlic (if using), reserved sage leaves, and Calabrian peppers, and cook over medium-high heat until the butter and sage begin to brown. Do not let them burn. Discard the garlic. Lightly brush the kebabs on all sides with this flavored butter (you will have some left in the pan—save it for basting) and season with salt and pepper.

**5.** Set up your grill for direct grilling and heat to medium-high, leaving a fire-free safety zone. Brush or scrape the grill grate clean and oil it well.

**6.** Arrange the kebabs on the grate. Grill until browned on all sides, the bacon is crisp, and the brussels sprouts are tender, 2 to 3 minutes per side. Baste the kebabs with some of the garlic-sage butter as they cook, 8 to 12 minutes in all. Note: The dripping bacon fat and basting mixture may cause flare-ups. Move the kebabs to the safety zone as needed to dodge them.

**7.** Transfer the kebabs to plates or a platter. Stir the honey into the remaining flavored butter in the saucepan and boil over medium-high heat until syrupy, about 1 minute. Spoon this mixture over the kebabs and dig in.

# GRILLED CARROTS
## WITH CARROT TOP PESTO

**YIELD** Serves 6 to 8

**METHOD** Direct grilling

**PREP TIME** 15 minutes

**GRILLING TIME** 12 to 20 minutes

Perhaps you've eaten at his restaurant, Charcoal Venice. (That's Venice, California, not Italy.) Perhaps you saw him on my *Project Fire* TV show when we profiled grill masters from Los Angeles. Josiah Citrin may be a multi-Michelin-starred chef, but when it comes to live fire, he's pure Prometheus, cooking solely over charcoal-burning grills, kamados, and ovens at the restaurant. So, when a pyromaniacal chef like Citrin chooses for the cover of his handsome book, *Charcoal*, a photo not of a charred steak or smoke-roasted chicken, but grilled carrots, you know this humble root has achieved serious star power. What you may not know is that carrot tops are not only edible, but delicious—especially when pureed with lemon and hazelnuts to make carrot top pesto. Grilling carrots intensifies their flavor and sweetness.

**GRILL/GEAR** Can be grilled over charcoal, gas, or wood. Ideally, you'll be grilling over a wood or wood-enhanced fire. If you're enhancing a charcoal or gas fire, you'll need hardwood chunks or chips (unsoaked), see page 8. Plus, you'll need a wooden toothpick or skewer and a rimmed sheet pan.

**WHAT ELSE** I like to use heirloom carrots of different colors—yellow, purple, and, of course, orange—ideally organic. Obviously, you'll want bunches of carrots with tops so you can save the greens for the pesto. Like all dense vegetables, carrots should be grilled over moderate heat—preferably a wood or wood-enhanced fire. You can make the pesto with any nut: I call for hazelnuts here, but other options include walnuts, pecans, almonds, macadamias, pistachios, and of course, the traditional pine nuts. When possible, choose an oil that matches the nut, but again, any oil will make a great pesto. Sometimes I add a handful of fresh mint or basil to pump up the flavor.

## INGREDIENTS

2 bunches carrots (about 2 pounds), green tops removed and reserved

¼ cup extra virgin olive oil, plus extra for basting

Coarse salt (sea or kosher) and freshly ground black pepper

Vegetable oil for oiling the grill grate

2 cloves garlic, peeled, skewered on a wooden toothpick

¼ cup fresh mint or basil leaves, roughly chopped (optional)

½ cup toasted hazelnuts, walnuts, or pine nuts

½ cup freshly and finely grated Parmigiano-Reggiano cheese, plus extra for sprinkling (optional)

1 teaspoon freshly and finely grated lemon zest

2 tablespoons fresh lemon juice, or to taste

¼ cup hazelnut or walnut oil (or more olive oil)

2 to 4 tablespoons warm water, or as needed

**1.** Scrub the carrots clean, but do not peel, and dry well. Lightly brush with olive oil and season with salt and pepper.

**2.** Set up your grill for direct grilling and heat to medium. Brush or scrape the grill grate clean and oil it well. If enhancing a charcoal fire, add the wood chunks or chips to the coals; if enhancing a gas fire, place the chunks or chips in your grill's smoker box or place chunks under the grate directly over one or more burners. Arrange the carrots and skewered garlic on the grate and grill until browned on all sides and just tender. Turn often so they grill evenly. This will take 3 to 5 minutes for the garlic—when it is done, transfer it to a rimmed sheet pan to cool, then unskewer it and roughly chop. The carrots will take 12 to 20 minutes.

**3.** While the carrots are cooking, make the pesto: Wash the reserved carrot tops well in cold water, shake dry, and discard the coarse stems. Roughly chop the leaves and measure 1 cup packed. (If you don't have enough, add fresh mint or basil.) Place the hazelnuts in a food processor and finely chop. Add the chopped garlic and the carrot tops and mint (if using), and process until finely chopped. Work in the cheese, lemon zest, and lemon juice. Gradually work in the ¼ cup of olive oil and the hazelnut oil. The pesto should be thick but pourable: Add warm water as needed to thin it. Add salt and pepper to taste: The pesto should be highly seasoned.

**4.** Spoon the pesto on a platter or plates and arrange the grilled carrots on top. Alternatively, arrange the carrots on a platter or plates and drizzle some of the pesto over them, serving the remainder in a bowl on the side. I wouldn't say no to a sprinkling of fresh cheese on top.

**NOTE:** This may make more pesto than you need for the carrots. Any leftover goes exceedingly well with other grilled vegetables or pasta. Store in a covered container in the refrigerator—it will keep for at least 3 days.

# VARIATION

## SMOKE-ROASTED CARROTS

Smoke-roasting (in an aluminum foil drip pan with wood smoke) is another great way to cook carrots.

**1.** Set up your grill for indirect grilling and heat to medium-high. Arrange the carrots and garlic in a single layer in a disposable aluminum foil drip pan. Drizzle with olive oil, rolling to coat each carrot and the garlic, and season generously on all sides with salt and pepper.

**2.** Place the carrots in the foil pan on the grill grate away from the heat. If enhancing a charcoal fire, add the wood chunks or chips to the coals; if enhancing a gas fire, place the chunks or chips in your grill's smoker box or place chunks under the grate directly over one or more burners. Close the grill lid. Smoke-roast the carrots until tender, about 30 minutes, turning with tongs a few times so they roast evenly. The garlic will be ready after 15 minutes. Remove it with tongs and use for making the pesto.

**3.** Move the foil pan with the carrots directly over one of the fires and grill until crusty and browned, 3 to 5 minutes, turning with tongs so they cook evenly.

# GRILLED CORN FIVE WAYS

**YIELD** Makes 4 ears and can be multiplied as desired

**METHOD** Direct grilling or ember-grilling

**PREP TIME** 10 minutes

**GRILLING TIME** 8 to 12 minutes

**GRILL/GEAR** Can be grilled over charcoal, gas, or wood. You'll also need butcher's string (optional); a sheet of aluminum foil folded in thirds like a business letter to make a grill shield to protect the husks; a rimmed sheet pan; and insulated gloves or a stiff-bristled brush (for Caveman Corn, page 145).

**WHAT ELSE** It used to be that to experience corn at its peak sweetness, you had to source it locally in August. While this is still best, new corn varieties, such as American Dream (a late-maturing variety) and Kickoff XR (an early-maturing variety), make it possible to enjoy sweet corn almost anywhere almost year-round.

When I was growing up, grilled corn was not on my radar. It wasn't until I started researching *The Barbecue! Bible* that I encountered charcoal-grilled corn basted with chandon beni butter (flavored with a cilantro-like herb called culentro) in Trinidad; corn grilled with coconut milk and fish sauce in Cambodia; and, of course, Mexico's now ubiquitous elote (grilled corn slathered with mayonnaise and dusted with piquant Cotija cheese and chili powder). Well, today, just about everyone grills corn—and with good reason, because there's nothing like the blast furnace heat of live fire to intensify its natural sweetness while imparting an irresistible smoky caramel flavor. Not to mention the leopard skin dappling of yellow and black that makes grilled corn so handsome to look at. And the popcorn-like snap, crackle, pop you hear as the corn grills. I've written about grilled corn a lot over the years, and I keep coming up with new ways of preparing it.

Corn grilled caveman style—right in the husk

# CAVEMAN CORN

Here's the Ur-corn—grilled the most primal way I know: directly on the embers. Unlike the other versions of grilled corn in these pages, you leave the husk and silk on. They serve as your smoking fuel, driving a sweet-scented corn smoke deep between the kernels.

## INGREDIENTS

4 ears of sweet corn, with husk and silk intact (do *not* soak)

4 tablespoons (½ stick) unsalted butter, melted

Coarse salt (sea or kosher) and freshly ground black pepper

**1.** Set up your grill for ember-grilling (caveman grilling). Rake out the coals in an even layer and fan off any loose ash.

**2.** Lay the corn on the coals. Grill until the husks and silk burn off completely and the kernels are dappled yellow and dark brown, about 2 minutes per side, about 8 minutes in all.

**3.** Transfer the corn to a rimmed sheet pan. Wearing insulated gloves or using a stiff-bristled brush, remove all the burnt husk, silk, and any ash.

**4.** Arrange the corn on a platter or plates and brush with the melted butter. Season the corn generously on all sides with salt and pepper. Corn doesn't get better this.

# EMILIA-ROMAGNA "ELOTE" (CORN GRILLED WITH GARLIC, BASIL, AND CHEESE)

Mexicans have been pairing grilled corn with cheese for centuries (see Esquites, on page 70). That set me thinking about what elote would taste like if it had been invented in Italy (and if Italians traditionally grilled corn, period, which they're finally starting to do). Imagine smoky-sweet grilled corn with sizzling garlic butter and fragrant basil. The only decision you need to make is whether to crust the corn with sweet Parmigiano-Reggiano or tangy-sharp sheep's milk Pecorino Romano. Whichever you choose, make sure you use a genuine imported Italian cheese.

## INGREDIENTS

Vegetable oil for oiling the grill grate

4 ears of sweet corn in the husk

4 tablespoons (½ stick) unsalted butter

1 clove garlic, peeled and minced

4 basil leaves, cut into thin slivers

Coarse salt (sea or kosher) and freshly ground black pepper

¾ cup freshly and finely grated Parmigiano-Reggiano or Pecorino Romano cheese

**1.** Set up your grill for direct grilling and heat to high. Brush or scrape the grill grate clean and oil it well.

**2.** Meanwhile, husk the corn: Cut the tapered ends off and strip back the husk as though you were peeling a banana. Strip them all the way back so you expose the entire ear, including the last inch at the bottom. Tie the husks back with butcher's string—the idea is to make a handle for eating the corn. Alternatively, use one or two strips of husk to tie off the handle. Pull off and discard any silk (the fine filaments between the husk and the ear). Skip this step if your corn comes already husked.

**3.** Melt the butter in a small saucepan. Stir in the garlic and basil, and cook over medium-high heat until fragrant, but not brown, about 2 minutes.

**4.** Lightly brush the corn on all sides with the garlic-basil butter and season with salt and pepper. Arrange the ears on the grate, sliding the foil grill shield under the tied-back husks to keep them from burning. Grill the corn until the kernels are darkly browned, rotating the ears every minute or so to ensure the ears cook evenly. You may hear some popcorn-like crackling— cool! Baste the corn with more garlic-basil butter as it grills. Total cooking time will be 8 to 12 minutes.

**5.** Transfer the corn to a platter or plates and brush one final time with the garlic-basil butter. Sprinkle the corn on all sides with the grated cheese and dig in.

# BALTIMORE GRILLED CORN WITH BROWN BUTTER AND OLD BAY SEASONING

This pays homage to the sweet corn from Maryland's Eastern Shore that I grew up with, and a unique seasoning piquant with pepper and fragrant mace that originated in Baltimore: Old Bay.

## INGREDIENTS

4 ears of sweet corn in the husk

4 tablespoons (½ stick) unsalted butter

Vegetable oil for oiling the grill grate

Old Bay seasoning, for sprinkling

1. Husk the corn: Cut the tapered ends off and strip back the husk as though you were peeling a banana. Strip them all the way back so you expose the entire ear, including the last inch at the bottom. Tie the husks back with butcher's string—the idea is to make a handle for eating the corn. Alternatively, use one or two strips of husk to tie off the handle. Pull off and discard any silk (the fine filaments between the husk and the ear). Skip this step if your corn comes already husked.

2. Fill a large bowl halfway with cold water and set it beside the stove. Melt the butter in a small saucepan over medium heat, then cook it until it turns nut brown, stirring with a wooden spoon, 5 to 8 minutes. Immediately take the pan off the heat and place the bottom in the cold water to keep the butter from burning. The French call this *beurre noisette* (hazelnut butter), and with a little imagination, it indeed acquires a nutty flavor.

3. Meanwhile, set up your grill for direct grilling and heat to high. Brush or scrape the grill grate clean and oil it well.

4. Lightly brush the corn with brown butter on all sides and season it with Old Bay seasoning. Arrange the ears on the grate, sliding the foil grill shield under the tied-back husks to keep them from burning. Grill the corn until the kernels are darkly browned, rotating the ears every minute or so to ensure the ears cook evenly. You may hear some popcorn-like crackling—cool! Baste the corn with more brown butter as it grills. Total cooking time will be 8 to 12 minutes.

5. Transfer the corn to a platter or plates and brush one final time with the brown butter. Sprinkle with a little more Old Bay seasoning. I wish someone had thought of grilling corn this way when I was growing up.

# GRILLED CORN
# WITH WASABI BUTTER AND SESAME

Grilled corn turns up at Japanese robatayaki (grill) parlors—especially when sweet Hokkaido corn is in season. Think of this one as corn channeling nigiri sushi.

## INGREDIENTS

Vegetable oil for oiling the grill grate

4 ears of sweet corn in the husk

2 teaspoons wasabi powder

4 tablespoons (½ stick) unsalted butter

2 teaspoons soy sauce

2 tablespoons toasted sesame seeds

1. Set up your grill for direct grilling and heat to high. Brush or scrape the grill grate clean and oil it well.

2. Meanwhile, husk the corn: Cut the tapered ends off and strip back the husk as though you were peeling a banana. Strip them all the way back so you expose the entire ear, including the last inch at the bottom. Tie the husks back with butcher's string—the idea is to make a handle for eating the corn. Alternatively, use one or two strips of husk to tie off the handle. Pull off and discard any silk (the fine filaments between the husk and the ear). Skip this step if your corn comes already husked.

3. Place the wasabi in a small bowl. Add 2 teaspoons of water and stir to a paste. Let it sit for 5 minutes for the wasabi to develop its flavor.

4. Melt the butter in a small saucepan over medium heat. Remove the pan from the heat and stir in the soy sauce and wasabi paste.

5. Lightly brush the corn with the wasabi butter on all sides. Arrange the ears on the grate, sliding the foil grill shield under the tied-back husks to keep them from burning. Grill the corn until the kernels are darkly browned, rotating the ears every minute or so to ensure the ears cook evenly. You may hear some popcorn-like crackling—cool! Baste the corn with more wasabi butter as it grills. Total cooking time will be 8 to 12 minutes.

6. Transfer the corn to a platter or plates and brush one final time with the wasabi butter. Sprinkle the corn on all sides with the sesame seeds and dig in.

# GRILLED CORN
# WITH THAI CURRY AND TOASTED COCONUT

This dish exists more in my imagination than what you'd find at a Thai street food center. I love the electrifying effect the red curry paste has on the sweet smoky corn. Look for canned or jarred Thai curry paste at an Asian market, in the international foods section of your local supermarket, or online.

## INGREDIENTS

Vegetable oil for oiling the grill grate

4 ears of sweet corn in the husk

1 tablespoon Thai red curry paste

½ cup unsweetened coconut milk

½ cup toasted, shredded, unsweetened coconut

**1.** Set up your grill for direct grilling and heat to high. Brush or scrape the grill grate clean and oil it well.

**2.** Meanwhile, husk the corn: Cut the tapered ends off and strip back the husk as though you were peeling a banana. Strip them all the way back so you expose the entire ear, including the last inch at the bottom. Tie the husks back with butcher's string—the idea is to make a handle for eating the corn. Alternatively, use one or two strips of husk to tie off the handle. Pull off and discard any silk (the fine filaments between the husk and the ear). Skip this step if your corn comes husked.

**3.** Place the curry paste and coconut milk in a small saucepan. Gradually bring to a boil over medium heat, whisking to dissolve the curry paste.

**4.** Lightly brush the corn on all sides with the red curry mixture. Arrange the ears on the grate, sliding the foil grill shield under the tied-back husks to keep them from burning. Grill the corn until the kernels are darkly browned, rotating the ears every minute or so to ensure the ears cook evenly. You may hear some popcorn-like crackling—cool! Baste the corn with more of the red curry mixture as it grills. Total cooking time will be 8 to 12 minutes.

**5.** Transfer the corn to a platter or plates and brush one final time with the red curry mixture. Sprinkle the corn on all sides with the toasted coconut and dig in.

# GREEK GRILLED LEEKS
## WITH SHEEP'S MILK CHEESE AND PRUNES

Greece boasts one of the world's oldest grilling traditions; there's even a grilled beef recipe in Homer's *Iliad*. You surely know such Greek grilled classics as souvlaki (shish kebab), paidakia (grilled baby lamb chops), and gyro. You may be less familiar with Greek grilled vegetables. Happily, Diane Kochilas is here to bring us up to speed. The American-born, Athens-based cooking authority hosts a terrific PBS series called *My Greek Table* (produced by Matt Cohen, who directs my *Project Fire* and *Project Smoke* TV shows). Her grilled leeks—adapted from a traditional Macedonian recipe—pairs the smokily charred allium with sweet prunes, salty cheese, and the Greek version of balsamic vinegar. Did I mention freshly grated lemon zest for brightness? There are two schools of thought when it comes to grilling a fibrous vegetable like leeks: The first (the Spanish method; see page 85) is to burn and discard the outer leaves, serving only the meltingly tender center. The second is to steam or boil the leeks long enough to make them tender, then sear them over the fire at the end. Diane uses the second method in her book *My Greek Table*—which inspired the recipe here.

**YIELD** Serves 4 as a starter or side dish

**METHOD** Direct grilling

**PREP TIME** 20 minutes

**GRILLING TIME** 4 to 6 minutes

**GRILL/GEAR** Can be grilled over charcoal, gas, or wood. You'll also need a deep pot and a steamer basket or a steamer and an aluminum foil drip pan or baking dish.

**WHAT ELSE** You'll want a sharp, salty cheese that's firm enough for shaving—Greek kasseri, kefalotyri, or aged mizithra come to mind. Or use a more readily available sheep's milk cheese, like Italian Pecorino Romano.

## INGREDIENTS

4 leeks, each 1 inch in diameter, trimmed and washed (see Note, page 87)

6 tablespoons extra virgin olive oil, preferably Greek

Coarse salt (sea or kosher) and freshly ground black pepper

2 tablespoons balsamic vinegar, preferably Greek

½ teaspoon freshly and finely grated lemon zest

1 tablespoon fresh lemon juice

4 pitted prunes, finely diced

Vegetable oil for oiling the grill grate

5 ounces firm sheep's milk cheese, such as kasseri, kefalotyri, aged mizithra, or Pecorino Romano

**1.** Fill a large pot or steamer with water to a depth of 1 inch and bring to a boil over high heat. Place the leeks in the steamer basket, cover, and steam until just tender, about 10 minutes.

Transfer to an aluminum foil drip pan or baking dish and drizzle with 3 tablespoons of the olive oil. Season generously with salt and pepper. The leeks can be steamed and seasoned up to a day ahead to this stage and refrigerated.

**2.** Meanwhile, combine the remaining 3 tablespoons of olive oil with the balsamic vinegar, lemon zest, and lemon juice in a small bowl and whisk to mix. Whisk in the diced prunes and salt and pepper to taste: The dressing should be highly seasoned. (It can be made several hours ahead and stored at room temperature.)

**3.** When ready to grill, set up your grill for direct grilling and heat to high. Brush or scrape the grill grate clean and oil it well.

**4.** Arrange the steamed leeks on the grate, running on the diagonal to the bars. Grill until browned with dark grill marks on both sides, 2 to 4 minutes per side, turning with tongs.

**5.** Arrange the leeks on a serving platter. Spoon the prune dressing over them. Shave or grate the cheese on top. You can serve the leeks warm or at room temperature.

**NOTE:** For a sharper, tangier dressing, use red wine vinegar instead of balsamic.

# DELICATA SQUASH RINGS
## GRILLED WITH BACON AND MAPLE SYRUP

**YIELD** Serves 4

**METHOD** Direct grilling

**PREP TIME** 10 minutes

**GRILLING TIME** 15 to 20 minutes

**METHOD** Direct grilling or plancha grilling

**GRILL/GEAR** Can be grilled over charcoal, gas, or wood.

Around the second week of October, our local farmers' market explodes with squash. Elongated butternuts. Crenellated acorns. Fire-orange kabochas. Turban squash that look like, well, turbans. And my favorite: delicata. Picture a handsome tan cylinder striated with dark green veins and with rounded ends. But it's the flavor that really grabs me—sweet, creamy, delicate (hence the name), with just a hint of sweet potato. You reinforce that sweetness with maple syrup and sautéed bacon—the latter providing a salty yang to the former's sweet yin. Grilling crisps the delicate edible skin, which contrasts nicely with the soft creamy flesh.

WHAT ELSE This recipe calls for delicata, but you could use other winter squash, such as acorn, dumpling, or kabocha. If you don't eat meat, you could substitute butter for the bacon and bacon fat, and if you don't eat dairy, mix the maple syrup with sesame oil or extra virgin olive oil. There are two ways to cook the squash: by direct grilling over a two-zone fire (moderate heat to cook the squash and high heat to sear in the glaze), or from start to finish on a plancha.

## INGREDIENTS

2 delicata squashes
(about 1½ pounds in all)

2 tablespoons butter

2 strips bacon, cut crosswise into
¼-inch slivers

Coarse salt (sea or kosher) and freshly
ground black pepper

Vegetable oil for oiling the grill grate

3 tablespoons maple syrup
(preferably dark)

**1.** Cut off and discard the rounded ends of the squash. (Take off about ¼ inch.) Cut the squash crosswise into ½-inch-thick rings—no more. Using a knife or spoon, scrape out and discard the stringy pulp and seeds. You can save the latter for roasting—see Note.

**2.** Melt the butter in a small skillet. Add the bacon and fry over medium-high heat until browned and crisp, about 3 minutes. Remove the pan from the heat.

**3.** Brush the squash rings on both sides with the melted butter and bacon fat, leaving the bacon bits in the pan. Season on both sides with salt and pepper.

**4.** Set up your grill for two-zone direct grilling. Heat one zone to medium and one zone to high. Brush or scrape the grill grate clean and oil it well.

**5.** Arrange the squash rings over the medium zone and grill until the squash is lightly browned and soft (test it with a bamboo skewer). This will take 5 to 8 minutes per side. Do not let it burn.

**6.** Meanwhile, stir the maple syrup into the bacon mixture. Brush the liquid part of this mixture over the tops of the squash rings, then invert and transfer to the hot zone. Brush the tops with more maple-bacon mixture. When the bottoms are sizzling and browned, invert the squash and baste the tops with more of the maple-bacon mixture.

**7.** Transfer the squash rings to a platter or plates. Spoon the remaining maple-bacon mixture (including the bacon bits) over the squash and serve at once.

**NOTE:** To roast squash seeds, rinse well, removing any stringy squash, then blot dry. Arrange the seeds in an aluminum foil pan and drizzle with a little olive oil. Season generously with salt and pepper and toss to mix. Set up your grill for indirect grilling and heat to medium-high. Indirect grill the seeds until browned and crisp, about 15 minutes or as needed, stirring from time to time.

# GRILLED FENNEL
## WITH GORGONZOLA

Cross celery with licorice and you get fennel. Cook fennel on the grill and you get a revelation. This anise-scented vegetable has the ability to absorb smoke and fire flavors without losing its satisfying crunch. And nobody grills it better than my Tuscan grill-master friend, Alfio Sapienza. Alfio grills fennel long enough to impart a char flavor, but briefly enough to keep its pristine crunch. He pairs it with Gorgonzola dolce, a creamy blue cheese from Lombardy that adds the perfect salty counterpoint to the sweet fennel. The optional pink peppercorns explode in your mouth with flavor.

### INGREDIENTS

2 medium fennel bulbs

2 tablespoons melted butter, preferably salted, or extra virgin olive oil (preferably Tuscan)

Coarse salt (sea or kosher) and freshly ground black pepper

Vegetable oil for oiling the grill grate

4 ounces Gorgonzola or Gorgonzola dolce cheese, thinly sliced (see What Else)

1 tablespoon minced fresh chives

1 teaspoon whole pink peppercorns (optional)

**1.** Slice the stalks off the fennel bulbs (save for tossing on the coals for a future grill session). Trim a thin slice off the root end and remove any blemished layers from the bulb. Stand the bulb on its root end and, starting at the top (the stalk end), cut the fennel lengthwise into broad ¼-inch-thick slices through the root end. Lightly brush each slice on both sides with the melted butter and season with salt and pepper.

**2.** Meanwhile, set up your grill for direct grilling and heat to medium-high. Brush or scrape the grill grate clean and oil it well. If enhancing a charcoal fire, add the wood chunks or chips to the coals; if enhancing a gas fire, place the chunks or chips in your grill's smoker box or place chunks under the grate directly over one or more burners.

**YIELD** Serves 4

**METHOD** Direct grilling

**PREP TIME** 10 minutes

**GRILLING TIME** 6 to 8 minutes

**GRILL/GEAR** Can be grilled over charcoal, gas, or wood. For even more flavor, grill over a wood or wood-enhanced fire. If you're enhancing a charcoal or wood fire, you'll need hardwood chunks or chips (unsoaked), see page 8.

**WHAT ELSE** Fennel is available in most supermarket produce sections. Look for firm white bulbs. If you're lucky enough to find fennel with the stalks and fronds attached, use the latter for stuffing fish or laying on your charcoal or wood fire to generate fennel-scented smoke. Note: There are two sorts of Gorgonzola—dolce and piccante. The former is soft and sweet, as its name implies; the latter is tangier and more pungent. Either will work.

**3.** Arrange the fennel slices on the grill, running diagonal to the bars of the grate. Grill until the bottoms are browned, giving each a quarter turn halfway through to lay on a crosshatch of grill marks, 3 to 4 minutes. If the fennel browns too slowly, notch up the heat.

**4.** Invert the fennel slices. Place a thin slice of Gorgonzola on each. Close the grill lid to hold in the heat to melt the cheese. Continue grilling until the bottoms are browned and the cheese starts to melt, giving each slice a quarter turn halfway through, another 3 to 4 minutes. Total grilling time will be 6 to 8 minutes.

**5.** Arrange the grilled fennel slices on a platter or plates. Sprinkle with the chives and pink peppercorns (if using). Serve immediately.

# SUNCHOKES BRAVAS
## (JERUSALEM ARTICHOKES WITH SPICY GRILLED TOMATO SAUCE)

Sunchokes (aka Jerusalem artichokes) may be the best-kept vegetable secret on Planet Barbecue. These lumpy tubers have a sweet taste that may remind you of the artichoke, only more earthy. They roast up crisp, like potatoes, and their porous flesh absorbs smoke and fire flavors like a sponge. Here, they get the papas bravas treatment, with a spicy grilled tomato and nut sauce from Catalonia. So where does Jerusalem fit in? Sunchokes are members of the sunflower family, the Italian word for which is *girasole*. From there it was a short aural leap to *Jerusalem*. That's it for today's etymology lesson. Let's eat.

**YIELD** Serves 4

**METHOD** Smoke-roasting (indirect grilling with wood smoke) or indirect grilling followed by direct grilling

**PREP TIME** 5 minutes

**GRILLING TIME** About 45 minutes

**GRILL/GEAR** Can be grilled on charcoal or gas, but you'll get a better smoke flavor on charcoal. You'll also need a stiff-bristle vegetable brush; a disposable aluminum foil drip pan (9 × 13 inches); and hardwood chunks or chips (soaked), see page 8.

## INGREDIENTS

2 pounds sunchokes

4 to 8 cloves garlic, unpeeled (optional—depends on how much you like garlic)

2 tablespoons extra virgin olive oil, preferably Spanish, or more as needed

Coarse salt (sea or kosher) and freshly ground black pepper

2 tablespoons chopped fresh flat-leaf parsley leaves, for serving

Salsa Brava (page 292)

Smoked Allioli (optional; page 296)

**1.** Scrub the sunchokes under cold running water with a stiff-bristle vegetable brush. (There is no need to peel them.) Blot dry with paper towels. Cut any large ones crosswise into quarters or halves so that all the sunchoke pieces are the same size.

**2.** Set up your grill for indirect grilling and heat to medium-high.

**3.** Arrange the sunchokes and garlic (if using) in a single layer in a disposable foil pan. Toss with the olive oil and season generously with salt and pepper.

**4.** Place the sunchokes in the foil pan on the grill grate away from heat. If enhancing a charcoal fire, add the wood chunks or chips to the coals; if enhancing a gas fire, place the chunks or chips in your grill's smoker box or place chunks under the grate directly over one or more burners. Close the grill lid.

**5.** Smoke-roast the sunchokes until browned and almost tender, about 40 minutes. Stir occasionally so they cook evenly.

**6.** Move the pan with the sunchokes directly over the fire and direct grill until the exteriors are darkly browned and crusty, 3 to 5 minutes more, stirring often.

**7.** Arrange the sunchokes in a shallow serving bowl or on plates and sprinkle with the parsley. Spoon the Salsa Brava over them or serve it alongside. If you're feeling really decadent, drizzle Smoked Allioli on top.

# GRILLED OKRA THREE WAYS

Okra, that polarizing finger-shaped pod, a relative of the mallow plant, is beloved in India, Louisiana (where it's an indispensable ingredient in gumbo), and other food cultures, but reviled by a seemingly equal number of partisans elsewhere. So what's the problem? Slime—that's what—because when you stew okra, it becomes slimy (which helps it thicken that gumbo). And anytime you cut okra and expose it to air, the sliminess becomes more pronounced. But what if there was a cooking method that minimized the offending texture? There is, and you guessed it: grilling. The high dry heat of the grill brings out okra's herbaceous flavor while retaining its vegetal crispness. Such is my affection for grilled okra, I won't just give you one way to prepare it.

## GRILLED OKRA WITH FIRE-ROASTED PIMENTO CHEESE

Here's a thoroughly Southern grilled okra with pimento cheese. Of course, I'm partial to homemade pimento cheese and you'll find a grilled version on page 48. In a pinch, use your favorite commercial brand.

### INGREDIENTS

Vegetable oil for oiling the grill grate

1 pound fresh okra (about 20 pods)

1 tablespoon melted butter, extra virgin olive oil, or bacon fat, or as needed

Coarse salt (sea or kosher) and freshly ground black pepper or your favorite barbecue rub

1 cup Fire-Roasted Pimento Cheese (page 48)

2 tablespoons finely chopped chives or scallion greens

**1.** Set up your grill for direct grilling and heat to high. Brush or scrape the grill grate clean and oil it well.

**2.** Meanwhile, lay 4 or 5 okra pods side by side, alternating stem ends and points. Pin them crosswise with 2 bamboo skewers to form rafts. Lightly brush the okra on both sides with the melted butter and season on both sides with salt and pepper.

**YIELD** Serves 4

**METHOD** Direct grilling

**PREP TIME** 15 minutes

**GRILLING TIME** 6 to 8 minutes

**GRILL/GEAR** Can be grilled over charcoal, gas, or wood. You'll also need small bamboo skewers or large wooden toothpicks.

**WHAT ELSE** As for all small slender vegetables (e.g., asparagus and green beans), when grilling okra, I use the Japanese raft technique. You lay 4 or 5 okra pods side by side and pin them crosswise with small skewers or large toothpicks to make a raft. It's a lot easier to grill and turn 5 rafts than 20 individual okra pods. When buying okra, choose pods that are roughly the same size, avoiding jumbo pods, which tend to be fibrous.

**3.** Arrange the okra rafts on the grate. Grill until well browned on both sides, about 3 minutes per side, turning with tongs.

**4.** Transfer the okra to a platter or plates. Place a spoonful of the pimento cheese on each okra raft. (The heat of the okra will partially melt it.) Sprinkle the cheese with chopped chives. Dig in while it's still hot (warn everyone to remove and discard the skewers).

# GRILLED OKRA
# WITH COCONUT CURRY SAUCE

Okra is also popular in Southeast Asia, where it's often paired with coconut milk and curry. You can serve the okra still pinned together in rafts with the sauce spooned over them. Or serve as individual pods, with a bowl or jar of coconut curry sauce for dipping.

## INGREDIENTS

2 tablespoons butter or vegetable oil

1 shallot, peeled and minced

1 tablespoon minced peeled fresh ginger

1 tablespoon curry powder or 2 tablespoons red or yellow Thai curry paste

1 cup unsweetened coconut milk

1 tablespoon Asian fish sauce or soy sauce

½ teaspoon freshly and finely grated lime zest

Coarse salt (sea or kosher) and ground white pepper

A few drops of fresh lime juice

Vegetable oil for oiling the grill grate

1 pound fresh okra (about 20 pods)

3 tablespoons chopped fresh cilantro leaves

3 tablespoons chopped toasted peanuts

**1.** Prepare the coconut curry sauce: Melt the butter in a small saucepan over medium heat. Add the shallot and ginger and cook until just beginning to brown, about 2 minutes, stirring often. Stir in the curry powder and cook until fragrant, about 1 minute more. Stir in the coconut milk, fish sauce, and lime zest and gently simmer until the sauce is richly flavored, about 3 minutes. Add salt and white pepper to taste and a few drops of lime juice for acidity: The sauce should be highly flavored. Set a couple of tablespoons of the sauce aside for basting the okra. Cover the remaining sauce and keep warm.

**2.** Set up your grill for direct grilling and heat to high. Brush or scrape the grill grate clean and oil it well.

**3.** Assemble the okra rafts as described on page 159. Brush both sides with the coconut curry sauce and season with salt and pepper. Arrange the okra rafts on the grate. Grill until well browned on both sides, about 3 minutes per side, turning with tongs. Baste with more sauce as the okra grills.

**4.** Transfer the okra to a platter or plates. Remove and discard the skewers. Spoon the coconut curry sauce over the okra. Sprinkle with the cilantro and peanuts and serve. Alternatively, serve the okra on a platter with a bowl or jar of the sauce for dipping. Dip and eat with your fingers.

# GRILLED OKRA
# WITH SESAME AND SHISO

I learned about grilling okra in rafts and seasoning it with sesame oil in the land of my birth: Japan. It's the simplest way I know to grill many vegetables and it remains one of the best. Note: Shiso (perilla leaf) is a popular Japanese herb that hints at mint and basil, but with an aromatic flavor that's unique. Once available only in Asian markets, it now turns up at a growing number of supermarkets, farmers' markets, and natural foods stores.

## INGREDIENTS

Vegetable oil for oiling the grill grate

1 pound fresh okra (about 20 pods)

1½ tablespoons sesame oil, or as needed

Coarse salt (sea or kosher) and freshly ground black pepper

3 tablespoons white or black sesame seeds

2 shiso or basil leaves, thinly slivered

**1.** Set up your grill for direct grilling and heat to high. Brush or scrape the grill grate clean and oil it well.

**2.** Assemble the okra rafts as described on page 159. Brush on both sides with the sesame oil and season on both sides with salt and pepper. Sprinkle on both sides with the sesame seeds. Arrange the okra rafts on the grate. Grill until well browned on both sides, about 3 minutes per side, turning with tongs.

**3.** Transfer the okra to a platter or plates. Remove and discard the skewers. Sprinkle the okra with shiso leaves and serve.

# SMOKE-ROASTED PARSNIPS
## WITH CRISPY CAPERS

**YIELD** Serves 4

**METHOD** Smoke-roasting (indirect grilling with wood smoke)

**PREP TIME** 10 minutes

**GRILLING TIME** 40 to 60 minutes

**GRILL/GEAR** Can be grilled over charcoal or gas but you'll get better smoke flavor on charcoal. You'll also need a disposable aluminum foil drip pan (9 × 13 inches) and hardwood chunks or chips (soaked), see page 8.

**WHAT ELSE** Parsnips look like white carrots, but there the resemblance ends. They're fatter at one end than carrots, which requires some knifework to make them equal in size. They're also a lot softer and sweeter, calling for salt and crunch (here, in the form of fried capers) to offset some of the sugar. Parsnips are available most of the year, but taste best in fall and winter.

"Fine words butter no parsnips," goes an old saying. But you can transform this sweet root vegetable into something fine indeed. You'll use a two-step process I often call for when grilling dense vegetables: First, indirect grill them in a foil pan to soften them. Then move the pan directly over the fire to crisp and caramelize the exterior. To this, add crispy salty capers and a gentle whiff of wood smoke, and these may be the most interesting parsnips you've ever experienced. Note: For even crispier parsnips, direct grill the parsnips from start to finish in their foil pan. This will take about 10 minutes, but you'll need to stir often with tongs.

## INGREDIENTS

2 pounds parsnips, ends trimmed

2 tablespoons extra virgin olive oil, or more as needed

Coarse salt (sea or kosher) and freshly ground black pepper

3 tablespoons unsalted butter

3 tablespoons drained brined capers

**1.** Peel the parsnips and cut in half crosswise. Cut the thicker end lengthwise into halves or quarters so all the pieces are about the same size.

**2.** Set up your grill for indirect grilling and heat to medium-high.

**3.** Arrange the parsnips in a single layer in a disposable foil pan. Drizzle with the olive oil and season generously with salt and pepper.

**4.** Place the parsnips in the foil pan on the grill grate away from the heat. If enhancing a charcoal fire, add the wood chunks or chips to the coals; if enhancing a gas fire, place the chunks or chips in your grill's smoker box or place chunks under the grate directly over one or more burners. Close the lid to hold in the smoke.

**5.** Smoke-roast the parsnips until barely tender, 30 to 40 minutes, turning with tongs a few times so they roast evenly.

**6.** Uncover the grill and move the foil pan with the parsnips directly over the fire. Grill, uncovered, until the parsnips are browned and crusty, 3 to 5 minutes, again turning with tongs so they cook evenly.

**7.** Meanwhile, fry the capers: Melt the butter in a small saucepan over medium-high heat. Add the capers and fry until crisp, about 3 minutes, stirring with a spoon.

**8.** Transfer the parsnips and their cooking juices to a platter (or serve them right in the foil pan). Spoon the fried capers and butter over them and dig in.

# GRILLED PLANTAINS
## WITH CANE SYRUP AND TURBINADO SUGAR

The plantain may be new to some readers, but it's hard to overestimate its importance as a staple and delicacy worldwide. They are eaten at every degree of ripeness—from hard and green (at which stage it tastes starchy, like a potato) to soft and black (think squishy ripe banana). The plantain you want here goes by the name *pinto* in Spanish, and you want it semi-ripe, with a yellow skin mottled with black—a stage at which it veers toward banana sweetness, while retaining a firmness that can stand up to the high heat of the grill. So if you're not already familiar with it, it's a fruit definitely worth knowing. Especially when brushed with artisanal cane syrup and smokily charred on the grill. To this, add fragrant cinnamon and a sprinkling of turbinado sugar and you'll wonder why you didn't fall in love with plantains sooner. Serve as a starter or side dish. Hell, you could even flambé it with dark rum and serve it topped with ice cream for dessert.

**YIELD** Makes 8 halves, enough to serve 4 to 8

**METHOD** Direct grilling

**PREP TIME** 10 minutes

**GRILLING TIME** 6 to 8 minutes

**GRILL/GEAR** Can be grilled over charcoal, gas, or wood.

## INGREDIENTS

Vegetable oil for oiling the grill grate

4 semi-ripe plantains (with yellow skins mottled with black)

4 tablespoons (½ stick) butter (preferably salted, but unsalted is okay, too)

4 tablespoons dark cane syrup, such as Steen's

½ teaspoon ground cinnamon, plus extra for sprinkling

4 tablespoons turbinado sugar

**1.** Set up your grill for direct grilling and heat the grill to high. Brush or scrape the grate clean and oil it well.

**2.** Trim the ends off the plantains, but do not peel. Slice each in half lengthwise.

**3.** Combine the butter, cane syrup, and cinnamon in a small saucepan and bring to a boil over medium-high heat. Lightly brush the cut sides of the plantains with this mixture.

**4.** Arrange the plantain halves on the grate, cut sides down, and grill until browned, rotating each 90 degrees to lay on a crosshatch of grill marks, about 3 minutes.

**5.** Turn the plantain halves over. Brush them with more syrup and sprinkle with the turbinado sugar. Lower the grill lid and continue grilling until the sugar is crusty and the plantains are soft (test with a toothpick). When cooked, the plantain flesh will have pulled away from the skin. This will take 3 to 5 minutes more.

**6.** Transfer the plantains to a platter or plates and pour any remaining butter and syrup over them. Cut and eat the plantain out of the skin, discarding the latter.

# VARIATION

## GRILLED PLANTAINS WITH CILANTRO, GARLIC, AND SCALLIONS

The plantain is one of those chameleon fruits/veggies that you can serve sweet as you would a side dish (think candied sweet potatoes) or savory (salty) as you would a starch (think roasted potatoes). Here it gets the garlic treatment, with scallions and cilantro to make it aromatic. Choose plantains with yellowish skins and very little black speckling.

### INGREDIENTS

Vegetable oil for oiling the grill grate

8 tablespoons (1 stick) unsalted butter or extra virgin olive oil

2 cloves garlic, peeled and minced

2 scallions, white and green parts trimmed and thinly sliced crosswise

½ cup chopped fresh cilantro leaves

Coarse salt (sea or kosher) and freshly ground black pepper

4 semi-ripe plantains

**1.** Heat the grill to high. Brush or scrape the grill grate clean and oil it well.

**2.** Melt the butter in a small saucepan over medium-high heat. Add the garlic, scallions, and ¼ cup of the cilantro and cook until the garlic is fragrant and just beginning to brown, about 2 minutes, stirring often. Add salt and pepper to taste.

**3.** Cut the plantains in half as described in Step 2 of the main recipe (Grilled Plantains with Cane Syrup and Turbinado Sugar). Brush the cut sides with some of the garlic herb butter.

**4.** Grill the plantains cut sides down, as described in Step 4 (see page 166). Turn and grill cut sides up, basting with more garlic herb butter. Test for doneness as described in Step 5 (see page 166).

**5.** Serve the plantains with any remaining garlic herb butter spooned over them and the remaining ¼ cup chopped cilantro sprinkled on top.

# ARMENIAN POTATO KEBABS

It's an idea so simple, you wonder why you didn't think of it earlier. Start with thick potato slices (think of them as potato chips on steroids). Brush them with mayonnaise (okay, I wouldn't have thought of that), season with vibrant Middle Eastern spices (that would be Aleppo pepper and sumac), and grill them over blazing charcoal. The result: crisp-edged, meltingly tender potatoes infused with fragrant spices and smoky grill flavors.

## INGREDIENTS

2 large baking potatoes, scrubbed (1½ pounds total)

¼ cup mayonnaise, or as needed, preferably Hellmann's or Best Foods

1 tablespoon extra virgin olive oil

2 teaspoons coarse salt (sea or kosher)

2 teaspoons freshly ground black pepper

2 teaspoons sweet or smoked paprika

2 teaspoons Aleppo pepper or hot paprika (or more sweet paprika)

1 teaspoon sumac (optional)

Vegetable oil for oiling the grill grate, if grilling directly on the grate

Finely and freshly grated lemon zest for garnish (optional)

**YIELD** Serves 2 to 4

**METHOD** Direct grilling

**PREP TIME** 10 minutes

**GRILLING TIME** 16 to 20 minutes

**GRILL/GEAR** Charcoal, gas, or wood (Armenians would use charcoal, but I like grilling over wood). You'll also need flat metal or bamboo skewers (ideally, ¼ inch wide) and a rimmed sheet pan.

You want large, firm potatoes for these kebabs, like Idaho bakers. To be strictly authentic, you'd use Aleppo pepper—a spicy hot red pepper originally from Syria—and sumac, a tart powder ground from a purplish dried berry. But don't worry if you can't find them: These grilled potatoes are pretty awesome seasoned with common paprika, salt, and pepper. Note: Armenians traditionally cook their kebabs on a grateless grill called a mangal. This eliminates the slight risk of the potatoes sticking to the bars of the grill grate. Should you wish to replicate the process on a Western grill (you don't need to), place two flat firebricks on the grate, one in front, one in the back, and balance the skewers between them. I grill the kebabs directly on the grate with no harm to the results.

**1.** Cut the potatoes crosswise into slices the thickness of a No. 2 pencil. Carefully skewer them sharply on the diagonal (through the cut sides) on metal skewers. The slices can butt up to one another or just barely overlap. The idea is to maximize the flat surface of the potato slices exposed to the fire.

**2.** Place the mayonnaise and olive oil in a small bowl and whisk to mix. Combine the salt, pepper, paprika, Aleppo pepper, and sumac (if using) in a small bowl and mix with your fingers to make a rub.

**3.** Working over a rimmed sheet pan, brush the potato kebabs on both sides with the mayonnaise mixture, then sprinkle with the rub. You may not need all of it, but it's nice to have extra for seasoning at the end.

**4.** Set up your grill for direct grilling and heat to medium-high. If grilling directly on the grate (see What Else), brush or scrape it clean and oil it well.

**5.** Arrange the potato kebabs on the grate. Grill until browned and tender, 8 to 10 minutes per side, turning several times.

**6.** Transfer the potatoes to a platter or plates and slide the slices off the skewers. (Never eat anything off a hot metal skewer.) You'll never think of potato chips quite the same way.

**NOTE:** Our food stylist Nora Singley likes to grate fresh lemon zest over the potatoes before serving. Just saying.

Skewer the potato slices sharply on the diagonal.

# UMAMI-FLAVOR CLUSTER MUSHROOMS

Mushrooms were put on this earth for grilling, being ready absorbers of butter-based basting sauces and wood smoke. Some cluster mushrooms grow so large, you could serve them as vegetable "roasts." All mushrooms are rich in umami—that complex blend of savory, earthy, meaty flavors associated with an amino acid called glutamate and found in such diverse foods as seafood, ripe tomatoes, and Parmigiano-Reggiano cheese. To reinforce that flavor, you'll baste the grilled mushrooms with my umami butter, a compound butter flavored with soy sauce and nori seaweed. Note: I like to serve one 4-ounce cluster per person.

## INGREDIENTS

1 pound cluster mushrooms
   (four 4-ounce packages)

Vegetable oil for oiling the grill grate

1 large sheet nori seaweed
   (or 4 sheets pre-toasted nori)

6 tablespoons (¾ stick) unsalted
   butter, at room temperature

2 teaspoons soy sauce, or to taste

1 tablespoon toasted sesame seeds
   or 1 teaspoon dark (toasted)
   sesame oil

⅓ cup freshly and finely grated
   Parmigiano-Reggiano (optional)

**1.** Trim the stem ends off the mushrooms, but leave the clusters intact.

**2.** Set up your grill for direct grilling and heat to medium-high. Brush or scrape the grill grate clean and oil it well.

**3.** If using a large sheet of nori, lay it on the grill and toast until crisp, a few seconds per side. Transfer to a wire rack over a rimmed sheet pan to cool.

**4.** Prepare the umami butter: Crumble the nori into a mixing bowl or finely chop it. Stir in the butter, soy sauce, and sesame seeds and beat until creamy.

**5.** Brush the mushroom clusters on all sides with umami butter. Place the mushrooms on the grate and grill until sizzling and browned, turning often with tongs, 6 to 8 minutes per side, or as needed. Baste the mushrooms as they grill and baste one final time with the remaining butter just before serving. Serve hot off the grill. If you like to mix metaphors (or culinary cultures, at least), sprinkle Parmigiano-Reggiano on top.

**YIELD** Serves 4

**METHOD** Direct grilling

**PREP TIME** 10 minutes

**GRILLING TIME** 6 to 8 minutes

**GRILL/GEAR** Can be grilled over charcoal, gas, or wood. You'll also need a wire rack set over a rimmed sheet pan.

**WHAT ELSE** Cluster mushrooms is my term for hen-of-the-woods (*Grifola frondosa*); enokis (*Flammulina velutipes*); beech mushrooms (*Hypsizygus tessellatus*); and other mushrooms that grow in bunches. But any mushroom tastes awesome grilled with this flavor-rich umami butter. (For that matter, so does steak.) One good brand of cluster mushrooms is Hokto Kinoko (sold in convenient 4-ounce packs)—available at Whole Foods and many supermarkets.

# CHAPTER 7
# VEGETABLE NOT-SO-SMALL PLATES

**T**his chapter brings us to the metaphorical "meat" of the matter—grilled dishes that are substantial enough to serve as a main course. A few contain meat, like the soulful Cajun Hobo Packs (studded with andouille sausage) and the Zucchini "Braciole" (lavished with pepperoni and bacon). Most are meat-free, from Romanesco with Romesco Sauce to my take on eggplant parmigiana—here grilled on a fire-charred cedar plank. Some offer twists on familiar favorites: fiery Nashville Hot Cauliflower, for example, and smoke-roasted acorn squash filled with a creamy Parmesan flan. The colorful Grilled Vegetable Paella is hearty enough to serve not only as a main course but as an entire meal. So fire it up: In this chapter good things come in not-so-small packages.

# RECIPES

# ROMANESCO
## WITH ROMESCO SAUCE

**YIELD** Serves 4

**METHOD** Direct grilling

**PREP TIME** 15 minutes

**GRILLING TIME** 6 to 9 minutes

**GRILL/GEAR** Can be grilled over charcoal, gas, or wood. (You'll get the most flavor over a wood fire.) Alternatively, enhance your charcoal or gas fire with hardwood chunks or chips (unsoaked), see page 8.

**WHAT ELSE** Look for romanesco at Whole Foods and other upscale supermarkets and at farmers' markets in season. If unavailable, grill broccoli or cauliflower the same way. This recipe is simple and straightforward, but it does require grilling the sauce ingredients as well as the romanesco, so plan your time accordingly. Or do as I often do: Make the sauce at a previous grill session.

Cross broccoli with cauliflower and you get romanesco. This newly fashionable vegetable—cone-shaped and green (make that chartreuse)—has a compelling flavor and some very interesting mathematics. The taste recalls its progenitors, but with more crunch and a little less brassica funk than either. The latter involves fractals and the Fibonacci sequence. A fractal, in case you're wondering, is a pattern that repeats at micro and macro levels. Huh? That means that if you look closely at the individual florets of a romanesco, they mirror the whole cluster of florets and so on. As for the Fibonacci sequence (named for a medieval Italian mathematician), it's the mathematical formula that describes the spiral form of a nautilus shell, the seeds in a sunflower, and yes, the spiral of florets in a head of romanesco. Which only enhances the pleasure you'll experience when you serve this earthly green vegetable grilled, with the rich Catalan grilled vegetable and roasted nut sauce, romesco. Note: Make the sauce ahead of time so you can concentrate on grilling the romanesco.

## INGREDIENTS

1½ to 2 pounds romanesco (2 to 3 heads)

Coarse salt (sea or kosher)

Vegetable oil for oiling the grill grate

Extra virgin olive oil

Freshly ground black pepper

Ground cumin

Romesco Sauce (recipe follows)

**1.** Trim the leaves off the base of the romanesco and cut the heads from top to bottom into quarters.

**2.** Bring 3 quarts of salted water to a boil in a large pot. Boil the romanesco for 2 minutes, then drain well in a colander, rinse under cold running water to cool, drain again, and blot dry on paper towels.

**3.** Set up your grill for direct grilling and heat to medium-high. Ideally, you'll grill over a wood fire. If enhancing a charcoal fire, add the wood chunks or chips to the coals; if enhancing a gas fire, place the chunks or chips in your grill's smoker box or place chunks under the grate directly over one or more burners. Brush or scrape the grill grate clean and oil it well.

**4.** Lightly brush the romanesco on all sides with olive oil and season generously with salt, pepper, and cumin. Arrange the romanesco on the grate and grill, turning with tongs, until tender and darkly browned all over, 6 to 9 minutes (2 to 3 minutes per side, figuring on 3 sides).

**5.** Spread the Romesco Sauce on plates or a platter. Arrange the grilled romanesco on top and dig in.

# ROMESCO SAUCE

**YIELD** Makes 3 to 4 cups (depending on the size of the tomatoes)

**METHOD** Direct grilling

**PREP TIME** 15 minutes, plus 30 minutes for soaking the peppers

**GRILLING TIME** 15 minutes

**GRILL/GEAR** Can be grilled over charcoal, gas, or wood. You'll also need a toothpick and a food processor.

**WHAT ELSE** Marconas are those round, fried almonds from Spain with a sweeter, more buttery flavor than that of California almonds. (The latter work in a pinch.) Chiles añoras (sometimes written *ñoras*) are dark, round, aromatic, but only mildly spicy dried peppers from Spain. Ancho or pasilla peppers make good substitutes.

You could call romesco the lifeblood of Catalonia—the essential sauce for calçots (the region's iconic grilled green onions; see page 85) and many other grilled vegetables. It's a sauce that's not only served with grilled foods of all sorts but whose ingredients themselves are grilled for extra flavor. Some versions are thick, like pesto, others thin, like salad dressing, but all ping-pong the sweet smoky flavors of fire-charred peppers, onions, and garlic off tart sherry vinegar and smoky dried chiles. Another distinctive feature is the texture—almonds and optional toasted bread (the latter used as a thickener) make this a sauce you bite into as well as savor. I serve the sauce here with romanesco, but it also goes great with grilled leeks, asparagus, artichokes, broccoli—actually, it's hard to imagine a grilled vegetable that doesn't shine in its presence.

## INGREDIENTS

3 añora peppers or 1 ancho or pasilla pepper

Vegetable oil for oiling the grill grate

4 medium ripe red tomatoes

2 red bell peppers

1 medium onion, peeled and quartered on a wooden toothpick

4 cloves garlic, peeled and skewered on a wooden toothpick

½ cup Marcona almonds or toasted almonds

2 teaspoons pimentón (Spanish smoked paprika) or sweet paprika

½ cup extra virgin olive oil, or as needed

2 tablespoons sherry vinegar, preferably Spanish, or rice vinegar, or to taste

Coarse salt (sea or kosher) and freshly ground black pepper

1. Place the dried añoras in a small bowl and add warm water to cover. Soak until soft, about 30 minutes, turning a couple times so they soften evenly. Drain the añoras, reserving the soaking liquid. Tear open and discard the stems and seeds. Tear the añoras into 1-inch pieces.

2. Meanwhile, set up your grill for direct grilling and heat to high. Brush or scrape the grill grate clean and oil it well.

3. Arrange the tomatoes, bell peppers, and onion on the grill grate and grill, turning with tongs, until charred all over, 2 to 3 minutes per side, 6 to 9 minutes in all. Grill the garlic until browned, 1 to 2 minutes per side. (Note: If the garlic cloves start to burn, slide a sheet of aluminum foil under them.) Remove the vegetables from the grill as they're done and transfer to a cutting board to cool.

4. Scrape the burnt skins off the peppers, tomatoes, and onion. (It's okay to leave a few black bits—they'll add color and flavor.) Stem and seed the peppers. Cut the stem ends out of the tomatoes and the root end off the onion and discard. Unskewer the garlic. Cut the vegetables into 1-inch pieces.

5. Place the almonds in a food processor and grind to a fine powder, running the machine in short bursts. Add the grilled vegetables, pimentón, and drained añoras and puree to a smooth paste. Gradually work in the olive oil, sherry vinegar, and enough of the reserved añora soaking liquid to obtain a thick but pourable sauce. Add salt, pepper, and additional vinegar to taste: The sauce should be highly seasoned.

6. Spoon the romesco sauce onto a platter or plates and serve the grilled romanesco on top of it. (Or spoon the sauce over the romanesco, serving any excess in a bowl on the side.) In the unlikely event you have any leftovers, store in a covered container in the refrigerator: The sauce will keep for at least 3 days.

# ROTISSERIE BRUSSELS SPROUTS
## WITH TURMERIC OIL AND CURRY LEAVES

**YIELD** Serves 8

**METHOD** Rotisserie grilling (spit-roasting)

**PREP TIME** 5 minutes

**COOKING TIME** 40 to 60 minutes

**GRILL/GEAR** Can be grilled over charcoal or gas using a rotisserie. You'll also need bare (uncoated) wire, a pastry brush; an aluminum foil drip pan; and hardwood chunks or chips (soaked), see page 8.

**WHAT ELSE** Your chief challenge will be affixing the brussels sprout stalk to the rotisserie spit. You won't be able to pierce the stalk, so you'll have to run the spit up between the sprouts, parallel and as close as possible to the stalk. Secure the ends with the rotisserie prongs. Then secure the center section with wire.

Just before Thanksgiving, whole stalks of brussels sprouts start, er, sprouting in the produce section of the supermarket. Picture a vertical stalk 20 inches long and the width of a broomstick, populated with green spheres the size of walnuts—brussels sprouts. (So *that's* how they grow!) The ensemble looks a little like the grapeshot fired from Civil War cannons. Are you thinking what I am? How cool would it be to cook a whole brussels sprouts stalk on a rotisserie? The fire would roast the individual sprouts to a crisp golden brown, while the gentle rotation would help them cook evenly. A couple of hardwood chunks or handful of chips added to the fire would bronze the sprouts with wood smoke. To counterpoint the cabbage-y funk of the sprouts, you'd baste them with golden turmeric oil. Extra points if you can find fresh curry leaves, which come from a subtropical tree native to India. The leaves have a tart, aromatic flavor (they're available at my local farmers' market); alternatively, use cilantro or mint.

## INGREDIENTS

1 brussels sprout stalk (about 20 inches long, 5 inches wide, and 3 to 5 pounds—it will hold 50 to 60 individual sprouts)

6 tablespoons extra virgin olive oil or vegetable oil

6 tablespoons unsalted butter

A 2-inch piece of fresh turmeric, scrubbed and finely grated, or 1 tablespoon turmeric powder

2 scallions, trimmed and thinly sliced crosswise

8 stemmed curry leaves or 3 tablespoons coarsely chopped fresh cilantro or mint

Coarse salt (sea or kosher) and freshly ground black pepper

**1.** Trim any blemished leaves off the brussels sprouts. Rinse the stalk under cold running water and drain. Run the rotisserie spit alongside the stalk between the individual sprouts, as close to the stalk as possible. (You may have to remove a few sprouts to accommodate the spit.) Secure the ends with the rotisserie prongs (remember to place the first prong on the spit before skewering the sprouts). Twist wire around the prongs and ends of the stalk to hold the sprouts in place as the spit turns. Wrap wire around the middle of the stalk to secure it to the spit. Breathe a sigh of relief: The hard part is over.

**2.** Make the turmeric oil: Heat the oil and butter in a medium saucepan over medium-high heat. When it sizzles, add the turmeric, scallions, and curry leaves. Fry the leaves until fragrant and crisp, about 4 minutes. Lay the brussels sprouts on their spit on a rimmed sheet pan or cutting board and brush on all sides with the turmeric mixture and season generously with salt and pepper.

**3.** Set up your grill for spit-roasting and heat to medium-high.

**4.** Place the spit with brussels sprouts on the grill with a foil drip pan beneath it. (This will capture any sprouts that fall off.) If enhancing a charcoal fire, add the wood chunks or chips to the coals; if enhancing a gas fire, place the chunks or chips in your grill's smoker box or place chunks under the grate directly over one or more burners. Lower the lid and spit-roast the brussels sprouts until handsomely browned and tender (they should be easy to pierce with a metal skewer), about 40 minutes or as needed, basting every 10 minutes or so with turmeric oil.

**5.** Transfer the brussels sprouts to a large platter and remove the spit. Using a large knife and fork, carve the individual sprouts off the stalk. Spoon any remaining turmeric oil over them and serve.

# GAUCHO BREAKFAST
## (GRILLED PORTOBELLOS WITH EGGS, CRISPY HAM, AND GOLDEN RAISIN CHIMICHURRI)

I'm not sure this robust breakfast has ever been served round a gauchos' campfire in the Argentine pampas. But this big-flavored mash-up of chimichurri-marinated grilled portobello mushrooms topped with fried eggs and crispy grilled country ham channels your inner cowboy any time of the day. Note the addition of sultanas (golden raisins) to chimichurri—an unexpected sweet note in Argentina's classic garlicky, vinegary parsley sauce for steak.

**YIELD** Serves 4

**METHOD** Direct grilling

**PREP TIME** 15 minutes, plus 15 minutes for marinating the portobellos

**GRILLING TIME** 15 minutes

## INGREDIENTS

### FOR THE CHIMICHURRI

¼ cup golden raisins

1 cup boiling water

About 1 cup extra virgin olive oil

1 bunch flat-leaf parsley, washed, shaken dry, and stemmed

¼ cup fresh oregano or cilantro leaves

3 cloves garlic, peeled and minced

3 tablespoons sherry vinegar, plus extra to taste

2 tablespoons fresh lemon juice

½ teaspoon hot red pepper flakes

Coarse salt (sea or kosher) and freshly ground black pepper

### FOR THE MUSHROOMS

4 large portobello mushrooms

4 ounces thinly sliced jamón Serrano or prosciutto

Extra virgin olive oil for brushing the jamón

Vegetable oil for oiling the grill grate

4 large eggs (preferably organic)

Your Basic Grilled Bread, slices or sticks, for serving (optional—page 98)

**GRILL/GEAR** Can be grilled over gas or charcoal, but for maximum flavor, grill over a wood or wood-enhanced fire. If you're enhancing a charcoal or gas fire, you'll need hardwood chunks or chips (unsoaked), see page 8. You'll also need an aluminum foil drip pan or baking dish.

**WHAT ELSE** You can certainly fry the eggs in a skillet. You probably will. But for maximum campfire cred, grill-fry the eggs in an egg spoon as described on page 242. If you don't eat meat, replace the grilled jamón Serrano with the Shiitakes Channeling Bacon, page 26. Or omit it entirely.

**1.** Make the chimichurri: Place the raisins in a heatproof bowl. Pour the boiling water over them and stir in 2 tablespoons of olive oil. Let the raisins soak until plump and soft, about 15 minutes.

**2.** Finely chop the parsley, oregano, and garlic in a food processor. Gradually work in ¾ cup olive oil, 3 tablespoons sherry vinegar, the lemon juice, and hot red pepper flakes. Drain the raisins well and add them to the chimichurri. Pulse the processor a few times to mix, but leave the raisins mostly whole. Add salt and pepper to taste and additional sherry vinegar as needed: The chimichurri should be highly seasoned.

**3.** Stem the portobellos and wipe the caps clean with a damp paper towel. Spoon 4 little mounds of chimichurri

in the bottom of an aluminum foil pan or baking dish. Place the portobello caps on top, rounded side down. Spoon a little more chimichurri onto each portobello, spreading it around with a spoon. (Save the rest for serving.) Let the portobellos marinate at room temperature for 15 minutes.

**4.** Lightly brush the jamón Serrano on both sides with olive oil.

**5.** Meanwhile, set up your grill for direct grilling and heat to medium-high. If enhancing a charcoal fire, add the wood chunks or chips to the coals; if enhancing a gas fire, place the chunks or chips in your grill's smoker box or place chunks under the grate directly over one or more burners. Brush or scrape the grill grate clean and oil it well.

Frying an egg in an egg spoon over a wood fire

**6.** Arrange the jamón Serrano slices on the grate and grill, turning once, until sizzling and lightly browned, 1 to 2 minutes per side. Transfer the jamón Serrano to a wire rack to cool: It will crisp as it cools.

**7.** Lift the portobellos from the marinade and grill them, gill sides down first, then rounded sides down, until sizzling, tender, and a little crisp at the edges, 2 to 4 minutes per side. Move to the edge of your grill and keep warm.

**8.** Place a heavy 10-inch skillet on the grate or your grill's side burner and heat it well (sprinkle in a few drops of water to test it; they should evaporate in 1 to 2 seconds). Add olive oil to a depth of ⅛ inch and heat until hot and shimmering. Add the eggs and fry until crisp at the edges and golden, 2 to 3 minutes. (If you like your eggs over easy, turn them after about 2 minutes.)

**9.** To serve, place the portobellos on plates or a platter, rounded side down. Slide an egg onto each grilled portobello. Spoon some chimichurri over the eggs and crumble the jamón Serrano on top. Serve with Your Basic Grilled Bread, if desired, for mopping up the eggs, and the remaining chimichurri on the side.

# CAJUN HOBO PACKS

**YIELD** Makes 4

**METHOD** Ember-grilling (caveman grilling) or direct grilling

**PREP TIME** 15 minutes

**GRILLING TIME** 8 to 10 minutes

**GRILL/GEAR** Can be grilled on charcoal, gas, or wood. You'll also need four 18 × 24-inch sheets of heavy-duty aluminum foil and a bamboo skewer (to test for doneness).

Once a staple of the traditional Scout cookout, the hobo pack is back—newly embraced by pedigreed pit masters like Pat Martin of Martin's Bar-B-Que Joint in Nashville. When Martin does a cookout, he goes all in, with fire pits, asado crosses, hanging chickens, hog rotisseries, and so on. Veggies (like okra, onions, peppers, and cherry tomatoes) get tucked into oversize foil envelopes to be roasted caveman-style—directly on the embers. This overcomes the one drawback of the traditional hobo pack—the tendency for the veggies to steam rather than roast. If you grill on charcoal or in a campfire, cook the hobo packs right on the coals. If using a gas grill, fire it up as hot as possible. For a refresher on building a campfire, see page 12.

## INGREDIENTS

6 tablespoons unsalted butter, at room temperature, or extra virgin olive oil

1 large sweet onion, peeled and cut crosswise into ¼-inch-thick slices

1 large red bell pepper, stemmed, seeded, and cut crosswise into ¼-inch-thick slices

1 large poblano pepper, stemmed, seeded, and cut crosswise into ¼-inch-thick slices

1 pound fresh okra (about 20 pods), trimmed

1 zucchini, cut crosswise into ¼-inch-thick slices

1 pint cherry tomatoes, halved

1 pound andouille or kielbasa sausage, thinly sliced crosswise, or tasso or other ham (optional)

Your favorite Creole or Cajun seasoning, such as Tony Chachere's

4 large sprigs fresh basil

4 sprigs fresh thyme or other herbs

**WHAT ELSE** You'll want heavy-duty aluminum foil for your hobo packs—the sort that comes in 18-inch-wide rolls. The filling of these packs is limited only by your imagination. I've used Cajun vegetables and seasonings for these, but any combination of veggies and herbs is fair game. Likewise, I've made meatless versions, but a few slices of tasso (Cajun ham) or andouille sausage would endear these hobo packs to carnivores. Your call.

**1.** Lay an 18 × 24-inch sheet of aluminum foil on your work surface, narrow side toward you. Smear a little butter in the center of the bottom half, leaving a 2-inch bare edge of foil. Mound the buttered section with a quarter of the sliced onions, peppers, okra, zucchini, cherry tomatoes, and andouille (if using). Season generously with Creole or Cajun seasoning and top with sprigs of basil and thyme. Smear the top half of the foil with more butter. Fold the top half over the bottom half and pleat/fold over each edge three times to make a hermetic seal. Repeat with the remaining ingredients and foil; you will have four packets.

**2.** Set up a charcoal grill for ember-grilling (caveman grilling). When the coals glow red, rake them out in an even layer and fan off any loose ash. Alternatively, build a campfire and let a portion of it burn down to embers. Or set up a gas grill for direct grilling and heat to high.

**3.** Lay the hobo packs on the coals (or on the grate of your gas grill). Grill until the foil is blackened and the vegetables are tender, 4 to 5 minutes per side, or as needed, turning with tongs. (Take care not to tear the foil.) To test for doneness, insert a bamboo skewer through the top of the foil packet—when you can pierce the okra and onions easily, the veggies are done.

**4.** Serve the hobo packs on large plates. Use a fork to open the packs and stay clear: The escaping steam is hot!

# MECHOUI CAULIFLOWER
## WITH MOROCCAN SPICES AND CHERMOULA

**YIELD** Serves 4 as a side dish or starter; 2 as an entrée

**METHOD** Spit-roasting/indirect grilling

**PREP TIME** 15 minutes

**GRILLING TIME** 1 to 1½ hours

**GRILL/GEAR** Charcoal, gas, or wood-burning rotisserie, or charcoal or gas grill.

**WHAT ELSE** Spit-roasting cauliflower this way gives it what I call a knife-and-fork consistency—firm enough to cut with silverware. I like my vegetables with some chew to them, but if you don't, you can blanch the cauliflower in lightly salted boiling water for 5 minutes before spit-roasting it. In this case, the rotisserie time will be more like 30 to 40 minutes. Note: If you don't have a rotisserie, use indirect grilling instead.

Talk about a success story. Ten years ago, cauliflower knocked around as a pallid side dish—unassuming and underappreciated. Today it turns up at trendy restaurants where it commands top dollar (I recently paid $19 for a single cauliflower!). Even more important, it has grabbed the attention of serious chefs. I believe that three things account for cauliflower's newfound fashionability. First, its shape and size: It's as close as a vegetable comes to a roast (think of it as the plant equivalent of a pork shoulder). Then, its texture—firm enough to hold up to spit-roasting and indirect grilling, the way few vegetables do. Finally, there's the taste—earthy, funky—quite different from broccoli or cabbage, but with enough family resemblance to let you know it's a brassica. Qualities that make it perfect for the mechoui treatment, which is traditionally reserved for lamb. Mechoui, of course, is Moroccan barbecue—whole lambs roasted on spits in underground fire pits or over a campfire. In this meat-free version, we flavor the cauliflower with traditional Moroccan spices and serve it with a spicy tomato vinaigrette called chermoula.

## INGREDIENTS

### FOR THE CAULIFLOWER AND RUB

1 large cauliflower, preferably organic

1 tablespoon coarse salt (sea or kosher)

1 tablespoon freshly ground black pepper

2 teaspoons ground turmeric

2 teaspoons ground cumin

2 teaspoons smoked paprika (such as Spanish pimentón) or sweet paprika

½ teaspoon cinnamon

½ cup extra virgin olive oil

### FOR THE CHERMOULA

1 clove garlic, peeled and minced

2 large luscious ripe red tomatoes

3 tablespoons finely chopped fresh cilantro or flat-leaf parsley leaves

½ teaspoon freshly and finely grated lemon zest

2 tablespoons fresh lemon juice, or to taste

½ cup extra virgin olive oil

Coarse salt (sea or kosher) and freshly ground black pepper to taste

**1.** Set up your grill for spit-roasting and heat to medium-high.

**2.** Pull any green leaves off the cauliflower. Trim the stem flush with the head. Thread the cauliflower onto the rotisserie spit (the spit should go from top to bottom through the stem). Note: It helps to make a starter hole through the cauliflower with a slender metal skewer. Secure the cauliflower on the spit with the rotisserie prongs.

**3. Make the rub:** Combine the salt, pepper, turmeric, cumin, paprika, and cinnamon in a small bowl and mix with a fork or your fingers. Set 2 teaspoons aside for the sauce. Stir the olive oil into the remaining rub. Brush the cauliflower with this spiced oil to coat all over.

**4.** Place the cauliflower on its spit on the grill and spit-roast until darkly browned on the outside and tender inside, 1 to 1½ hours. (Sorry for the wide range: Every cauliflower and grill cooks differently.) Baste it every 15 minutes with the spiced oil.

**5. Meanwhile, make the chermoula:** Place the garlic in a mixing bowl with 1 teaspoon of the reserved rub. Mash to a paste with the back of a wooden spoon. Cut the tomatoes in half crosswise and grate them, seeds and all, on the coarse side of a box grater into the garlic mixture. Discard the spent tomato skins. Stir in the remaining rub, cilantro, lemon zest, and lemon juice. Whisk in the olive oil in a thin stream. Correct the seasoning, adding salt and pepper if necessary (the rub contains salt and pepper, so you may not need them). Right at the end, whisk in any unused basting mixture.

**6.** When the cauliflower is cooked (it should pierce easily with a metal skewer), carefully remove it from the spit and place on a platter, stem side down. Cut it into slices, wedges, or florets and serve it with the chermoula spooned on top.

Rotisserie cauliflower—it's so tasty, you might want to cook two.

# NASHVILLE HOT CAULIFLOWER

Nashville hot chicken is one of America's iconic regional dishes (see What Else). While the notion of transforming it into cauliflower might seem heretical to some Tennesseans, cauliflower is roughly the size and shape of a chicken—perfect for smoke-roasting—and the scorching paste of cayenne and garlic goes uncannily well with its earthy funk. Besides, why should chicken have all the fun? Warning: There is a serious amount of cayenne pepper in this recipe. I give you a range, but even at the lower end, it's hot. Dial it up or down to suit your taste.

## INGREDIENTS

1 large cauliflower, preferably organic

**FOR THE MARINADE (OPTIONAL)**

2 cups buttermilk

2 tablespoons cayenne pepper, or to taste

1 tablespoon sweet paprika

2 teaspoons garlic powder

2 teaspoons onion powder

2 teaspoons coarse salt (sea or kosher)

2 teaspoons freshly ground black pepper

2 tablespoons vegetable oil , plus extra for oiling the grill grate

**FOR THE BASTE**

2 tablespoons cayenne pepper, or to taste

2 teaspoons brown sugar (light or dark—your choice)

1 teaspoon sweet paprika

1 teaspoon garlic powder

1 teaspoon onion powder

1 teaspoon coarse salt (sea or kosher)

1 teaspoon freshly ground black pepper

½ cup extra virgin olive oil or vegetable oil

2 tablespoons unsalted butter, melted (or more olive oil)

**YIELD** Serves 2 to 4

**METHOD** Smoke-roasting (indirect grilling with wood smoke)

**PREP TIME** 10 minutes, plus 4 to 12 hours for marinating the cauliflower

**GRILLING TIME** 1 to 1½ hours

**GRILL/GEAR** Can be grilled over charcoal or gas. You'll also need an aluminum foil drip pan and hardwood chunks or chips (soaked), see page 8.

**WHAT ELSE** Nashville hot is associated with the popular Prince's Hot Chicken Shack (where I ate perhaps the most painfully incendiary poultry dish of my life). Proprietor André Prince credits its invention with her great uncle, Thorton, who had a reputation as a ladies' man. One morning Thorton returned home after a night out on the town. To punish him, his girlfriend blasted his fried chicken breakfast with massive doses of cayenne pepper. But Mr. Price saw not pain, but opportunity, and turned the fiery fried chicken into a thriving business. The long waiting lines outside the shack attest to his masochism—and his foresight—to this day. Tradition calls for marinating Nashville chicken (here cauliflower) in buttermilk for 12 hours prior to cooking. This certainly adds a layer of flavor, but it also adds a day to the preparation time. I've made it optional. For softer cauliflower, parboil it in lightly salted water for 5 minutes before grilling.

**1.** Pull any green leaves off the cauliflower and trim the bottom ⅛ inch off the stem.

**2.** If using the marinade, prick the cauliflower all over with a fork or metal skewer (this fosters the absorption of the marinade) and place the cauliflower in a jumbo resealable plastic bag or deep bowl. Combine the buttermilk, cayenne, paprika, garlic powder, onion powder, salt, pepper, and oil in a mixing bowl and whisk to mix. Pour the marinade into the bag over the cauliflower. Seal the bag and marinate the cauliflower for at least 4 hours, preferably overnight, in the refrigerator, turning it a few times so it marinates evenly.

**3.** Set up your grill for indirect grilling and heat to medium-high. Brush or scrape the grill grate clean and oil it well.

**4. Meanwhile, make the baste:** Place the cayenne, sugar, paprika, garlic powder, onion powder, salt, and pepper in a small bowl and whisk to mix. Whisk in the olive oil and melted butter. The baste should be thick, but pourable.

**5.** If you marinated the cauliflower, drain it well. Place the cauliflower on the grill grate over the drip pan away from the heat. If enhancing a charcoal fire, add the wood chunks or chips to the coals; if enhancing a gas fire, place the chunks or chips in your grill's smoker box or place chunks under the grate directly over one or more burners.

**6.** Indirect grill the cauliflower until browned and tender, 1 to 1½ hours, brushing with the baste every 20 minutes. Transfer the cauliflower to a platter and spoon the remaining baste mixture over it. Cut into slices, wedges, or florets for serving.

# CEDAR-PLANKED EGGPLANT PARMIGIANA

**YIELD** Serves 4

**METHOD** Direct grilling/ indirect grilling

**PREP TIME** 15 minutes, plus the time it takes to make the smoked tomato sauce

**GRILLING TIME** 2 to 4 minutes for charring the plank, plus 4 to 6 minutes for the eggplants, plus 10 to 15 minutes for finishing the parmigiana

Raichlen's Rule states that if something tastes great baked, fried, or sautéed, it probably tastes better grilled. Which brings us to a dish I never imagined I'd cook on the grill: eggplant parmigiana. Another rule of mine states that if grilling doesn't measurably improve a dish you might bake, fry, or sauté, you should stick with the traditional method. (Just because you *can* cook virtually everything on the grill, it doesn't mean you should.) Well, grilling benefits eggplant parmigiana in at least four ways. First, you eliminate a lot of the oil and oil-soaked breading. Second, you can introduce an interesting smoke flavor by using the Smoked Tomato Sauce (page 290). Third, there's the charred cedar plank, which adds another layer of flavor and cool factor. Finally, my grilled version is a lot quicker, easier, and less messy to make than traditional eggplant parm, and it tastes cleaner, too.

## INGREDIENTS

1 medium or 2 small eggplants (about 12 ounces in all—you'll need 12 slices)

Extra virgin olive oil for brushing and drizzling

Coarse salt (sea or kosher) and freshly ground black pepper

Dried oregano flakes, preferably Italian

Vegetable oil for oiling the grill grate

12 ounces fresh burrata, sliced (cream reserved), or mozzarella

2 cups Smoked Tomato Sauce or your favorite chunky tomato sauce

½ cup freshly and finely grated Parmigiano-Reggiano cheese

4 basil leaves, thinly slivered (optional)

½ cup dried plain breadcrumbs, preferably homemade, or panko (optional)

**1.** Set up your grill for direct grilling and heat to high. Char the cedar planks on one side, about 2 minutes—long enough for them to darken and smoke, but not so long they catch fire. Set aside and let cool on a heatproof surface.

**2.** Meanwhile, cut the eggplant crosswise into ¼-inch-thick slices. Lightly brush each on both sides with olive oil and season on both sides with salt, pepper, and oregano.

**3.** Brush or scrape the grill grate clean and oil it well.

**4.** Arrange the eggplant slices on the grate. Grill until well browned on both sides and soft in the center, 2 to 3 minutes per side, turning with tongs. Alternatively, you can grill the eggplant on a preheated plancha. Transfer the eggplant slices to a rimmed sheet pan and let cool.

**5.** Assemble the parmigianas: Place a slice of eggplant on each plank (2 slices if using long planks). Top each slice with a slice of burrata (spoon on some of the cream as well), followed by a generous dollop of tomato sauce. Sprinkle with Parmigiano-Reggiano and a tuft of slivered basil (if using). Build the second layer of eggplant, burrata, tomato sauce, Parmigiano-Reggiano, and basil. Crown with a slice of eggplant. If you like a crispy top, sprinkle the top eggplant slice with breadcrumbs and drizzle with olive oil. The eggplant parmigianas can be assembled and refrigerated several hours ahead of time and grilled at the last minute.

**6.** Return the parmigianas on their planks to the grill (but now away from the heat). Indirect grill until the tomato sauce is bubbling, the cheese is melted, and the tops are browned, 10 to 15 minutes. Serve the parmigianas on their planks.

# THE RAICHLEN BAKER
# (ITALIAN SMOKED STUFFED POTATOES)

The baked stuffed potato is as American as, well, pick your metaphor. I came up with this Italian version while taping a grilling show for Italian television. (It's called *Steven Raichlen Grills Italy*, and it aired on the Italian food network, Gambero Rosso.) The premise was simple: Travel around Italy with a TV crew documenting local grill masters and their specialties. Then, repair to a villa in Tuscany to create Raichlen versions of the dishes I experienced on tour. Whence these potatoes, smoke-roasted in the best American tradition, but stuffed with such traditional Italian flavorings as guanciale, basil, and Taleggio cheese. (For a meatless version, omit the pork and use 1 tablespoon melted butter or olive oil to brush the potatoes before baking.) Think the comfort of a baked potato, the soulful succulence of Italian salumi and cheese, and the campfire goodness of wood smoke.

## INGREDIENTS

Vegetable oil for oiling the grill grate

4 large baking potatoes
  (12 to 14 ounces each)

6 ounces smoked or regular guanciale,
  smoked pancetta, or bacon, cut
  crosswise into ¼-inch slivers

Coarse salt (sea or kosher) and
  freshly ground black pepper

5 tablespoons cold butter

2 scallions, trimmed, white and green
  parts thinly sliced crosswise

12 fresh basil leaves, rolled up and
  thinly slivered crosswise

8 ounces cold Taleggio or provolone
  cheese, cut into ½-inch dice

½ cup sour cream or crème fraîche

¼ cup freshly and finely grated
  Parmigiano-Reggiano (optional)

**1.** Set up your grill for indirect grilling and preheat to medium-high. Brush or scrape the grill grate clean and oil it well.

**2.** Scrub the potatoes on all sides with a stiff-bristle vegetable brush. Rinse well and blot dry with paper towels. Prick the potatoes in several places with a fork.

**YIELD** Serves 4

**METHOD** Smoke-roasting (indirect grilling with wood smoke)

**PREP TIME** 15 minutes

**GRILLING TIME** 1½ hours

**GRILL/GEAR** Can be grilled over charcoal or gas. You'll need a stiff-bristle vegetable brush; hardwood chunks or chips (soaked), see page 8; a 10-inch skillet; and an aluminum foil drip pan.

**WHAT ELSE** You'll need to know about a few special Italian ingredients that may be new to your pantry. Guanciale is cured pork jowl (think of it as turbocharged bacon). Look for it at Italian markets (if you look hard enough, you can find smoked guanciale). Alternatively, substitute pancetta (Italian cured pork belly), prosciutto, or American bacon, or leave it out. Taleggio is a semisoft, washed-rind cow's milk cheese named for the Taleggio Valley in Lombardy in northern Italy. Think creamy texture, piquant flavor, with a funky finish. Other good options (although with different flavor profiles) include aged provolone, Pecorino Romano, or cave-aged Gruyère.

**3.** Cook the guanciale: Place it in a cold 10-inch skillet and fry over medium-high heat until browned and crisp, about 3 minutes. Transfer the guanciale pieces to a large mixing bowl. Leave the fat in the skillet.

**4.** Brush the potatoes on all sides with the reserved guanciale fat and season generously with salt and pepper.

**5.** Place the potatoes on the grill over the drip pan away from the heat. If enhancing a charcoal fire, add the wood chunks or chips to the coals; if enhancing a gas fire, place the chunks or chips in your grill's smoker box or place chunks under the grate directly over one or more burners. Close the grill lid. Smoke-roast the potatoes until tender, about 1 hour. To test for doneness, pierce a potato through the top with a slender metal or bamboo skewer. It should pierce easily. Transfer the potatoes to a cutting board.

**6.** Cut each potato in half lengthwise. Using a spoon, scrape out most of the potato flesh, leaving a ¼-inch-thick

layer next to the skin. (Note: It's best to scoop the potatoes when still very warm.) Very roughly chop the scooped potato and place in the mixing bowl with the guanciale.

**7.** Cut 4 tablespoons of the butter into small cubes and add it to the potato. Add the scallions, basil, and cheese, and gently stir to mix. Using a rubber spatula, gently fold in the sour cream and salt and pepper to taste: The mixture should be highly seasoned. Stir as little as possible so as to leave some texture to the potatoes.

**8.** Stuff the potato mixture back into the potato skins, mounding it in the center. Sprinkle each potato with the Parmigiano-Reggiano (if using), and top with a thin slice of butter (from the remaining 1 tablespoon). The potatoes can be prepared up to 24 hours ahead to this stage, covered, and refrigerated.

**9.** Just before serving, reheat the potatoes on your grill (still set up for indirect grilling) until browned and bubbling, 20 to 30 minutes. Serve hot off the grill.

# EMBER-GRILLED SWEET POTATOES
## WITH DUKKAH AND LEMON YOGURT

Grilled sweet potatoes turn up across Planet Barbecue. In Korea, they're eaten out of hand with sesame soy dipping sauce. Spanish uber chef and humanitarian José Andrés tops them with ice cream to make a charred sweet potato sundae for dessert. Appropriately, this dish reaches across continents, featuring an intensely aromatic Egyptian nut and spice blend called dukkah (pronounced doo-kuh) and yogurt flavored with Moroccan preserved lemons. The contrast of textures and flavors is stunning.

**YIELD** Serves 4

**METHOD** Ember-grilling (caveman grilling), direct grilling, or indirect grilling

**PREP TIME** 15 minutes

**GRILLING TIME** 20 to 60 minutes (depending on the method)

**GRILL/GEAR** If ember-grilling (caveman grilling), use a charcoal grill; you'll also need an aluminum foil drip pan. If indirect grilling, you can use charcoal or gas. If direct grilling, you can grill over charcoal, gas, or wood. If enhancing a charcoal or gas fire, you'll also need hardwood chunks or chips (soaked), see page 8.

## INGREDIENTS

### FOR THE SWEET POTATOES

4 sweet potatoes (8 to 10 ounces each)

Vegetable oil for oiling the grill grate (optional)

### FOR THE DUKKAH

¼ cup hazelnuts

¼ cup almonds

¼ cup hulled pumpkin seeds

¼ cup sesame seeds

1 teaspoon freshly ground black pepper

1 teaspoon ground coriander

1 teaspoon ground cumin

1 teaspoon coarse salt (sea or kosher), or to taste, plus salt for the yogurt

¼ teaspoon ground cinnamon

### FOR THE LEMON YOGURT

1 cup plain yogurt or sour cream

2 tablespoons chopped preserved lemon with 1 tablespoon preserved lemon juices (or 1 teaspoon freshly and finely grated lemon zest plus 2 tablespoons fresh lemon juice and salt to taste)

**1. To ember-grill the sweet potatoes:** Rake out the coals in an even layer and fan off any loose ash. Arrange the spuds on top. Grill until the skins are charred and the flesh is tender (a skewer inserted in the thickest part will pierce them easily), 15 to 20 minutes, or as needed. Turn often with tongs. Transfer the grilled sweet potatoes to an aluminum foil drip pan and let cool slightly, then brush off any loose ash with a crumpled paper towel or pastry brush.

**WHAT ELSE** There are three
ways to grill the sweet potatoes:
ember-grilling, which gives
you the smokiest flavor; direct
grilling, which gives you a
slightly smoky flavor; and
indirect grilling, which requires
no special attention. Dukkah
(an Egyptian nut rub) can be
made with a wide range of nuts
and seeds. I call for a blend of
almonds, hazelnuts, pumpkin
seeds, and sesame seeds, but
you could also use peanuts,
pistachios, and/or walnuts.
Preserved lemon is a Moroccan
citrus pickle. Look for it at North
African markets and a growing
number of supermarkets, or
online. Freshly grated lemon
zest and juice will work in a
pinch.

**To direct grill the sweet potatoes:** Heat your grill to medium-high. Arrange the spuds on the grate (nestle them lengthwise between the bars of the grates). Grill until the skins are dark and the flesh is tender, 6 to 8 minutes per side, 20 to 30 minutes in all, turning often with tongs.

**To indirect grill the sweet potatoes:** Heat your grill to medium-high. Brush or scrape the grill grate clean. Arrange the sweet potatoes on the grate away from the heat. Indirect grill until the skins are browned and the flesh is tender, 40 to 60 minutes. For extra smoke flavor, add hardwood chunks or chips to the coals; if enhancing a gas fire, place the wood chunks or chips in the smoker box or under the grate directly over one or more burners.

**2.** Meanwhile, make the dukkah: Roast the hazelnuts and almonds in a dry skillet over medium-high heat until fragrant, 1 to 2 minutes. Add the pumpkin seeds, sesame seeds, pepper, coriander, cumin, salt, and cinnamon, and continue roasting until the sesame seeds are lightly browned, about 1 minute. Transfer the mixture to a shallow bowl and let cool.

**3.** Place the dukkah mixture in a food processor and grind to a coarse powder, running the machine in short bursts. Don't overprocess: You want a powder, not a paste. Correct the seasoning, adding any spice or salt to taste. Note: This makes more dukkah than you may need, but you can store any excess in a covered jar at room temperature—it will keep for several weeks and tastes great sprinkled on just about everything.

**4.** Make the lemon yogurt: Place the yogurt in a bowl and whisk in the preserved lemon with juices. The yogurt should be richly flavored.

**5.** To serve, make a deep lengthwise cut in each sweet potato (you want to cut into it but not all the way through the skin on the bottom). Push in at the ends to open the potatoes. Place a dollop of lemon yogurt in each and sprinkle with dukkah.

# SMOKED ACORN SQUASH
## WITH PARMESAN FLAN

H ere's a stunning meatless entrée that doubles as a vegetable side dish. It starts with one of the most ubiquitous winter squashes: acorn. Sure, you could grill it sliced or in rings (see page 154), but I like smoke-roasting it in halves, which are perfect for stuffing. The following plays the squash's sweetness against the mild cheesy tang of a Parmesan flan, with wood smoke perfuming both vessel and filling.

## INGREDIENTS

### FOR THE SQUASHES

2 acorn squashes
(about 1½ pounds each)

Extra virgin olive oil for brushing

Coarse salt (sea or kosher) and freshly ground black pepper

### FOR THE FLAN

2 large eggs, preferably organic

1½ cups heavy cream or half-and-half

1 cup (4 ounces) freshly and finely grated Parmigiano-Reggiano

1 tablespoon minced fresh chives

Coarse salt (sea or kosher) and freshly ground black pepper to taste

**1.** Set up your grill for indirect grilling and heat to medium-high. If using a salt slab, heat it as well. If enhancing a charcoal fire, add the wood chunks or chips to the coals; if enhancing a gas fire, place the chunks or chips in your grill's smoker box or place chunks under the grate directly over one or more burners.

**2.** Cut each squash widthwise in half. Cut an ⅛-inch slice off the rounded bottom of each half so the squash sits straight without wobbling. Scoop out and discard the seeds. Brush the cavities and edges of the squash with olive oil and season with salt and pepper.

**YIELD** Makes 4 halves, enough to serve 2 as an entrée or 4 as a side dish

**METHOD** Smoke-roasting (indirect grilling with wood smoke)

**PREP TIME** 15 minutes

**GRILLING TIME** 1¼ hours, or as needed

**GRILL/GEAR** Works best on a charcoal grill, but can be cooked on a gas grill. You'll also need hardwood chunks or chips (soaked), see page 8; a salt slab or four 3 × 12-inch strips of aluminum foil, each crumpled and twisted into a 2-inch ring.

**WHAT ELSE** There are several ways to cook the squash prior to stuffing. I like grilling the halves on a salt slab (cut sides down), which adds a nice salty tang to the vegetable's natural sweetness. Or roast the halves cut sides up on rings of crumpled aluminum foil—handy for holding the squash halves and filling upright. Note: Avoid grilling on salt slabs in very cold weather. When you open the grill lid, cold air can cause a salt slab to explode.

**3.** Set each squash half, cut side down, on the salt slab. Alternatively, set each squash half, cut side up, on a foil ring and place on the grate over the drip pan away from the heat. Indirect grill until semi-tender, 30 to 40 minutes. If grilling on a salt slab, invert the squash halves so the cut sides are up.

**4.** Meanwhile, make the Parmesan flan: Whisk the eggs in a mixing bowl until smooth. Whisk in the heavy cream, followed by the grated Parmigiano-Reggiano and chives. Season with salt and pepper.

**5.** Pour the cheese mixture into the squash halves. Continue indirect grilling until the tops of the flans are golden, the center is set (an inserted toothpick will come out clean), and the squash itself is tender (the sides will be squeezably soft), 15 to 20 minutes more.

**6.** Transfer the squash to a platter or plates and dig in.

# TWICE-GRILLED SQUASH
## WITH PUMPKIN SEED PRALINE

**YIELD** Serves 2 to 4

**METHOD** Smoke-roasting (indirect grilling with wood smoke)

**PREP TIME** 15 minutes

**GRILLING TIME** 50 minutes

**GRILL/GEAR** Can be grilled over charcoal or gas; charcoal is preferable. If you're enhancing a charcoal or gas fire, you'll also need hardwood chunks or chips (soaked), see page 8. For the praline, you'll need a rimmed sheet pan and a food processor outfitted with a metal chopping blade.

Butternut squash is what I call a "roast" vegetable, meaning it's large enough to grill whole and slice at the table, as you would a pork or beef roast. This one involves a two-step process: You roast the squash whole until soft, then halve, seed, and direct grill it to lay on a sizzling dark crust. The squash gets a crackling crust in the form of a crumbled pumpkin seed praline. Burnt sugar? Crunchy seeds? Sweet squash? It's autumn in a single bite.

### INGREDIENTS

1 large butternut squash (2½ to 3 pounds)

3 tablespoons unsalted butter

3 tablespoons honey

½ teaspoon ground cinnamon

Vegetable oil for oiling the grill grate

Coarse salt (sea or kosher) and freshly ground black pepper

½ cup Pumpkin Seed Praline (recipe follows), for topping

Smoked Acorn Squash
with Parmesan Flan

**WHAT ELSE** You have several options for squash here: butternut, Honeynut, or delicata, to name a few. Likewise, you could make the praline with pecans or almonds instead of pumpkin seeds. Note: You can make the honey butter and praline ahead of time (store the butter and praline at room temperature) until you're ready to grill.

**1.** Set up your grill for indirect grilling and heat to medium-high. Place the squash on the grate over the drip pan away from the heat. If enhancing a charcoal fire, add the wood chunks or chips to the coals; if enhancing a gas fire, place the chunks or chips in your grill's smoker box or place chunks under the grate directly over one or more burners. Close the lid and indirect grill the squash until tender (it will be easy to pierce with a skewer), about 45 minutes.

**2.** Transfer the squash to a cutting board and cut it in half lengthwise. Scrape out the seeds and pulp. (If you have the patience to separate the former from the latter, you can roast them later—see Note on page 154.)

**3.** Meanwhile, make the honey butter: Melt the butter in a small saucepan. Add the honey and cinnamon and boil for 30 seconds. The squash and butter can be prepared ahead to this stage.

**4.** Just before serving, set up your grill for direct grilling and heat to high. (On a charcoal grill, simply rake the coals from indirect grilling into a shallow pile in the center.) Brush or scrape the grill grate clean and oil it well. Brush the cut sides of the butternut squash with the honey butter and season with salt and pepper.

**5.** Place the squash on the grill, cut sides down, slightly on the diagonal to the bars of the grate, directly over the fire. Grill until darkly browned, 3 to 5 minutes, giving the squash a quarter turn halfway through to lay on a crosshatch of grill marks.

**6.** Transfer the squash to a platter. Spoon the remaining honey butter on top. Sprinkle with the Pumpkin Seed Praline and serve.

# VARIATION

### SALT SLAB–ROASTED SQUASH WITH PUMPKIN SEED PRALINE

Place a salt slab on the grate and heat it as you preheat your grill. Cut the squash in half lengthwise. Place the 2 halves cut sides down on the salt slab. Roast until tender, about 45 minutes. Baste, season, and direct grill the squash as described in Steps 4 and 5. Note: Avoid grilling on salt slabs in very cold weather. When you open the grill lid, cold air can cause a salt slab to explode.

# PUMPKIN SEED PRALINE

**YIELD** About ¾ cup

## INGREDIENTS

2 teaspoons vegetable oil

½ cup sugar

½ cup hulled pumpkin seeds

½ teaspoon ground cinnamon

**1.** Lightly oil a rimmed sheet pan with vegetable oil and set aside. Place the sugar in a small heavy saucepan. Cook it over medium-high heat until the sugar melts and turns golden, swirling the pan from time to time so it cooks evenly.

**2.** Stir in the pumpkin seeds and continue cooking until the sugar is medium to dark brown (the darker, the more bitter-smoky). But don't let it burn. Immediately pour the sugar mixture onto the oiled sheet pan and let it cool to room temperature.

**3.** Pry the cooled brittle off the sheet pan and break it into 1-inch pieces. Place these and the cinnamon in a food processor. Grind the brittle until it resembles coarse breadcrumbs, running the processor in short bursts. It will take a few minutes and make a lot of noise to grind the brittle: This is normal. Do not over-process: You want a coarse powder, not a paste.

**NOTE:** This may make more brittle than you'll need for the squash, but it's killer delicious and you'll want to sprinkle it over Ember-Grilled Sweet Potatoes (page 193), ice cream, and grilled or smoked desserts. Store in an airtight container away from heat and light.

# BUTTERNUT SQUASH
## WITH THAI SWEET CHILI TERIYAKI

**YIELD** Serves 4

**METHOD** Indirect grilling/ direct grilling

**PREP TIME** 15 minutes

**GRILLING TIME** About 50 minutes

**GRILL/GEAR** Can be grilled on charcoal or gas or a wood-enhanced fire. If you're enhancing a charcoal or gas fire, you'll need hardwood chunks or chips (soaked), see page 8. You'll also need a large aluminum foil pan or baking dish.

**WHAT ELSE** I call for butternut squash here—I love the look of the long slender quarters— but you could certainly use another squash, like rings of acorn squash or dense orange kabocha. (If using the latter, cut it into wedges.) One good brand of Thai chili sauce is Mae Ploy. Note: You can omit the ginger and garlic if you wish. They add more flavor, but your squash will still be very tasty without them.

I love the sweet-salty yin and yang of Japanese teriyaki. And I love the gentle garlicky heat of Thai chili sauce. They come together in this simple grilled butternut squash dish, which plays the smoky sweetness of charred squash against Japan's classic barbecue sauce. I suggest indirect grilling in a foil pan to cook the squash most of the way, followed by a quick direct grill to char the sauce into the sweet butternut flesh. Note: Wood smoke is not widely used when grilling vegetables in Asia, but you could certainly deepen the flavor by adding hardwood chunks or chips to the coals (see page 8).

## INGREDIENTS

**FOR THE SQUASH**

1 large or 2 small butternut squashes (2½ to 3 pounds total)

Vegetable oil for oiling the grill grate

**FOR THE SAUCE**

3 tablespoons soy sauce

3 tablespoons sake or mirin

3 tablespoons dark (toasted) sesame oil

3 tablespoons pure maple syrup

3 tablespoons sweet Thai chili sauce

1 scallion, trimmed, white part cut in half, green part thinly sliced crosswise and reserved for serving

3 slices peeled fresh ginger, each ¼ inch thick

1 clove garlic, peeled

2 tablespoons toasted sesame seeds (optional)

**1.** Set up your grill for indirect grilling and heat to medium-high. If enhancing a charcoal fire, add the wood chunks or chips to the coals; if enhancing a gas fire, place the chunks or chips in your grill's smoker box or place chunks under the grate directly over one or more burners.

**2.** Cut the large squash lengthwise into 6 wedges. Cut the small squashes lengthwise into quarters. Scoop out and discard the strings and seeds.

**3.** Make the sauce: Pour the soy sauce, sake, sesame oil, maple syrup, and chili sauce into the foil pan and whisk to mix. Gently flatten the scallion white, ginger, and garlic with the side of a cleaver or chef's knife. Stir them into the sauce. Add the squash pieces, turning each several times to coat all sides.

**4.** Place the squash, cut sides down, in its foil pan on the grill grate away from the heat. Indirect grill the squash until almost tender, about 30 to 45 minutes, turning the pieces with tongs a couple of times so they cook evenly.

**5.** Brush or scrape the grill grate clean (the portion directly over the fire) and oil it well. Using tongs, lift the squash pieces out of the pan with the teriyaki sauce and arrange directly over one of the fires, cut sides down. Move the foil pan with the sauce over the other fire.

**6.** Direct grill the squash pieces until sizzling and darkly browned on all sides (the two cut sides and the skin side), 1 to 2 minutes per side, 3 to 6 minutes in all. If you like, give each a piece a quarter turn after 1 minute to lay on a crosshatch of grill marks. Meanwhile, boil the teriyaki sauce in its pan until thick, brushing it on the squash pieces as they grill.

**7.** Transfer the squash to a platter or plates. Spoon any remaining teriyaki sauce over them. (I leave the ginger and garlic in, but you can certainly discard them if you are so inclined.) Sprinkle with the scallion greens and sesame seeds (if using), and dig in!

# ZUCCHINI "BRACIOLE"
## WITH PEPPERONI, PROVOLONE, AND SAGE

This is a book about vegetable-forward grilling, not vegetarian grilling, and one of the commitments I made when I started it was that if a little meat could make a good grilled vegetable taste even better, then meat it would have. Which brings me to this braciole—made with one of the quintessential veggies of summer: zucchini. Traditional Italian braciole (from the Italian word *brace*, "embers," over which the meat was traditionally grilled) consists of thin slices of meat rolled around a stuffing of cheese and vegetables. This one turns the traditional braciole architecture inside out: The veggie is now on the outside; the meat (sliced pepperoni or spicy salami), along with provolone cheese, becomes the stuffing.

### INGREDIENTS

4 medium-size zucchini (about 10 ounces each)

Coarse salt (sea or kosher) and freshly ground black pepper

8 strips bacon, pancetta, or guanciale

6 ounces thinly sliced aged provolone cheese

6 ounces thinly sliced pepperoni or spicy salami

1 bunch fresh sage, stemmed

Vegetable oil for oiling the grill grate

**1.** Cut each zucchini in half lengthwise. (Keep the halves in pairs.) Season the cut sides with salt and pepper.

**2.** Lay four 8-inch lengths of butcher's string parallel to one another on your work surface. The distance between the outside strings should be 1 inch less than the length of the zucchini.

**3.** Assemble the braciole: Lay a strip of bacon on top of and perpendicular to the strings so it bisects them. Lay a zucchini half, cut side up, on top of the bacon. Top it with sliced provolone, trimming the cheese to fit the cut side of the zucchini. Top with pepperoni slices and sage leaves, and top with its matching zucchini half, cut side down. Lay another strip of bacon on top. Bring the ends of the strings over the zucchini and tie to make a compact log. Assemble the remaining braciole the same way.

**YIELD** Makes 4, enough to serve 2 to 4

**METHOD** Smoke-roasting (indirect grilling with wood smoke)

**PREP TIME** 20 minutes

**GRILLING TIME** 20 minutes

**GRILL/GEAR** Can be cooked on a gas or charcoal grill, but you'll get the best smoke flavor with charcoal. You'll also need butcher's string, and if you're enhancing the fire, hardwood chunks or chips (soaked), see page 8.

**WHAT ELSE** Like most simple recipes, this one will be good or great depending on the ingredients. To be strictly Italian, you'd use pancetta (cured pork belly) or guanciale (cured pork jowl) instead of bacon, but the latter gives you more smoke flavor. The provolone—preferably piccante (aged for at least 4 months and prized for its sharp flavor)—should be imported from Italy. Alternatively, you could use a smoked cheese, like Italian scamorza affumicata. To make a meatless version of this dish, replace the pepperoni with roasted red bell peppers or piquillo peppers and omit the bacon.

**4.** Meanwhile, set up your grill for indirect grilling and heat to high. Brush or scrape the grill grate clean and oil it well. Arrange the zucchini on the grate over the drip pan away from the heat. If enhancing a charcoal fire, add the wood chunks or chips to the coals; if enhancing a gas fire, place the chunks or chips in your grill's smoker box or place chunks under the grate directly over one or more burners. Close the lid.

**5.** Indirect grill the braciole until the bacon is crisp and brown, the zucchini is tender (test it with a toothpick), and the cheese is melted, about 20 minutes, or as needed. Transfer the braciole to a platter or plates. Snip off the strings and serve.

Halve the zucchini lengthwise.

Lay a strip of bacon down the center of four pieces of string.

Top the bacon with the bottom half of the zucchini.

Layer provolone—cut to fit—on top.

Next, add a few slices of pepperoni.

Add the fresh sage leaves.

Top with the upper half of the zucchini.

Drape a final strip of bacon on top, and tie the strings to hold the filling in place.

# FIRE-SEARED POLENTA
## WITH MUSHROOM MIXED GRILL

Polenta is to Italy what grits are to the American South, but unlike the latter, this Italian cornmeal mush is often cooked firm enough to be cut into slabs and cooked *ai ferri*, on the grill (literally "on iron"). Do it right and your polenta will come out crusty on the outside and meltingly soft in the center. The secret is to oil the grill grate well and oil or butter the polenta even better. The toppings are limited only by your imagination. Here I suggest an exotic mushroom mixed grill. Alternatively, try topping it with butter-fried sage leaves and Italian fontina cheese. For that matter, the Smoked Tomato Sauce on page 290 would make an awesome polenta topping. So would the Wood Fire Eggs (Egg Spoon Eggs) on page 242.

**YIELD** Serves 3 or 4 as an entrée

**METHOD** Direct grilling

**PREP TIME** 15 minutes

**GRILLING TIME** 20 minutes

**GRILL/GEAR** Can be grilled over charcoal or gas, but for the best flavor, grill over wood. You'll also need a plancha, vegetable grilling grid, or grill wok. If you're enhancing the fire, you'll need hardwood chunks or chips (unsoaked), see page 8.

**WHAT ELSE** It used to be that to grill polenta you had to make polenta—a lengthy process of boiling and stirring that left your arm spatter-burned and feeling like it had run a marathon. You can now buy ready-made, shelf-stable polenta in tubes, and while it doesn't quite measure up to what an Italian grandmother would make, it's firm enough to hold together on the grill, which makes it a win in my book. (Two good brands are Ancient Harvest and San Gennaro. They're usually found in the pasta aisle.) As for the mushrooms, I like to grill them on a plancha—this holds in the moisture while crisping the edges. You have lots of options for mushrooms (see the ingredients list); when available, fresh porcini are quintessentially Italian.

## INGREDIENTS

- 1 pound mixed mushrooms, including porcinis, chanterelles, shiitakes, hen-of-the-woods, oyster mushrooms, and/or button mushrooms
- 1 clove garlic, peeled and minced
- 1 shallot, peeled and minced, or 1 scallion, trimmed, white and green parts thinly sliced crosswise
- 3 tablespoons chopped fresh sage or flat-leaf parsley leaves

- 2 tablespoons extra virgin olive oil or melted butter, plus extra for the polenta
- Coarse salt (sea or kosher) and freshly ground black pepper
- 1 tube (18 ounces) prepared polenta, cut crosswise into eight ¾-inch-thick slices
- 2 tablespoons grappa or cognac (optional; see Note)
- Vegetable oil for oiling the grill grate

**1.** Set up your grill for direct grilling and heat to high. Place a plancha, vegetable grilling grid, or grill wok on one side of the grate and heat it as well. When properly heated, a drop of water dripped on the hot metal will evaporate in 1 or 2 seconds.

**2.** Meanwhile, trim the stem ends off the mushrooms. Wipe the caps clean with a damp paper towel. Cut any large mushrooms in halves or quarters—you want uniform pieces about 1 inch in size. Just before grilling, place the mushrooms in a large mixing bowl. Toss with the garlic, shallot, sage, 2 tablespoons of olive oil, and salt and pepper.

**3.** Oil the plancha or vegetable grate well. If enhancing a charcoal fire, add the wood chunks or chips to the coals; if enhancing a gas fire, place the chunks or chips in your grill's smoker box or place chunks under the grate directly over one or more burners. Add the mushrooms and grill over a hot fire until browned, crisp at the edges, and cooked through, 4 to 6 minutes, or as needed, turning with a spatula. Move the mushrooms to a corner of the grill to keep warm.

**4.** Meanwhile, generously brush the polenta slices on both sides with olive oil and season with salt and pepper. Arrange the polenta on the grate and grill until the bottoms are sizzling and browned, 5 to 8 minutes. Using a thin-bladed spatula, invert the polenta and grill the other side the same way. Alternatively, grill the polenta on the plancha—you won't get grill marks, but you'll eliminate the risk of sticking.

**5.** Arrange the grilled polenta slices on a platter or plates. Spoon the mushroom mixed grill on top and serve.

**NOTE:** For extra drama, warm the grappa in a small saucepan. It should be body-temperature warm: Do not let it boil, or you'll evaporate the alcohol. Touch a long, lit match to the grappa to light it. Carefully pour the flaming grappa over the polenta and mushrooms and serve at once. For safety's sake, make sure your sleeves are rolled up and there's nothing else but the grappa that can catch on fire.

# GRILLED VEGETABLE PAELLA

**YIELD** Serves 4 to 6

**METHOD** Direct grilling

**PREP TIME** 30 minutes

**GRILLING TIME** 50 minutes

Forget everything you think you know about paella. You make it with seafood, right? No, traditional paella, as prepared in its birthplace—Spain's Valencia province—contains just two proteins: rabbit and snails. Like many of the world's great rice dishes (pilaf comes to mind), you cook it on the stove or in the oven. Wrong again: The authentic way to cook paella is over an open orange wood or grapevine fire. (The wood subtly smokes the rice, adding flavor nuances you simply can't achieve indoors.) The good news is that the process translates easily to a grill or campfire. Here's a plant-based paella bursting with bright Spanish flavors. The chickpeas provide the protein. Yes, I know, tradition calls for cooking the veggies right in the paella pan, not directly on the grill, but live fire intensifies their color and flavor.

## INGREDIENTS

**FOR THE GRILLED VEGETABLES**

1 large or 4 small artichokes

½ lemon

1 large sweet onion, peeled

12 ounces broccolini or zucchini

8 ounces green beans or snow peas, ends snapped off and strings removed

2 ears of sweet corn, husked, silk removed

6 ounces Padrón or shishito peppers, stemmed

12 cherry tomatoes

2 to 3 tablespoons extra virgin olive oil

Coarse salt (sea or kosher) and freshly ground black pepper

Vegetable oil for oiling the grill grate

**TO FINISH THE PAELLA**

3 to 4 tablespoons extra virgin olive oil, plus extra as needed

1 large onion, peeled and finely chopped

1 large red bell pepper, stemmed, seeded, and cut into ¼ × 2-inch strips

2 cloves garlic, peeled and thinly sliced

3 tablespoons finely chopped flat-leaf parsley leaves

1 large luscious ripe tomato, seeded and cut into ¼-inch dice

Coarse salt (kosher or sea) and freshly ground black pepper

3 cups Valencia-style rice, such as bomba or Calasparra

1 teaspoon saffron threads, soaked in 1 tablespoon warm water for 5 minutes

1 cup dry white wine, preferably Spanish

8 to 10 cups vegetable stock, preferably homemade, or as needed

1 cup drained cooked chickpeas

Lemon wedges, for garnish (optional)

**GRILL/GEAR** Can be grilled over charcoal or gas, but tastes best grilled over wood or a wood-enhanced fire. If you're enhancing a charcoal or gas fire, you'll need hardwood chunks or chips (unsoaked), see page 8. You'll also need wooden toothpicks; a wire grill basket or vegetable grate; a 16-inch paella pan or large cast-iron skillet; and a long-handled stirring implement, like a grill hoe.

**WHAT ELSE** This recipe may sound complicated, but actually, it's a series of simple steps. For the best results, you'll want to use a Valencia-style rice, like Calasparra or bomba (find them at some supermarkets or at Latienda.com). These are short-grained rice varieties that don't become mushy when simmered. For vegetables, I'd use what's fresh and in season. Use the ingredients list as a guideline; you'll need 6 to 8 cups in all. The traditional fuel for grilling paella is orange tree wood or grapevines. Just saying.

**1.** Prepare the vegetables, using the instructions here as a general guideline: If using an artichoke, cut the points off the leaves. Trim ⅛ inch off the bottom of the stem. Cut the artichoke from crown to stem into 6 wedges (if using small artichokes, cut them in half). Cut out and discard the fibrous choke. Rub the cut sides with the half lemon to keep them from discoloring. Blanch the artichoke wedges or halves in boiling salted water for about 3 minutes, then drain in a colander and blot dry.

**2.** If using the onion, cut it from top to bottom into 6 wedges. Pin each crosswise with a toothpick (this keeps the wedges from falling apart).

**3.** If using broccolini, trim off the ends and separate it into stalks. If using zucchini, cut it in half lengthwise.

Grilling paella over a wood fire

**4.** Lightly brush the artichokes, onion, broccolini (or zucchini), green beans, corn, Padrón peppers, and cherry tomatoes with the olive oil and season with salt and pepper.

**5.** Meanwhile, set up your grill for direct grilling and build a hot fire. Ideally, you'll work over a grapevine or orange wood fire. If enhancing a charcoal fire, add the wood chunks or chips to the coals; if enhancing a gas fire, place the chunks or chips in your grill's smoker box or place chunks under the grate directly over one or more burners. Brush or scrape the grill grate clean and oil it well.

**6.** Arrange the oiled seasoned vegetables on the grill (smaller vegetables like green beans, shishitos, and cherry tomatoes should be in a grill basket or on a vegetable grate) and grill until darkly browned on all sides, 2 to 4 minutes per side. Don't worry about cooking them through—they'll finish cooking in the paella.

**7.** Transfer the vegetables to a cutting board. Remove the toothpicks from the onions. Cut the broccolini or zucchini into 2-inch pieces. Cut the corn crosswise into 1-inch rounds with a chef's knife or cleaver. The veggies can be grilled and prepped ahead to this stage. Cover and refrigerate for up to 1 day.

**8.** To finish the paella, place the paella pan over the fire. Add 3 to 4 tablespoons of olive oil and heat until shimmering. Add the onion and bell pepper and cook over high heat, stirring with a long-handled

implement, like a grill hoe or long-handled wooden spoon, until the onions begin to brown, about 4 minutes. Add the garlic, parsley (save 1 tablespoon for garnish), diced tomato, 1 teaspoon of salt, and ½ teaspoon of pepper and cook for 2 minutes more. Add oil as needed. If the mixture—called a sofrito—starts to burn, slide the pan to a cooler part of the grill. Note: The Spanish wouldn't brown the sofrito, but you'll get more flavor if you do.

**9.** Stir in the rice and sauté until the grains look shiny, about 1 minute. Stir in the soaked saffron (with its liquid) and wine and boil for 2 minutes.

**10.** Stir in 6 cups of stock, or more as needed to cover the rice with liquid. Adjust the heat (by moving the paella pan closer to or farther away from the hot part of the fire) to obtain a gentle simmer. Gently simmer the rice for 10 minutes.

**11.** Stir in the artichokes and corn and simmer for 5 minutes. Stir in the remaining grilled vegetables and the chickpeas. Continue cooking the paella until the rice is al dente, about 20 minutes in all, stirring occasionally. Add more stock (½ cup at a time) as needed. Add salt and pepper to taste: The paella should be highly seasoned.

**12.** If you get it right, all the liquid will cook out and the bottom of the rice will turn into a crisp savory crust called socarrat. Sprinkle the paella with the remaining parsley, garnish with lemon wedges (if using), and serve straight from the pan.

# CHAPTER 8
# VEGETABLE SIDES

**T**ravel the world's barbecue trail and you'll find grilled plant foods on every continent. From ember-grilled artichokes in Sicily to grilled onigiri (rice cakes) in the land of my birth: Japan. This chapter on vegetable "side dishes" takes you on a vegetable grilling tour of Planet Barbecue: from Korean-inflected grilled cabbage and English breakfast–inspired grilled tomatoes to creamy corn with a Mexican twist. Barbecued onions and grilled bok choy with shichimi togarashi sound a traditional note, while smoked carrots with toasted yeast and zucchini "burnt ends" take you to barbecue's cutting edge. That hoary French classic, green beans almondine, gets a live-fire makeover with Marcona almonds. And, yes, there will be a sweet potato casserole for Thanksgiving—smoke-roasted, of course (I couldn't resist). This may be a chapter on vegetable side dishes, but you might well want to grill some of these as the star of the show.

# RECIPES

# PLUM TOMATOES
## GRILLED IN THE STYLE OF ENGLISH BREAKFAST

**YIELD** Makes 8 halves (serves 4)

**METHOD** Indirect grilling

**PREP TIME** 10 minutes

**GRILLING TIME** 10 to 15 minutes

**GRILL/GEAR** Can be grilled over charcoal or gas. If you're enhancing a charcoal or gas fire, you'll need hardwood chunks or chips (unsoaked), see page 8. You'll also need wooden toothpicks.

**WHAT ELSE** Use thin-cut bacon for wrapping the tomatoes. For cheese, I'd use a well-aged English cheddar.

The broiled tomato is a staple of the English breakfast (joining bacon, sausage, eggs, and toast). My grilled version focuses on the tomato, topping it with cheddar cheese and sliced hard-cooked eggs and wrapping it with bacon. (The eggs are optional—they add a step—but they definitely up the flavor and deliciousness.) Breakfast is just a start.

### INGREDIENTS

4 plum tomatoes, preferably organic

Coarse salt (sea or kosher) and freshly ground black pepper

2 hard-cooked eggs or smoked eggs (see page 245), peeled and thinly sliced (optional)

3 ounces cheddar cheese, cut into ¼-inch-thick slices the size of the tomatoes

8 strips bacon (preferably thin-cut)

¼ cup breadcrumbs, preferably homemade

Extra virgin olive oil or melted butter, for drizzling

Vegetable oil for oiling the grill grate

Fresh oregano leaves, for garnish (optional)

**1.** Cut the tomatoes in half lengthwise. Cut a thin slice off the rounded bottom of each half so the tomatoes stand without tipping. Generously season each half on the large cut side with salt and pepper. Shingle the sliced eggs (if using) on top of the tomatoes and arrange the sliced cheese on top. Wrap each tomato crosswise with a strip of bacon, securing it with a toothpick. Sprinkle the tomatoes with the breadcrumbs and drizzle with olive oil.

**2.** Meanwhile, set up your grill for indirect grilling and heat to high. Brush or scrape the grill grate clean

and oil it well. If enhancing a charcoal fire, add the wood chunks or chips to the coals; if enhancing a gas fire, place the chunks or chips in your grill's smoker box or place chunks under the grate directly over one or more burners.

**3.** Arrange the tomatoes, cut sides up, on the grate over the drip pan away from the heat. Indirect grill the tomatoes until the bacon and breadcrumbs are sizzling and brown and the cheese is melted, 10 to 15 minutes. Garnish with oregano leaves (if using). Serve hot.

# ARTICHOKES SICILIAN STYLE

**YIELD** Makes 4 and can be multiplied as desired

**METHOD** Ember-grilling (caveman grilling) or direct grilling

**PREP TIME** 15 minutes

**GRILLING TIME** 15 to 30 minutes (depending on the artichokes)

**GRILL/GEAR** Must be cooked on a charcoal or wood-burning grill. You'll also need a metal skewer; heatproof gloves; and a rimmed sheet pan.

**WHAT ELSE** When buying artichokes for this dish, choose large flowers (for, botanically speaking, that's what an artichoke is). I call for ember-grilling here, which gives the artichokes a pronounced smoke flavor. But direct grilling, also practiced in Sicily, delivers remarkable artichokes, too (instructions follow). Note the striking technique of smashing the artichokes against a hard surface to tenderize them and spread open the leaves. I now use it whenever I prepare artichokes.

To say Italians love grilled artichokes is like stating that plants naturally grow toward sunlight. You find them from one end of the peninsula to the other—grilled with olive oil in Portofino, flame-charred and marinated with herbs at delicatessens in Rome, sizzled on giant grills in the middle of the street in the Sicilian city of Catania. But for sheer novelty, nothing tops the Sicilian grilled artichokes of Fabrizio Calamia. Owner of La Brace Smokehouse American Bbq Restaurant in Partanna near Trapani, Fabrizio stuffs the artichokes with chopped garlic and fresh mint, drizzling them with peppery Nocellara del Belice olive oil prior to grilling them right on the embers. Scrape off the burnt part, and you'll experience artichokes of supernatural smokiness and sweetness. The cool factor is off the charts.

## INGREDIENTS

4 large artichokes

2 cloves garlic, peeled and minced

⅓ cup packed fresh mint leaves, stemmed and finely chopped

Extra virgin olive oil, preferably Sicilian, for drizzling during grilling and for serving

Coarse salt (sea or kosher) and freshly ground black pepper

**1.** Trim the stem off each artichoke. Using kitchen scissors, cut the points off the leaves. (This is optional and most Sicilians don't bother, but it does remove the sharp prickles.) Turn each artichoke upside down (stem end up) and smash it against your work surface a half dozen times to spread open the leaves.

**2.** Stuff each artichoke with the garlic and mint, forcing both between the leaves. Generously—and I mean generously—drizzle each artichoke with olive oil and season with salt and pepper.

**3.** Meanwhile, set up your grill for ember-grilling. Rake out the coals in an even layer and fan off any loose ash.

**4.** Stand the artichokes on the embers on their stem ends. Grill until the bottoms are charred and the flesh is tender. Using long-handled tongs, rotate the artichokes from time to time so they cook evenly. Turn them on their sides to char the outside leaves. Total grilling time will be 15 to 30 minutes. Use a metal skewer to test for doneness: It should pierce the artichokes easily.

**5.** Transfer the artichokes to a rimmed sheet pan. Using heatproof gloves and a paring knife, scrape any really burnt parts off the bottom and remove any really charred outside leaves. Transfer the artichokes to wide shallow bowls, drizzle with more olive oil, and dig in.

# VARIATION

### DIRECT GRILLED ARTICHOKES

Equally common in Sicily, if not more so, are direct grilled artichokes, opening this amazing preparation to gas grillers. You'd think the artichokes would dry out. They don't. You'd think the leaves would taste burnt. They don't. What you get is a dry-roasted artichoke that's delectably different.

Set up your grill for direct grilling and heat to high. Prep and stuff the artichokes as described in Steps 1 and 2. Stand the stuffed artichokes upright on the grate. Direct grill until the bottoms and sides are darkly browned, even charred, and the flesh is tender, 20 minutes or as needed, turning with tongs. Be sure to grill the sides. If your grill has a lid, lower it to hold in the heat and speed up the cooking. I wouldn't say no to melted butter for serving.

Artichokes grilled Sicilian style—roasted in the embers

# WOOD-GRILLED BROCCOLINI
## WITH CHILI OIL AND GOLDEN RAISINS

**YIELD** Serves 3 to 4

**METHOD** Direct grilling

**PREP TIME** 15 minutes

**GRILLING TIME** 6 to 10 minutes

**GRILL/GEAR** Can be grilled over charcoal, gas, or wood. You'll need a rimmed sheet pan or baking dish.

**WHAT ELSE** Broccolini is one of my favorite brassicas for grilling. It possesses a milder flavor than broccoli, and its slender stalks and lacy heads crisp when exposed to the fire. The topping triangulates sweet golden raisins, nutty almonds, and spicy chili oil—it's a combination that works great with almost any grilled vegetable, from asparagus to zucchini. Note: Chili oil consists of vegetable oil heated and infused with fiery Chinese chilies and sometimes ginger, garlic, and Sichuan peppercorns. Look for it at Asian markets and many supermarkets.

Jon Shook and Vinny Dotolo launched their Los Angeles restaurant empire with a meat- and offal-centric restaurant called Animal. So, the irony is not lost that some of the best dishes at their casual Italian restaurant, Jon & Vinny's, are plant-based. Like fire-charred sugar snap peas doused with house-made ranch dressing. Or grilled asparagus tarted up with lemon and shaved Parmigiano-Reggiano. Which brings me to what may be their most interesting grilled vegetable of all—broccolini doused with a bright nutty vinaigrette of golden raisins and toasted almonds, with chili oil to notch up the heat.

## INGREDIENTS

### FOR THE BROCCOLINI

1 pound broccolini

Extra virgin olive oil for brushing and basting

Coarse salt (sea or kosher) and freshly ground black pepper

Vegetable oil for oiling the grilling grate

### FOR THE CHILI OIL VINAIGRETTE AND TOPPING

¼ cup golden raisins

½ cup boiling water

1½ tablespoons sherry vinegar, or to taste

3 tablespoons extra virgin olive oil

3 tablespoons Chinese chili oil

¼ cup toasted chopped Marcona (Spanish) almonds or California almonds (see What Else, page 228)

**1.** Trim the ends off the broccolini. Prick the stems in a few places with a fork. Arrange the broccolini on a rimmed sheet pan or in a baking dish. Brush generously with olive oil and season with salt and pepper.

**2.** Make the vinaigrette: Place the golden raisins in a mixing bowl and add the boiling water. Let the golden raisins soften for about 5 minutes, then drain off the water. Add the sherry vinegar, olive oil, and chili oil, and whisk to mix. Whisk in salt and pepper to taste: The vinaigrette should be richly flavored.

**3.** Meanwhile, set up your grill for direct grilling and heat to medium-high. Brush or scrape the grill grate clean and oil it well.

**4.** Arrange the broccolini stalks on the grate and grill until nicely browned on the outside and fork tender, 3 to 5 minutes per side, turning often with tongs. If the broccolini starts to

dry out, baste it with a little of the vinaigrette.

**5.** Transfer the broccolini to a platter or plates. Re-whisk the vinaigrette to mix, then spoon it over the broccolini. Sprinkle with toasted almonds and serve.

# SAVOY CABBAGE BULGOGI

Bulgogi is one of Korea's national dishes and culinary treasures—wafer-thin rib steaks marinated in a sweet-salty-nutty mixture of sugar, soy sauce, and sesame oil. And garlic, lots of garlic. It's one of those flavor quadrangles that makes any food taste better. And best of all, you boil the marinade down to create a barbecue sauce. That set me thinking about a vegetable bulgogi you could make with "steaks" cut from savoy cabbage.

## INGREDIENTS

1 savoy cabbage (about 2 pounds)

3 cloves garlic, peeled and minced

1 tablespoon minced peeled fresh ginger

2 scallions, trimmed, white parts minced, green parts thinly sliced on the diagonal

⅓ cup brown sugar (white sugar or honey are okay, too), or to taste

1 teaspoon freshly ground black pepper

⅔ cup soy sauce

½ cup rice wine or sake

⅓ cup dark (toasted) sesame oil, plus 2 tablespoons for basting

3 tablespoons gochujang (optional; see What Else)

3 tablespoons unsalted butter, cubed

Vegetable oil for oiling the grill grate

¼ cup toasted sesame seeds, for sprinkling

**1.** Cut the cabbage from stem to crown into 1-inch wedges. Insert 1 or 2 bamboo skewers through each wedge

to hold it together during grilling. Arrange the cabbage wedges in a single layer in a baking dish.

**YIELD** Serves 4 to 6

**METHOD** Direct grilling

**PREP TIME** 15 minutes, plus 2 to 4 hours for marinating

**GRILLING TIME** 6 to 10 minutes

**GRILL/GEAR** Korean tradition calls for grilling over charcoal, but you can also use gas or wood. You'll also need bamboo skewers and a wire rack set over a rimmed sheet pan.

**WHAT ELSE** I've beefed up the marinade with one untraditional but thoroughly Korean flavoring: gochujang. This flavorful paste of fermented chilies, garlic, and rice has an uncanny way of electrifying any sauce or marinade. I've made it optional, but I think you'll like the kick it adds to the bulgogi. Look for it at the supermarket or online. Note: I often make this with napa cabbage or brussels sprouts instead of savoy cabbage. Also, if you're crunched for time, you can skip the marinade.

**2.** Make the marinade: Place the garlic, ginger, scallion whites, brown sugar, and black pepper in a mixing bowl. (Reserve the scallion greens for a garnish.) Pound together with a pestle or the back of a wooden spoon until fragrant. Whisk in the soy sauce, rice wine, ⅓ cup of the sesame oil, and gochujang (if using).

**3.** Pour the marinade over the cabbage wedges, turning to coat both sides. Marinate in the refrigerator for 2 to 4 hours, turning the wedges a few times so they marinate evenly.

**4.** Remove the cabbage wedges from the marinade (reserve the marinade) and drain on a wire rack set over a rimmed sheet pan. Pour the reserved marinade into a small saucepan. Scrape any marinade that collects on the sheet pan into the saucepan. (If you're feeling fancy, you can strain the marinade into the pan—I rather like pieces of garlic and ginger, so I leave them in.) Boil the marinade until syrupy, sauce-like, and richly flavored, about 3 minutes. Whisk in the butter and remove from the heat. Keep the sauce warm.

**5.** Meanwhile, set up your grill for direct grilling and heat to medium-high. Brush or scrape the grill grate clean and oil it well.

**6.** Brush the cabbage wedges on both sides with the 2 tablespoons of sesame oil. Arrange on the grate and grill until both sides are darkly browned and the cabbage is cooked through, 2 to 4 minutes per side, or as needed. Baste the wedges with some of the sauce as they grill.

**7.** Transfer the cabbage wedges to a platter or plates. Remove and discard the skewers. Pour any remaining sauce over the cabbage and sprinkle with sesame seeds and the reserved scallion greens.

## VARIATIONS

### BULGOGI OF NAPA CABBAGE

Cut a napa cabbage crosswise into 1-inch "steaks." Insert 1 or 2 small bamboo skewers through the side of each to hold the cabbage together. Marinate and grill as described in Steps 2 to 7.

### BULGOGI OF BRUSSELS SPROUTS

**1.** Cut trimmed brussels sprouts in half through the stem ends. Lay the sprout halves flat side down on a cutting board and thread them onto bamboo skewers so the skewers pass through the rounded sides and run parallel to the cutting board.

**2.** Arrange the resulting kebabs in a baking dish and pour the marinade over them. Marinate as described in Steps 3 and 4, turning several times so the brussels sprouts marinate evenly.

**3.** Grill the kebabs as described in Steps 5 to 7, basting with sesame oil. Sprinkle with sesame seeds and scallion greens before serving.

# GRILLED BOK CHOY
## WITH JAPANESE PEPPER RUB

**YIELD** Serves 4

**METHOD** Direct grilling

**PREP TIME** 10 minutes

**GRILLING TIME** 4 to 8 minutes

**GRILL/GEAR** Can be grilled over charcoal, gas, or wood.

**WHAT ELSE** You'll need to know about one special ingredient: the Japanese spice mix shichimi togarashi. Blends vary from manufacturer to manufacturer, but the traditional flavorings include ground red chilies, roasted orange peel, dried ginger, poppy seeds, hemp seeds, black and white sesame seeds, pulverized nori seaweed, and sanshō pepper. The latter—*Zanthoxylum piperitum*, also known as Japanese prickly ash—is a reddish peppercorn-like berry with a distinctively aromatic, pine-like flavor. (The flavor may remind you of Sichuan peppercorns, to which the plant is related.) You can buy shichimi togarashi at an Asian market or well-stocked supermarket or order it online. Two good brands are Yoshi and Spiceology. Note: Yuzu is a Japanese citrus fruit with a haunting, perfumed flavor. Lemon zest gets you on the dance floor.

If ever there was a vegetable ripe for grilling, it's bok choy—a Chinese cabbage with succulent pale green stems and delicate dark green leaves. Its high water content (95 percent) keeps it moist during grilling. Its herbaceous flavor (milder than most members of the cabbage family) marries well with soy sauce, mirin, dark sesame oil, and the Japanese pepper spice mix known as shichimi togarashi. (For an interesting variation, replace the latter with "everything bagel" seasoning.) Bok choy is rich in vitamins A, C, and K, not to mention folate and calcium—all the more reason it belongs on your grill.

### INGREDIENTS

4 small bok choy (1 to 1¼ pounds in all)

¼ cup dark (toasted) sesame oil

¼ cup tamari or soy sauce

¼ cup mirin or sake (if using sake, add 2 teaspoons sugar)

½ teaspoon freshly and finely grated yuzu or lemon zest (optional)

Vegetable oil for oiling the grill grate

1 tablespoon shichimi togarashi, or to taste

**1.** Cut each bok choy in half lengthwise.

**2.** Combine the sesame oil, tamari, mirin, and yuzu zest (if using) in a small bowl and mix with a fork. Brush the bok choy on all sides with this basting mixture.

**3.** Set up your grill for direct grilling and heat to high. Brush or scrape the grill grate clean and oil it well.

**4.** Arrange the bok choy, cut sides down, on the grate, running on the diagonal to the bars of the grate. Grill until the cut sides are browned, 2 to 4 minutes. Brush the rounded sides of the bok choy with the basting mixture.

**5.** Turn the bok choy over and continue grilling until the rounded sides are browned, another 2 to 4 minutes, brushing the cut sides again with the basting mixture. Do not overcook; the bok choy should remain crisp in the center.

**6.** Transfer the bok choy to a platter, cut sides up. Spoon any remaining basting mixture on top. Sprinkle the grilled bok choy with shichimi togarashi and serve. It's that easy.

## VARIATION

For even more briny umami flavor, replace the shichimi togarashi with furikake, a flaky Japanese seasoning composed of sesame seeds, chopped nori seaweed, bonito (dried cured tuna), sugar, and salt.

# SMOKED CARROTS
## WITH TOASTED YEAST

Jeremy Umansky is a master meat curer from Cleveland, Ohio, where he runs a New Wave deli called Larder. New Wave? The guy serves smoked carrots and burdock root "meat sticks" alongside house-cured pancetta, pastrami, and bresaola. And don't get him talking about koji—the miracle spore used by the Japanese to turn soybeans into soy sauce and miso. (His passion for, and dare I say obsession with, koji runs so deep, he gave a whole TED talk on the topic.) Most of his veggie charcuterie involves a complex curing, smoking, and aging process that can last weeks, plus fermentation with koji. But these carrots can be smoked from start to finish in about an hour. The toasted yeast rub gives them an otherworldly flavor that's smoky, malty, and absolutely unique.

**YIELD** Serves 4 to 6

**METHOD** Hot-smoking

**PREP TIME** 10 minutes

**SMOKING TIME** 1 hour

**GRILL/GEAR** Best cooked in a charcoal grill or smoker. (If using a gas grill, see page 13.) You'll also need hardwood chunks or chips (soaked), see page 8. Note: Umansky uses shagbark hickory.

**WHAT ELSE** Just as you can't make a silk purse out of the proverbial sow's ear, you can't make great-tasting smoked carrots if you start with industrially farmed vegetables. If your carrots don't taste sweet and carroty, neither will your final dish. As for yeast, two good commercial brands are Fleishmann's and Red Star.

## INGREDIENTS

### FOR THE CARROTS AND YEAST RUB

Vegetable oil for oiling the grill grate

2 pounds carrots, preferably organic, or from your garden or local farmers' market, trimmed and scrubbed (there is no need to peel)

3 tablespoons active dry yeast (preferably from a jar—it's easier to measure)

2 teaspoons freshly ground black pepper

1 teaspoon unsweetened cocoa powder

1 teaspoon cumin seeds

1 teaspoon caraway seeds

5 juniper berries, lightly crushed with the side of a cleaver

### FOR SERVING

3 tablespoons pure maple syrup, or to taste

3 tablespoons extra virgin olive oil or vegetable oil

Coarse salt (sea or kosher)

¼ cup chopped celery leaves or fresh flat-leaf parsley leaves, for garnish (optional)

**1.** Set up your smoker following the manufacturer's instructions and heat to medium-low. Alternatively, set up your charcoal grill for indirect grilling and heat to medium-low, using half the normal amount of charcoal (you need less charcoal to keep the heat low). If enhancing a charcoal fire, add the wood chunks or chips to the coals; if enhancing a gas fire, place the chunks or chips in your grill's smoker box or place chunks under the grate directly over one or more burners. Brush or scrape the grill grate clean and oil it well. Close the grill lid.

**2.** Smoke the carrots until pliable but still al dente. This will take 45 minutes to 1 hour. (To test for doneness, bend a carrot into a horseshoe shape from the ends. If you can bring the ends to within 2 inches of each other without the carrot breaking, they're ready.)

**3.** Meanwhile, make the toasted yeast rub: Heat a dry cast-iron skillet over medium-low heat. Add the yeast, pepper, cocoa powder, cumin, caraway seeds, and juniper berries. Toast, shaking the pan and stirring the mixture often with a wooden spoon to keep the yeast from scorching, until the yeast darkens a few shades to chestnut brown and the spices are fragrant, 5 to 8 minutes. Transfer the mixture to a shallow mixing bowl and let cool.

**4.** Add the hot-smoked carrots to the yeast mixture and toss to coat. Stir in the maple syrup and olive oil and mix well. Add salt to taste. Let the carrots rest to absorb the yeast and spice flavors and to cool, 10 to 15 minutes. Sprinkle with the chopped celery leaves (if using), and serve at room temperature. Umansky recommends eating them with your fingers.

Char Siu Yams, page 224

# CHAR SIU YAMS

**YIELD** Serves 4

**METHOD** Smoke-roasting (indirect grilling with wood smoke)/direct grilling to finish

**PREP TIME** 10 minutes

**GRILLING TIME** 40 to 50 minutes

**GRILL/GEAR** Can be grilled over charcoal or gas. You'll also need an aluminum foil drip pan and, if you're enhancing the fire, hardwood chunks or chips (soaked), see page 8.

**WHAT ELSE** While a typical char siu consists of barbecued meat, this recipe calls for a technique I call pan grilling. You start by indirect grilling a vegetable (usually a root) in a foil pan, adding wood to the fire to lay on smoke flavor. The last 5 minutes, you switch to direct grilling (you slide the pan over one of the mounds of coals or directly over one of the burners). This sears the outside of the vegetable, sizzling the sauce to a shiny glaze. Note: Oyster sauce is a thick briny gravy traditionally made from oysters. Many brands contain more oyster flavoring than actual oysters. A vegetarian or vegan could safely use the Wan Ja Shan brand.

Char siu (from the Cantonese words for "fork roast") is Chinese barbecue—traditionally pork—glazed with a dark thick sauce sweetened with honey and hoisin sauce and made salty with oyster sauce and soy sauce. (The licorice undertones come from star anise—a primary ingredient in Chinese five-spice powder.) It turns out that the char siu glaze works wonders with grilled root vegetables—among them parsnips, carrots, sweet potatoes, and my favorite: garnet yams, sometimes called garnet sweet potatoes—how's that for confusing? (For more on the difference between yams and sweet potatoes, see What Else, page 226.) To mimic the look of a char siu pork loin, you could smoke-roast a whole yam. But I like the crisp edges that come with roasting the yams in quarters. Use this recipe as a general guide for turning your favorite root vegetable into char siu.

## INGREDIENTS

### FOR THE YAMS

2 pounds garnet yams or your favorite sweet potato variety (try to choose yams with a smooth, even, tapered, cylindrical shape)

1 tablespoon dark (toasted) sesame oil, plus 1 tablespoon for the glaze

2 tablespoons melted unsalted butter

### FOR THE GLAZE AND GARNISH

3 tablespoons honey

3 tablespoons soy sauce

2 tablespoons oyster sauce

2 tablespoons Chinese rice wine or sake

1 tablespoon hoisin sauce

1 tablespoon dark (toasted) sesame oil

½ teaspoon Chinese five-spice powder

2 tablespoons thinly sliced scallion greens or chives, for garnish

**1.** Set up your grill for indirect grilling and heat to medium-high.

**2.** Scrub the yams. Cut each one lengthwise in quarters. Arrange the yams in a single layer in a disposable aluminum foil drip pan. Toss with the sesame oil and add the melted butter.

**3.** Place the yams in their foil pan on the grill grate away from heat. If enhancing a charcoal fire, add the wood chunks or chips to the coals; if enhancing a gas fire, place the chunks or chips in your grill's smoker box or place chunks under the grate directly over one or more burners. Close the grill lid.

**4.** Smoke-roast the yams until almost tender, 30 to 40 minutes. Test with a skewer: It should pierce the yams easily. Stir a few times so they cook evenly.

**5. Meanwhile, make the glaze:** Combine the honey, soy sauce, oyster sauce, rice wine, hoisin sauce, sesame oil, and five-spice powder in a small bowl and whisk to combine.

**6.** Move the pan with the yams directly over the fire and direct grill until the exteriors are browned and crusty, about 3 minutes, stirring often.

**7.** Stir in the glaze and continue direct grilling until the glaze boils and thickens and coats the yams on all sides in a shiny lacquer, 2 to 4 minutes.

**8.** Arrange the yams in a shallow serving bowl or on plates. Sprinkle with the scallion greens and serve.

# SMOKED SWEET POTATO CASSEROLE
## WITH BROWN SUGAR AND MAPLE SYRUP

Thanksgiving wouldn't be complete without a sweet potato casserole. And sweet potatoes wouldn't be complete without butter, brown sugar, and maple syrup. What sets this one apart is a flavor that's simultaneously familiar and unexpected: wood smoke. Happy T-Day!

### INGREDIENTS

6 sweet potatoes (3 to 3½ pounds)

1 tablespoon unsalted butter, at room temperature, for the baking dish, plus 4 tablespoons (¼ cup) cold butter for the topping

1 tablespoon dark rum (optional)

⅓ cup pure maple syrup

⅓ cup dark brown sugar, or to taste

1 tablespoon thinly slivered fresh chives (optional)

**YIELD** Serves 8

**METHOD** Smoke-roasting (indirect grilling with wood smoke)

**PREP TIME** 15 minutes

**GRILLING TIME** 40 to 60 minutes for smoke-roasting the potatoes, plus 20 to 30 minutes for browning

**GRILL/GEAR** Can be grilled over gas, but you'll get a better flavor from charcoal. You'll also need a 9 × 13-inch baking dish or aluminum drip pan; a stiff-bristle vegetable brush; and hardwood chunks or chips (soaked), see page 8.

Sweet potatoes come in more than 6,500 varieties, including the popular Japanese sweet potato (purple skin, cream-colored flesh) and the Okinawa (tan skin, purple flesh). But for the fourth Thursday in November, you want a good old-fashioned orange-fleshed sweet potato, sometimes (and incorrectly) called a yam. To the extent possible, choose spuds that are more cylindrical and less football-shaped. Organic is always a plus.

**1.** Set up your grill for indirect grilling and heat to medium-high. Grease the bottom and sides of the baking dish with 1 tablespoon of butter.

**2.** Meanwhile, scrub the sweet potatoes in their skins with a stiff-bristle vegetable brush. Dry well, then prick each sweet potato 10 or 12 times with a fork. (This allows the steam to escape so the potatoes don't explode, and lets the smoke penetrate the flesh.) Arrange the sweet potatoes on the grate over the drip pan away from the heat. If enhancing a charcoal fire, add the wood chunks or chips to the coals; if enhancing a gas fire, place the chunks or chips in your grill's smoker box or place chunks under the grate directly over one or more burners. Close the grill lid.

**3.** Smoke-roast (indirect grill) the sweet potatoes until tender, 40 to 60 minutes. Use a bamboo skewer to test for doneness: It should pierce the spud easily. Transfer the sweet potatoes to a cutting board to cool. The sweet potatoes can be smoke-roasted at a previous grill session up to a day ahead; cover and refrigerate.

**4.** Cut each sweet potato crosswise into ½-inch slices. (I leave the skins on, but you can certainly peel the potatoes if you like.) Shingle the slices in rows to fill up the buttered baking dish. If you like rum, stir it into the maple syrup and pour the mixture evenly over the sweet potatoes. Sprinkle the brown sugar on top. Thinly slice the cold butter on top. The sweet potatoes can be prepared up to a day ahead to this stage and refrigerated.

**5.** Set up your grill for indirect grilling and heat to medium-high. Indirect grill the sweet potatoes until the butter is melted, the brown sugar is bubbling, and the sweet potatoes are darkly browned, 20 to 30 minutes, or as needed. Sprinkle with the chives (if using). Serve right out of the baking dish.

# VARIATION

So, you're probably wondering what happened to the marshmallows. If your Thanksgiving sweet potatoes are unthinkable without them, buy mini marshmallows or slice large ones (preferably artisanal) and arrange them on top of the sweet potatoes over the brown sugar. Smoke-roast as described above until the marshmallows are melted, browned, and smoky.

# MEXICAN GRILLED CREAMED CORN

This flavorful dish is a sort of creamed corn made with ingredients similar to those found in Esquites (see page 70), but combined and heated to a completely different effect. Inspired by the Los Angeles Mexican fusion restaurant Broken Spanish, this owes its lush texture to a combination of Mexican crema and mayonnaise.

## INGREDIENTS

Vegetable oil for oiling the grill grate

4 ears of sweet corn, husked

1½ tablespoons extra virgin olive oil or melted butter

Coarse salt (sea or kosher) and freshly ground black pepper

1 large poblano pepper (optional)

2 ounces Cotija, queso fresco, feta, Pecorino Romano, or other piquant cheese, crumbled

3 tablespoons crema (Mexican sour cream) or sour cream

3 tablespoons heavy cream (or more crema)

½ teaspoon freshly and finely grated lime zest

1 tablespoon fresh lime juice, or to taste

⅓ cup chopped fresh cilantro leaves

2 tablespoons mayonnaise, preferably Hellmann's or Best Foods

**1.** Set up your grill for direct grilling and heat to high. Brush or scrape the grill grate clean and oil it well.

**2.** Meanwhile, lightly brush the corn with the olive oil and season generously with salt and pepper.

**3.** Grill the corn and poblano (if using), turning with tongs until darkly browned on all sides. For the corn, this will take 2 to 3 minutes per side, 8 to 12 minutes in all; for the poblano, 3 to 4 minutes per side, 12 to 16 minutes in all. Transfer the corn and poblano to a cutting board to cool.

**4.** Cut the kernels off the cobs using broad strokes with a sharp chef's knife. (The easiest way to do this is to lay the corn flat on the cutting board.) Scrape any burnt skin off the poblano. Cut the poblano into ½-inch dice, discarding the seeds and veins. Place the corn and poblano in a medium-size saucepan.

**5.** Stir the cheese, crema, heavy cream, lime zest, lime juice, and half the cilantro into the corn and poblano in the pan. Simmer the mixture over medium heat until thick and creamy, about 5 minutes. Remove the pan from the heat and whisk in the mayonnaise and salt and pepper to taste. Transfer to a serving bowl, sprinkle with the remaining cilantro, and serve.

**YIELD** Serves 4

**METHOD** Direct grilling

**PREP TIME** 20 minutes

**GRILLING TIME** 12 to 16 minutes

**GRILL/GEAR** Can be grilled over charcoal, gas, or wood.

**WHAT ELSE** The recipe calls for two Mexican ingredients that may be unfamiliar: crema (similar to sour cream, but thinner and a little sharper) and queso Cotija (named for a town in the state of Michoacán in southwest Mexico famed for its sharp salty cheese). Sour cream makes a fine substitute for the former; queso fresco, feta, or Italian Pecorino Romano for the latter.

# NEW SCHOOL GREEN BEANS ALMONDINE
## WITH MARCONA ALMONDS AND BROWN BUTTER

**YIELD** Serves 4

**METHOD** Pan grilling

**PREP TIME** 15 minutes

**GRILLING TIME** 8 to 12 minutes

**GRILL/GEAR** Can be grilled over charcoal, gas, or wood. If you're enhancing a charcoal or gas fire, you'll need hardwood chunks or chips (unsoaked), see page 8. Depending on the cooking method, you'll also need a large skillet or large aluminum foil drip pan; a grilling grid; wooden toothpicks; or a wire-mesh grill basket.

**WHAT ELSE** You have several options for the green beans: slender French haricots verts, classic green, or even yellow beans, wax beans, or broad beans. Marcona almonds from Spain are rounder and sweeter than California almonds with buttery overtones of macadamia nut. Look for them in well-stocked supermarkets, Iberian grocery stores, or online. If unavailable, California almonds will work.

It's hard to get more old school than green beans almondine—that age-old French side dish consisting of boiled or steamed haricots verts dressed with slivered almonds and butter. Well, here's the new school version, and it involves—you guessed it—the grill. Actually, there are four ways to grill the green beans: smoke-roasted in a pan (the technique offered here); direct grilled on a grilling grate or skewered into rafts (like the okra on page 159); or caveman-style on the embers (the latter three methods offered as variations). Each produces a subtly different texture, but all beat boiling hollow. For nuts, you'll use Spanish Marcona almonds, which you'll bolster with sherry vinegar and brown butter (beurre noisette). Which just goes to show how grilling can breathe new life into an old chestnut—or in this case, into old school green beans.

## INGREDIENTS

**FOR THE GREEN BEANS**

1½ pounds haricots verts or other green beans, ends snapped off and strings removed

1 tablespoon extra virgin olive oil or melted butter

Coarse salt (sea or kosher) and freshly ground black pepper

**FOR THE SAUCE**

3 tablespoons unsalted butter

3 tablespoons Marcona almonds, coarsely chopped

3 tablespoons roughly chopped fresh flat-leaf parsley leaves

1 tablespoon sherry vinegar, or to taste

Coarse salt (sea or kosher) and freshly ground black pepper

**1.** Set up your grill for direct grilling and heat to high. Optional: If enhancing a charcoal fire, add the wood chunks or chips to the coals; if enhancing a gas fire, place the chunks or chips in your grill's smoker box or place chunks under the grate directly over one or more burners.

**2.** Place the green beans in a large skillet with a heatproof handle or 1 or 2 aluminum foil drip pans. (The beans should be layered no deeper than ½ inch.) Toss with the olive oil and season with salt and pepper. Grill the beans in the pan until browned and tender, 3 to 5 minutes, turning with tongs. Don't overcook. You want the beans to have some crunch. Transfer the beans to a platter.

**3.** Make the sauce: Return the skillet to the heat (or to your grill's side burner). Add the 3 tablespoons of butter and cook until it melts and begins to brown (the sizzling will subside just before browning), about 2 minutes. Stir in the Marcona almonds and parsley and cook until browned, about 1 minute. Stir in the sherry vinegar and salt and pepper to taste. Pour this mixture over the beans and serve.

# VARIATIONS

### DIRECT GRILLING METHOD— ON A VEGETABLE GRILLING GRID

Follow Step 1 above. Heat the vegetable grilling grid as well. Toss the beans with oil and season with salt and pepper. Grill on the grilling grid until browned and tender, 2 to 4 minutes per side. Follow the remaining steps.

### DIRECT GRILLING METHOD— IN RAFTS

Follow Step 1. Lay 6 to 8 green beans side by side and skewer together crosswise with wooden toothpicks to make rafts (see photo on page 161). Lightly brush with olive oil and season with salt and pepper. Direct grill the green beans until browned and tender, 2 to 4 minutes per side. Follow the remaining steps.

### EMBER-GRILLING (CAVEMAN GRILLING) METHOD

Here's a way cool technique I observed at the celebrated wood-burning-hearth restaurant The Dabney, in Washington, D.C., where James Beard Award–winning chef Jeremiah Langhorne grills his green beans in a wire-mesh grill basket directly in the embers. The result: charred smoky beans that retain their primal crunch. You'll need a charcoal grill for this one.

**1.** Rake out the coals in an even layer and fan off any loose ash.

**2.** Place the beans in a wire-mesh grill basket. Set the basket directly on the coals. Grill the beans until browned and evenly charred, turning with tongs and shaking the basket. This will take 2 to 4 minutes. Transfer the beans to a platter and proceed with Step 3.

# ZUCCHINI "BURNT ENDS"
## WITH HERB BUTTER AND LEMON

Your first zucchini of the season delights, as does your second, but by the fourth or fifth, you wonder why so many people have planted so much of a vegetable that is mild (almost bland) in flavor, soft in texture, and moist to the point of being watery. Russ Faulk knows why. Russ is the head designer at Kalamazoo Outdoor Gourmet and, as such, is responsible for some of the most stylish grills on the planet. He has also devised one of the world's most ingenious ways to grill zucchini. He slices it paper-thin on a mandoline (a necessary tool for this recipe unless you have mad knife skills), then accordions the slices on bamboo skewers. (This recipe was inspired by his stunning cookbook *Food + Fire*.) This turns the notoriously limp vegetable into a series of crisp burnt edges. The result looks cool as all get-out. Add a lemon herb butter, and you may just find yourself planting extra zucchini next summer.

**YIELD** Serves 4

**METHOD** Direct grilling

**PREP TIME** 15 minutes

**GRILLING TIME** 8 minutes

**GRILL/GEAR** Can be grilled over charcoal, gas, or wood, but for the best flavor, work over a wood or wood-enhanced fire. If you're enhancing a charcoal or gas fire, you'll need hardwood chunks or chips (unsoaked), see page 8. You'll also need a rimmed sheet pan; a mandoline; and 8 flat (12-inch-long) bamboo skewers or 16 round bamboo skewers.

**WHAT ELSE** You'll need a special tool called a mandoline, which is a flat slicer with a razor-sharp blade you can adjust to slice vegetables as thinly as you desire. (The back-and-forth action of slicing the vegetable mimics the strumming of a mandolin: hence the name.) Choose small zucchini—6 to 8 inches long and 6 to 8 ounces. Use flat skewers or parallel bamboo skewers, which keeps the zucchini slices from spinning when you attempt to turn them.

## INGREDIENTS

8 tablespoons (1 stick) unsalted butter or extra virgin olive oil

2 cloves garlic, peeled and slightly flattened with the side of a knife

1 teaspoon freshly and finely grated lemon zest

3 tablespoons stemmed, chopped fresh dill or mint leaves, plus 3 tablespoons for serving

½ teaspoon hot red pepper flakes (optional)

8 small zucchini (6 to 8 ounces each)

Coarse salt (sea or kosher) and freshly ground black pepper

Vegetable oil for oiling the grill grate

**1.** Make the lemon herb butter: Melt the butter in a small saucepan over medium heat. Add the garlic, lemon zest, 3 tablespoons of chopped dill, and the hot red pepper flakes (if using). Cook until fragrant, about 3 minutes.

Remove the pan from the heat and let it cool. Discard the garlic.

**2.** Cut off and discard the ends of the zucchini. Using a mandoline (preferably one equipped with a finger guard) thinly slice one zucchini lengthwise. (The slices should be the thickness of a quarter.) Lay the slices flat on a rimmed sheet pan. Lightly brush the slices on both sides with the lemon herb butter and season with salt and pepper.

**3.** Fold a zucchini slice into an accordion shape (like multiple Ws) and thread it onto a flat skewer. Don't worry if a few of the slices break—skewer the pieces back to back. Continue threading until all the slices from a single zucchini are on the skewer. The green skin should be on the top and bottom. If using round bamboo skewers, insert a second skewer parallel to the first. (This keeps the zucchini slices from spinning.) Slice, butter, season, and skewer the remaining zucchini the same way. You should wind up with 8 kebabs. It's best to skewer the zucchini right before grilling.

**4.** Meanwhile, set up your grill for direct grilling and heat to high. If enhancing a charcoal fire, add the wood chunks or chips to the coals; if enhancing a gas fire, place the chunks or chips in your grill's smoker box or place chunks under the grate directly over one or more burners. Brush or scrape the grill grate clean and oil it well.

**5.** Arrange the zucchini kebabs, skin side down, on the grate and grill until darkly browned, even singed, at the edges, 3 to 4 minutes. Turn and grill the other side, skin side down the same way, 6 to 8 minutes in all. Baste the zucchini skewers with the lemon herb butter as they grill. Transfer to a platter or plates for serving and spoon any remaining butter over them. Serve immediately.

Cut the zucchini into wafer-thin slices on a mandoline.

Weave the zucchini slices onto bamboo skewers.

# THE ULTIMATE SMOKED BAKED BEANS

Baked beans are an indispensable side dish for any barbecue or cookout. In this version, they become the barbecue itself. That's right: By smoking the baked beans on your grill or in your smoker, you add a depth of smoky flavor that turns the lowly baked bean from side dish to star attraction. Traditional American baked beans are made with a single variety—typically navy beans. You're going to up the ante by using four different types of beans.

**YIELD** Serves 8

**PREP TIME** 15 minutes

**METHOD** Indirect grilling or smoking

**GRILLING/SMOKING TIME** 2 hours (plus another ½ hour if using a smoker)

**GRILL/GEAR** Can be cooked over charcoal or gas or in a smoker. If using a grill, you'll also need hardwood chunks or chips (soaked), see page 8. Optional: a large aluminum foil roasting pan.

**WHAT ELSE** The purist may wish to start with dried beans (you'll need ⅔ cup of each), which would be soaked overnight, then boiled until tender. At my house, we usually use organic canned beans with no serious diminution of pleasure. I've made the bacon optional: Folks who don't eat meat can omit it. Obviously, if you use it, your baked beans will taste all the richer. I also call for optional liquid smoke, which, despite its questionable reputation in barbecue circles, is a natural product made from distilled real hardwood smoke. It will definitely reinforce the smoke flavor.

## INGREDIENTS

4 strips thick-cut bacon, preferably artisanal, cut crosswise into ½-inch slivers (optional), or 3 tablespoons unsalted butter or extra virgin olive oil

1 large onion, peeled, cut into ½-inch dice

1 poblano pepper, stemmed, seeded, and cut into ½-inch dice

1 red or yellow bell pepper, stemmed, seeded, and cut into ½-inch dice

2 jalapeño peppers, stemmed, seeded, and cut into ½-inch dice (for spicier baked beans, leave the seeds in)

2 cloves garlic, peeled and minced

¼ cup chopped fresh cilantro or flat-leaf parsley leaves

1 can (15 ounces) black beans, preferably organic

1 can (15 ounces) red kidney beans, preferably organic

1 can (15 ounces) navy beans, preferably organic

1 can (15 ounces) chickpeas, preferably organic

1 cup of your favorite sweet red barbecue sauce, or to taste

¾ cup brown sugar (light or dark—your choice), or to taste

½ cup molasses (light or dark—your choice)

⅓ cup Dijon mustard

2 tablespoons Worcestershire sauce

2 teaspoons of your favorite hot sauce

½ teaspoon liquid smoke (optional)

Coarse salt (sea or kosher) and freshly ground black pepper

**1.** Place the bacon (if using) in a large Dutch oven or heavy pot. Place over medium-high heat on your stovetop or the side burner of your grill and cook, stirring occasionally, until sizzling and golden, about 5 minutes.

**2.** Add the onion, poblano, bell pepper, jalapeños, garlic, and cilantro to the pot and cook until lightly browned, about 4 minutes.

**3.** Stir the beans with their juices into the bacon-vegetable mixture. Stir in the barbecue sauce, sugar, molasses, mustard, Worcestershire sauce, hot sauce, and liquid smoke (if using). Add salt and pepper to taste; the baked beans should be highly seasoned. You'll smoke the beans in the Dutch oven, or if you prefer, transfer them to a large aluminum foil roasting pan.

**4.** To smoke the beans on your grill, set it up for indirect grilling and heat to medium. If enhancing a charcoal fire, add the wood chunks or chips to the coals; if enhancing a gas fire, place the chunks or chips in your grill's smoker box or place chunks under the grate directly over one or more burners. If using a smoker, set it up following the manufacturer's instructions and heat to 275°F. Smoke-roast the beans, uncovered, until thick, concentrated, and richly flavored, about 2 hours (this may take another ½ hour in a smoker). Note: You cook the beans uncovered to concentrate the flavor and juices. But take care not to dry the beans out. If they start to dry out, add a little water and put the lid on the Dutch oven or cover the pan with aluminum foil.

**5.** Correct the seasoning, adding salt, pepper, barbecue sauce, or brown sugar to taste: The beans should be sweet and savory. Dig in!

# EMBER-GRILLED BARBECUED ONIONS

**YIELD** Serves 4

**METHOD** Ember-grilling (caveman grilling) or direct grilling

**PREP TIME** 15 minutes

**GRILLING TIME** 45 minutes, plus 5 to 8 minutes for reheating the onions

**GRILL/GEAR** Best grilled on charcoal. You'll also need a metal skewer; a rimmed sheet pan; and latex gloves (optional).

Onions loom large on the barbecue landscape—sliced raw on brisket sandwiches, diced raw in pico de gallo for tacos, grilled on shish kebabs, sautéed to make barbecue sauce, etc. In the following recipe, they become the barbecue itself. The idea comes from Andrew Brady, chef-owner of Field & Vine restaurant in Somerville, Massachusetts, where a massive wood-burning grill dominates the kitchen and vegetables dominate the menu. Brady cooks onions slowly in butter, then fortifies them with barbecue sauce. You'll take the process even further, roasting the onions in the embers to impart a smokiness you never suspected an onion could possess. And talk about cool factor: I like to serve the barbecued onion mixture in the charred hollowed-out onion shells. Note: Handling the charred onion shells can be messy. You can certainly skip this step and serve the creamy onions as they are.

## INGREDIENTS

4 large onions (each about the size of a baseball), unpeeled

2 tablespoons of your favorite barbecue sauce, or to taste

3 tablespoons unsalted butter

Coarse salt (sea or kosher) and freshly ground black pepper

1 tablespoon honey (optional)

Sprigs of fresh thyme or 2 teaspoons minced fresh chives, for garnish

**1.** Set up your grill for ember-grilling (caveman grilling). Rake out the coals and fan off any loose ash. Alternatively, set your grill up for direct grilling and heat it as high as it will go.

**2.** Lay the onions on the coals (or on the hot grill grate) and roast them in their skins until charred black on the outside and very tender inside, turning with tongs so they roast evenly. The whole process will take about 45 minutes—a little more or a little less, depending on the size of your onions. Use a metal skewer to test for doneness: It should pierce the onions easily. Transfer the grilled onions to a rimmed sheet pan, brushing off any loose embers. Let cool to room temperature.

**3.** Cut each onion in half from the top to the root end. (Wear latex gloves to keep the black char off your fingers.) Using a spoon, scrape out the soft center. Save the charred onion shells for serving (optional). Roughly chop the scooped onion and transfer it to a medium-size saucepan. Stir in the barbecue sauce and butter.

**4.** Set the pan on your grill (replace the grate) or on your grill's side burner or on the stovetop over medium heat. Simmer the onions in the sauce until richly flavored, 5 to 8 minutes. Correct the seasoning, adding salt and pepper and the honey (if using), for extra sweetness.

**5.** To serve, spoon the barbecued onion mixture back into the charred onion shells. Or spoon it directly into a bowl or onto plates. Top with thyme sprigs and you're in business.

**WHAT ELSE** You have many options for onions: sweet onions, like Vidalias or Walla Wallas; red onions, like Brunswick or Flamencos; torpedo onions; commonplace yellow; and more. All acquire splendid sweetness and smoke on the embers. You'll want a sweet smoky barbecue sauce for the onions: I'd reach for my Project Smoke Lemon Brown Sugar or Chipotle Molasses. Serve these barbecued onions as a side dish or condiment.

# SMASHED POTATOES

**YIELD** Serves 4

**METHOD** Indirect grilling/
plancha grilling

**PREP TIME** 5 minutes

**GRILLING TIME** 45 minutes,
plus 5 minutes for plancha
grilling the smashed potatoes

**GRILL/GEAR** Can be grilled
over charcoal or gas. You'll
also need a plancha or large
cast-iron skillet and, if you're
enhancing the fire, hardwood
chunks or chips (soaked), see
page 8.

**WHAT ELSE** Any potato
can be roasted and smashed,
from Idaho bakers to purple
potatoes from Peru. I like the
creamy texture and buttery
taste of Yukon Golds, and I
like to smash halved potatoes
so you get a crisp side with
skin and a softer side with
pure potato. Fingerling and
baby potatoes (Dutch Yellows)
are also great for smashing,
with the added advantage of
maximizing the ratio of crusty
skin to potato. Note: I call for
oiling the potatoes with extra
virgin olive oil, but bacon or
duck fat produce wondrous
smashers, too.

Smashed potatoes combine the creamy texture of the best baked spud with the crunch of a well-executed French fry. I first experienced them at a beachside restaurant called Parador La Huella in José Ignacio, Uruguay, where the potatoes were roasted in a wood-burning oven, then griddled. From there, it's a short leap to the grill—a leap worth taking because it enables you to amplify the smoke flavor by adding wood chunks or chips to the fire. Once the potatoes are smashed, you can lavish them with your favorite toppings: sour cream, grated cheese, scallions, bacon, chopped toasted walnuts, anchovies—your imagination is the only limit.

## INGREDIENTS

4 large Yukon Gold potatoes

Extra virgin olive oil (or bacon fat or duck fat), for brushing

Coarse salt (sea or kosher) and freshly ground black pepper

Pimentón (Spanish smoked paprika; optional)

3 tablespoons unsalted butter, extra virgin olive oil, or— why not?—bacon fat

Your favorite potato toppings, such as sour cream, chopped fresh chives or scallions, crumbled bacon, grated cheese, and so on

**1.** Set up your grill for indirect grilling and preheat to medium-high. Place a plancha or large cast-iron griddle, grill pan, or skillet in the center and heat it as well.

**2.** Scrub the potatoes clean, blot dry with paper towels, and prick each in a few places with a fork. Brush the potatoes on all sides with olive oil and season generously with salt, pepper, and pimentón (if using).

**3.** Arrange the potatoes on the plancha. If enhancing a charcoal fire, add the wood chunks or chips to the coals; if enhancing a gas fire, place the chunks or chips in your grill's smoker box or place chunks under the grate directly over one or more burners. Close the grill lid.

**4.** Smoke-roast (indirect grill) the potatoes until tender, about 45 minutes. (Turn the potatoes once or twice so they roast evenly.) Use a metal skewer to test for doneness: It should pierce a potato easily.

**5.** Transfer the roasted potatoes to a cutting board and cut each one in half crosswise. Increase the heat under the plancha to high. (If using charcoal, rake it directly under the plancha; if using gas, turn the burner under it to high.)

**6.** Melt half the butter on the plancha, spreading it around with a spatula. Place the potato halves, cut sides down, on the plancha. Using a grill press, potato masher, scaloppini pounder, or other flat heavy object, smash the potatoes and flatten to a thickness of ¼ inch. Fry on the hot plancha until crusty and brown on the bottom, about 3 minutes.

**7.** Melt the remaining butter on the plancha between the smashed potatoes. Flip the smashed potatoes onto the butter and fry the other side the same way—you'll need about 2 minutes.

**8.** Transfer the smashed potatoes to a platter or plates. They're delicious as is, or dollop with sour cream and sprinkle with pimentón, chives, or any other topping you fancy.

# GRILLED ONIGIRI
## (JAPANESE RICE CAKES)

**YIELD** Makes 6 (1 or 2 per person) and can be multiplied as desired

**METHOD** Direct grilling

**PREP TIME** 10 minutes (plus the time it takes to cook the rice and make the optional sauce)

**GRILLING TIME** 6 to 10 minutes

**GRILL/GEAR** Can be grilled over charcoal, gas, or wood.

**WHAT ELSE** I usually make onigiri when I have leftover sticky (glutinous) white rice or brown rice. For even more flavor, start with sushi rice, which is seasoned with rice vinegar and lightly sweetened with sugar or honey. (Make your own or buy it from your local sushi parlor.) Note: Miso, umeboshi (pickled plum) paste, and sweet red bean paste can be found at Asian markets and many supermarkets, such as Whole Foods, or online.

If you want a singular food experience in a land replete with singular food experiences, order lunch from a vending machine in a Japanese train station. Among the offerings are what, at first glance, look like Jewish hamantaschen (triangular pastries associated with the Purim holiday). On closer inspection, they turn out to be grilled rice cakes. Onigiri (literally "rice balls") are a popular Japanese snack, lunch, or side dish at robatayaki (grill) parlors. At their simplest, onigiri consist of unembellished grilled sticky rice. More elaborate versions might conceal a dab of miso or sweet red bean paste in the center. Or come glazed with sweet-salty teriyaki sauce (see the variation that follows). Here, I make them round, not triangular—they're easier to form. Use the following recipe as a broad guide, customizing the flavorings to suit your taste. Note: I call for direct grilling, but you can also sear the onigiri on a hot, well-oiled plancha, griddle, or cast-iron skillet. Advantage? Less risk of sticking.

### INGREDIENTS

3 cups cooked sticky white or brown rice, or sushi rice

4 tablespoons white or red miso, umeboshi paste (pickled plum paste), or sweet red bean paste, for filling

Vegetable oil for oiling the grill grate

2 tablespoons dark (toasted) sesame oil or vegetable oil, or as needed

About 2 tablespoons toasted white or black sesame seeds (optional)

1 scallion, trimmed, greens thinly sliced crosswise (save the white part for another use)

**1.** Cover a plate with plastic wrap. Wet your hands with cold water to keep the rice from sticking. Take ½ cup rice and roll it between your hands to form a ball. Make a depression in the center and spoon in about 2 teaspoons of the miso. Pinch the top to encase the filling, then pat the ball into a flat disk about 2½ inches in diameter and ¾ inch thick. Place on the prepared plate and cover with plastic wrap. Refrigerate until you're ready to grill: The onigiri can be prepared several hours ahead to this stage.

**2.** Set up your grill for direct grilling and heat to high. Brush or scrape the grill grate clean and oil it well (alternatively, preheat a well-oiled plancha).

**3.** Brush the onigiri on both sides with the sesame oil. Arrange them on the grate (or plancha) and grill until the bottoms are crusty and browned, 3 to 5 minutes. Brush the tops with more oil. Using a thin-bladed metal spatula, gently turn the onigiri and grill the other side the same way.

**4.** Sprinkle with the sesame seeds (if using) and/or chopped scallions and serve.

## VARIATION

To glaze the onigiri, use the Thai sweet chili teriyaki sauce (page 200), brushing it on the onigiri on both sides before placing them on the grill, then again while the onigiri are grilling. Spoon a little sauce over the cooked onigiri and serve at once.

# CHAPTER 9

# GRILLED EGGS & CHEESES

Eggs are a food few people think of grilling. Cheese is something almost all of us eat grilled, although most "grilled cheese" is actually cooked on a griddle or in a sandwich press. This chapter aims to give both foods their barbecue bona fides. We start, appropriately, with breakfast: eggs grilled over a smoky wood fire in an impossibly cool tool called an egg spoon. From there, it's on to a grilled vegetable frittata from Italy, smoked eggs from Japan, and eggs grilled directly in the shell, as they do in Vietnam. Eyes will pop and jaws will drop when you serve my take on Cambodian grilled egg kebabs—a dish that spans seven centuries and two continents. And while we're on the subject of kebabs, in this chapter you'll find garlicky Brazilian cheese kebabs, honey and rosewater halloumi kebabs, and a cheese and veggie shawarma flavor-blasted with Middle Eastern spices. You've surely heard of planked salmon; how about Brie cheese grilled on a flame-charred cedar plank, complete with fig jam and walnuts? Or tandoori-style grilled cheese and pepper kebabs and cheese-grilled portobellos flambéed with cognac? Eggs and cheese, meet grill. What are you waiting for?

# RECIPES

# WOOD FIRE EGGS
## (EGG SPOON EGGS)

**YIELD** Makes 1 egg and can be multiplied as desired

**METHOD** Direct grilling

**PREP TIME** 2 minutes

**GRILLING TIME** 2 to 4 minutes

**GRILL/GEAR** Can be grilled over charcoal or gas, but tastes best grilled over wood (as in your fireplace or over a campfire). You'll also need an egg spoon.

**WHAT ELSE** For the full effect, you'll need the titular utensil—basically a giant cast-iron spoon with a small deep bowl at one end and a long slender handle at the other. Two good sources are Wayfarer Forge and The Egg Spoon. If you don't have an egg spoon, use a long-handled cast-iron or carbon steel skillet. The trick with the skillet is to tip it on an angle so the oil pools at the far edge. Cook the egg in that pool and continue to spoon the hot oil over it. That way, the egg will deep-fry rather than pan-fry. Note: The egg spoon was designed to be used over a wood fire, but you can certainly use it on a charcoal or gas grill.

Most of my recipes are inspired by ingredients and dishes I've enjoyed on my travels. Some come from new grills or specialized grilling techniques. This one was inspired by a grilling accessory, the egg spoon—used in European fireplace cooking and more recently popularized by Alice Waters of Chez Panisse. You might think the egg spoon functions like a skillet, but it delivers a different effect. Thanks to its deep bowl and narrow dimensions (just large enough for one egg), you wind up deep-frying the egg, which produces a luscious crusty exterior. And because you're working over live fire, you perfume the egg with wood smoke. Use a high-quality fruity olive oil for frying—preferably Spanish.

## INGREDIENTS

1 large egg, preferably organic

2 tablespoons extra virgin olive oil, or as needed

Your Basic Grilled Bread (page 98), for serving (optional)

Coarse salt (sea or kosher) and freshly ground black pepper

**1.** Build your fire or light your grill. If working on a wood grill, over a campfire, or in the fireplace—the dream scenario—start grilling while some of the logs are still flaming. (There's more smoke in a flaming fire than in an ember fire.) If using a gas or charcoal grill, heat to high.

**2.** Crack the egg into a small bowl. Place the oil in the egg spoon and heat it over the fire. (On a gas grill, heat the spoon right on the grate.) When the oil is shimmering hot, about 2 minutes, carefully slide the egg into it and put it back over the fire. Fry until the outside of the egg is crisp and brown, swirling the spoon to coat the sides with hot oil. Using a wooden spoon, gently turn the egg over to fry the top. Total cooking time will be about 2 minutes.

**3.** Slide the egg onto a plate (or better yet, onto a slice of grilled bread). Season with salt and pepper. Repeat again. And again.

**NOTE:** Sometimes I add a couple of slices of garlic or jalapeño to the oil while heating it and frying the egg. Just saying.

# SMOKED EGGS
## WITH JAPANESE SEASONINGS

You've probably experienced ajitsuke tamago even if you've never heard of them. They're the topaz-colored eggs floating in bowls of ramen soup. Soy sauce makes them salty; mirin and sugar, a little sweet; and they're about to become even more amazing by the addition of a flavoring near and dear to the heart of this barbecue community: wood smoke. Tip o' the hat to Frank Thornton, a self-described army brat, foodie, and English teacher living in Hiroshima, who often makes these sweet, smoky eggs to serve at parties. (We became acquainted through my Steven Raichlen Facebook fan page.) Thanks, Frank!

### INGREDIENTS

8 large eggs, preferably organic

1 cup mirin

1 cup soy sauce

2 tablespoons granulated sugar

3 coins (each ¼ inch thick) unpeeled fresh ginger, smashed with the side of a chef's knife

Shichimi togarashi (Japanese pepper rub—see page 220), for serving (optional)

Vegetable oil for oiling the wire rack

**YIELD** Makes 8 eggs, enough to serve 4

**METHOD** Smoke-roasting (indirect grilling with wood smoke)/smoking

**PREP TIME** 15 minutes, plus 8 to 12 hours for marinating

**SMOKING TIME** 10 to 15 minutes (possibly longer if using a smoker—follow the manufacturer's instructions)

**GRILL/GEAR** If smoke-roasting, work over charcoal. If smoking, any sort of smoker will do—outdoor or indoor (see What Else). You'll also need a wire rack set over a rimmed sheet pan; hardwood chunks or chips (unsoaked), see page 8; and an aluminum foil drip pan filled with ice.

**1.** Boil the eggs: Place the eggs in a large saucepan with cool water to cover by a depth of 2 inches. Bring to a boil over medium-high heat, then reduce the heat and gently simmer the eggs for 11 minutes for hard-cooked yolks, or 7 to 8 minutes for softer, jammier yolks. (This is at sea level; increase the cooking time if you live at high altitude.) Pour off the hot water and fill the pot with cold water. When the eggs are cool enough to handle, but still warm, carefully peel, then let cool to room temperature.

**2.** Combine the mirin, soy sauce, and sugar in a deep bowl and whisk until the sugar dissolves. Add the ginger and the peeled eggs and marinate, refrigerated, for 8 to 12 hours, stirring occasionally so they marinate evenly.

**3.** Drain the eggs and discard the marinade. Place the eggs on a wire rack over a rimmed sheet pan or baking pan in the refrigerator until the surface feels tacky, about 1 hour.

eggs are cooked to a stage between soft-cooked and hard-cooked (for 7 to 8 minutes at sea level). The yolk should remain bright orange and just barely set—a texture often referred to as "jammy." You may want to go longer if the eggs are to be served as a pass-around. Mirin is Japanese sweet rice wine. If unavailable, use sake and up the sugar by 2 teaspoons. Note: Some people like to smoke the eggs in the shells (as pictured on page 244). This delivers a more subtle smoke flavor but looks really cool.

**4.** Set up your grill for smoking (indirect grilling) and heat to medium-low. To achieve this low temperature, use only half or a third as much charcoal as you normally would for indirect grilling. If enhancing a charcoal fire, add the wood chunks or chips to the coals; if enhancing a gas fire, place the chunks or chips in your grill's smoker box or place chunks under the grate directly over one or more burners.

**5.** Coat a wire rack with oil and set it over an aluminum foil pan full of ice. Cut the boiled eggs in half, lengthwise or widthwise—your choice—and arrange them cut sides up on the rack (the eggs should not touch the ice). The ice keeps the eggs from overcooking and becoming rubbery.

**6.** Place the eggs on the wire rack over the ice on the grill. Close the grill lid and smoke the eggs until lightly bronzed with smoke, 10 to 15 minutes. (Rub an egg with your fingertip—you should be able to taste smoke.)

**7.** Let the eggs cool to room temperature, then refrigerate until serving; you can make the eggs up to 1 day ahead. Frank says the smoked eggs taste even better refrigerated overnight. (I can never wait that long.) Serve as is or sprinkled with shichimi togarashi.

## VARIATION

### SMOKED EGGS PLAIN AND SIMPLE

Boil and peel the eggs as described in Step 1. Skip the marinating (Steps 2 and 3). Chill and smoke the eggs as described.

# SMOKED DEVILED EGGS
## WITH WASABI

**YIELD** Makes 16 halves, enough to serve 4 to 6

**METHOD** Indirect grilling/ smoking

**PREP TIME** 15 minutes

**GRILLING TIME** 10 to 15 minutes on a grill

I first smoked eggs on my *Project Smoke* TV show. It was love at first bite. I loved how wood smoke utterly transformed a simple, almost boring food you've eaten all your life. How commonplace hard-cooked eggs took on bigger-than-life barbecue flavors normally reserved for chicken or spare-ribs. I loved the versatility: how smoked eggs could be transformed into egg salad of uncommon distinction or deviled eggs that, once you tasted them, you'd never want any other way. Here they are reborn—using wasabi for firepower.

## INGREDIENTS

8 large eggs, preferably organic

1 tablespoon wasabi powder

3 tablespoons mayonnaise, or to taste, preferably Hellmann's or Best Foods

1 teaspoon soy sauce, or to taste

Freshly ground black pepper

A drop or two of fresh lemon juice or rice vinegar (optional)

Kimchi or salmon caviar, for garnish (optional)

**1.** Hard-cook the eggs: Place the eggs in a large saucepan with cool water to cover by a depth of 2 inches. Bring to a boil over medium-high heat, then reduce the heat to a simmer and cook the eggs for 11 minutes (a few minutes longer if you live at a high altitude). Pour off the hot water and fill the pot with cold water. When the eggs are cool enough to handle but still warm, carefully peel, then let cool to room temperature.

**2.** Meanwhile, set up your grill for smoking (indirect grilling) and heat to medium-low. To achieve this low temperature, use only half or a third as much charcoal as you normally would for indirect grilling. If enhancing a charcoal fire, add the wood chunks or chips to the coals; if enhancing a gas fire, place the wood chunks or chips in the smoker box or under the grate directly over one or more burners. If using a smoker, heat it to medium-low, following the manufacturer's instructions.

**3.** Cut the hard-cooked eggs in half, lengthwise or widthwise—your choice. Arrange them cut sides up on a wire rack over a foil pan full of ice (the eggs should not touch the ice). The ice keeps the eggs from overcooking and becoming rubbery.

**4.** Place the eggs on the wire rack over the ice on the grill or in the smoker. Close the grill or smoker and smoke the eggs until lightly bronzed with smoke, 10 to 15 minutes. (Rub an egg with your fingertip—you should be able to taste smoke.)

**5.** Meanwhile, place the wasabi powder in a small bowl and add 1 tablespoon of water. Stir to form a paste and let it stand for 5 minutes to develop the flavor.

**6.** Make the filling: Scoop out the egg yolks and place in a food processor (a small one works best). Add the wasabi paste and process to mix. Work in the mayonnaise, soy sauce, and pepper to taste: The filling should be highly seasoned. You may want to add a drop or two of fresh lemon juice or rice vinegar (if using), for tartness.

**7.** Spoon the filling into the egg white halves, or for folks with a penchant for embellishment, pipe it into the cavities in decorative swirls using a piping bag. Don't own a piping bag? Use a small resealable plastic bag with one of the lower corners clipped off. For an extravagant touch, crown each egg with a sliver of kimchi or a spoonful of salmon caviar (if using).

**GRILL/GEAR** If grilling, you'll need a charcoal grill. If smoking, any sort of smoker will do—outdoor or indoor. You'll also need hardwood chunks or chips (unsoaked), see page 8; a wire rack; an aluminum foil drip pan; and a food processor.

**WHAT ELSE** There are many ways to smoke eggs: on a charcoal grill; in an outdoor smoker or pellet grill; or using a stovetop or handheld smoker indoors. Grilling is the fastest. The secret is the pan of ice to keep the eggs cool so they don't become overcooked and rubbery.

### SMOKED DEVILED EGGS WITH MAYO AND MUSTARD

These smoky eggs have the mayo-mustard flavor profile associated with traditional American deviled eggs. Chipotles bolster the smoke flavor. For an interesting twist, replace the mustard with miso.

For the filling, combine the smoked egg yolks with 3 tablespoons mayonnaise, 1 tablespoon Dijon mustard, 1 teaspoon Worcestershire sauce, 1 teaspoon minced canned chipotles or chipotle-flavored hot sauce, and coarse salt and freshly ground black pepper to taste. Garnish the filled eggs with pimentón (Spanish smoked paprika) or sweet or hot paprika.

# SMOKED EGG SALAD

**YIELD** Serves 4 to 6

There is egg salad and there is egg salad. Once you've tasted this one—made with smoked eggs and fiery chipotles—it's hard to imagine egg salad any other way. I've made the caramelized shallots optional as they add an extra step. For me, the extra flavor is worth it. (You can use scallion whites instead, if you prefer.)

### INGREDIENTS

**FOR THE CARAMELIZED SHALLOTS (OPTIONAL)**

2 tablespoons butter (unsalted or salted) or extra virgin olive oil

1 large shallot or 1 small onion, minced

**FOR THE SALAD**

8 Smoked Eggs Plain and Simple (page 246), peeled

6 tablespoons mayonnaise, preferably Hellmann's or Best Foods, or to taste

2 tablespoons Dijon mustard, or to taste

1 to 2 teaspoons minced canned chipotle or chipotle-flavored hot sauce

1 scallion, trimmed, white part minced, green part thinly sliced on the diagonal (optional)

Coarse salt (sea or kosher) and freshly ground black pepper to taste

Your Basic Grilled Bread (page 98) or Plancha Pita (page 102), for serving

**1.** If adding the caramelized shallots, melt the butter in a small frying pan. Add the shallot and cook over medium heat until golden brown, 3 to 5 minutes, stirring often. Lower the heat as needed to keep the shallots from scorching.

**2.** Place the eggs and caramelized shallots in a food processor and roughly chop, running the processor in short bursts. (Alternatively, chop the eggs by hand or coarsely mash with a fork or pastry blender.) Work in the mayonnaise, mustard, chipotle, scallion white (if using), and salt and pepper to taste: The mixture should be highly seasoned. Sprinkle with the scallion greens (if using). Serve with the grilled bread.

# GRILLED EGGS
## WITH VIETNAMESE FLAVORS

I first experienced these eggs in Hanoi, where they were grilled on a brazier (ingeniously fashioned from an old car wheel rim) by an ancient grill mistress squatting on a sidewalk. As a guy who likes to grill everything, I was mesmerized by this singular way to cook eggs. It turns out that fire-roasting eggs in the shell gives them a very different texture and flavor than you get with conventional boiling. Combine that with the traditional Vietnamese way of serving grilled foods—wrapped in lettuce leaves and piled with fragrant mint, Thai basil, fresh cilantro, fiery chilies, and crisp bean sprouts, then dipped in the classic sweet-tart-salty table sauce known as nuoc cham—and grilled eggs become not just a novelty, but a revelation.

**YIELD** Makes 8 eggs, enough to serve 4

**METHOD** Direct grilling

**PREP TIME** 20 minutes

**GRILLING TIME** 10 minutes

**GRILL/GEAR** In Vietnam, these eggs would be grilled over charcoal in a sort of hibachi. You can use charcoal, gas, or wood.

**WHAT ELSE** The key to grilling eggs is to work over a gentle fire or at the edge of the fire. The trick to cutting those hair-thin strands of carrot—so essential for nuoc cham—is to use a vegetable peeler, then a sharp knife (see Step 1).

## INGREDIENTS

**FOR THE DIPPING SAUCE (NUOC CHAM)**

1 carrot, trimmed and peeled

1 clove garlic, peeled and minced

2 tablespoons granulated sugar

½ teaspoon freshly ground black
  pepper

¼ cup fish sauce

¼ cup fresh lime juice

1 tablespoon rice vinegar
  (or more lime juice)

1 Thai chili or serrano pepper, very
  thinly sliced crosswise

**FOR GRILLING AND SERVING THE EGGS**

1 large or 2 small heads Boston
  lettuce, broken into leaves, washed
  and spun dry

1 bunch fresh mint, washed, shaken
  dry, and stemmed

1 bunch fresh basil (preferably Thai),
  washed and shaken dry

1 bunch fresh cilantro, washed,
  shaken dry, and stemmed

1 to 2 jalapeño or serrano peppers,
  stemmed and thinly sliced crosswise

2 cups fresh mung bean sprouts

8 large eggs, preferably organic

**1.** Make the dipping sauce: Using a vegetable peeler, cut a 2-inch section of the thickest part of the carrot lengthwise into paper-thin slices. (Hold the carrot by the slender end and save the remainder for another use.) Arrange 3 or 4 carrot slices in a stack, and, using a sharp knife, cut them lengthwise into paper-thin slivers. Repeat with the remaining carrot slices. Phew! The hard part is over.

**2.** Place the minced garlic in a mixing bowl and add 2 teaspoons of the sugar and the black pepper. Mash well with the back of a wooden spoon. Add the slivered carrots and remaining sugar and gently toss to mix. Let the carrots marinate for about 5 minutes: They will soften.

**3.** Add the fish sauce, lime juice, and vinegar, and stir until the sugar is dissolved. Add enough water to mellow the sauce, starting with ¼ cup (you may need up to ⅓ cup). The sauce can be prepared several hours ahead. Just before serving, pour it into 4 small bowls for dipping and sprinkle the thinly sliced Thai chili on top.

**4.** Arrange the lettuce leaves, mint, basil, cilantro, sliced jalapeños, and mung bean sprouts on a platter.

**5.** Meanwhile, light your grill. Set it up for direct grilling and heat to medium. Be sure to leave a fire-free safety zone. Brush or scrape the grill grate clean. (There is no need to oil it.)

**6.** Grill the eggs until the shells are browned and the eggs are cooked through, turning frequently with tongs. This will take about 10 minutes (2½ minutes per side). If the shells start to crack or burst, your heat is too high: Move the eggs to the edge of the fire or the fire-free safety zone. So how do you know when the eggs are cooked? Spin one on a flat surface: If it spins easily without wobbling, the egg is cooked. Transfer the eggs to a platter and let cool.

**7.** To serve, have each eater shell the eggs and cut lengthwise into quarters. Place an egg quarter or two on a lettuce leaf. Add mint, basil, and cilantro leaves, jalapeño slices, and bean sprouts for crunch. Roll the lettuce leaf around the egg and garnishes. Dip it in the nuoc cham sauce and pop it into your mouth.

# GRILLED EGG KEBABS (REALLY!)
## WITH CAMBODIAN SEASONINGS

**YIELD** Makes 12 eggs, enough to serve 4 to 6

**METHOD** Indirect grilling/direct grilling

**PREP TIME** 40 minutes

**GRILLING TIME** 15 to 30 minutes for indirect grilling or steaming, plus 6 to 8 minutes for direct grilling

**GRILL/GEAR** Can be grilled over charcoal, gas, or wood. You'll also need 4 to 6 metal skewers (10 to 12 inches); a large sewing or darning needle; a wine cork; a small funnel with a narrow neck; a bamboo steamer and wok (optional); a cardboard egg carton; a wire rack; and bamboo skewers.

I first encountered grilled eggs in a fourteenth-century cookbook—*Le Viandier* ("The Victualer")—written by France's first celebrity chef, Guillaume Tirel, better known by his professional name, Taillevent ("wind-slicer"). (Yes, the legendary Paris restaurant is named for him.) The medieval chef instructed you to poke small holes in the ends of the shells, blow the eggs out into a bowl, beat them with herbs, stuff them back in the shells, and grill them on skewers. The preparation sounded so preposterous, I chalked it up to the theatrics that characterized so much medieval cooking: all show, but totally impractical. Until, that is, I encountered modern grilled eggs—a popular street food in Cambodia and Thailand. I did a double take: Picture whole eggs threaded lengthwise on bamboo skewers, their shells cracked and darkened by charcoal fire. I was captivated by their flavor—sweet with sugar, salty with fish sauce, aromatic with cilantro and garlic—but I still had no idea how they got raw eggs onto skewers to grill them. As it turns out, the technique hews closely to Taillevent's recipe written 600 years earlier: The secret involves a narrow-neck funnel. The preparation is a little involved—sorry—but people will be gobsmacked by the results. Tip o' the hat to Sasha Martin, who elucidates the method on Globaltableadventure.com.

## INGREDIENTS

12 large eggs, preferably organic

2 to 3 tablespoons finely minced fresh cilantro leaves

1 clove garlic, peeled and finely minced

1 Thai chili or serrano pepper, stemmed, seeded, and finely minced (optional)

1½ tablespoons fish sauce, or to taste

1 tablespoon brown sugar (light or dark—your choice), or to taste

1 teaspoon freshly ground black pepper

**1.** Stick the eye end of the needle into the cork. (The cork gives you a handle for working with the needle.) Carefully poke a small hole in the narrow end of each egg, gyring the needle to widen that hole to a diameter of about ⅟₁₆ inch.

**2.** Now, use the needle to prick a half dozen holes in the opposite (wide) end of the egg to form a circle about ¼ inch in diameter. Gently use the tip of a bamboo skewer or paring knife to open this second hole. Insert the tip of the bamboo skewer in this hole and gently move it back and forth a few times to scramble the egg a little and break up the yolk.

**3.** When you finish puncturing the egg, put the narrow end of the shell to your mouth or use an egg blower (yes, there really is such a thing, and they're available online) and blow the raw egg into a large mixing bowl. (It will shoot out in a viscous squirt.) Take care not to crack or break the eggshells. Repeat with the other eggs.

**4.** Dry off the empty eggshells with a paper towel and stand upright in an egg carton (cardboard, please), wide holes at the top. If you don't have a cardboard egg carton, arrange the eggs on a shellfish rack or other rack that will hold them securely upright. (Don't worry—the holes in the bottom of the shells are so tiny, the egg won't really seep out when you pour it back in.)

**5.** Using a spoon, remove any stray pieces of shell from the eggs in the bowl. Add the cilantro, garlic, Thai chili (if using), fish sauce, brown sugar, and black pepper and beat well. Using a funnel, pour the egg mixture back into the shells, dividing it evenly among them.

**6.** Meanwhile, set up your grill for indirect grilling and heat to medium. Alternatively, set up a bamboo steamer over a wok and fill it with 1½ inches of hot water.

**WHAT ELSE** Cambodian grilled eggs involve a clever two-step cooking process. First, you steam the beaten flavored eggs in their shells until firm. This enables you to thread them onto a bamboo skewer for direct grilling just before serving. You can also precook the eggs by indirect grilling instead of steaming. Guess which method I prefer. Note: Buy eggs in a cardboard carton. You'll see why in Step 4.

**7.** If indirect grilling, place the eggs in their cardboard carton or rack on the grate away from the heat. Lower the lid and indirect grill the eggs until the filling is just set, 20 to 30 minutes. Use a bamboo skewer to test for doneness: If it comes out clean, the eggs are cooked. Note: If the eggs start to leak and stick to the carton, gently loosen them with a skewer. If using a steamer, bring the water in the wok or pot to a boil. Place the steamer on top and the eggs (in their carton or rack) inside. Steam the eggs until the filling is set, 15 to 20 minutes. Note: Work over low heat, or the cooked eggs will spill out over the shell.

**8.** Once the filling is cooked, place the eggs upright on a wire rack or in a clean egg carton and let them cool to room temperature, then refrigerate until serving. The eggs can be prepared up to 2 days ahead to this stage, but bring them to room temperature before grilling.

**9.** Just before serving, set up your grill for direct grilling and heat to medium-high. Skewer the eggs from end to end on bamboo skewers, 2 or 3 eggs to a skewer. Arrange the resulting kebabs on the grill grate and grill until the eggshells are browned and the filling is hot, about 2 minutes per side, 6 to 8 minutes in all, turning so all sides grill evenly.

**10.** Transfer the kebabs to a platter or plates and serve. Obviously, each eater removes the eggs from the skewers and shells the eggs before eating.

# VARIATION

### TUSCAN-FLAVOR GRILLED EGGS

In Step 5, replace the cilantro, Thai chili, fish sauce, and brown sugar with 3 tablespoons slivered basil, 3 tablespoons finely grated Parmigiano-Reggiano, 2 tablespoons heavy cream, 1 tablespoon minced chives or scallion greens, and salt wand pepper to taste.

# DOUBLE-GRILLED SUMMER VEGETABLE FRITTATA

Grilling 24/7 is one of my bywords and that means firing up the grill for breakfast and brunch as well as for dinner. Which brings me to a dish that's welcome pretty much anytime, day or night—double-grilled vegetable frittata. Frittata is a cross between an omelet and a quiche, of course, and the first grilling (direct) imparts a smoky char to the vegetables. The second grilling (indirect) cooks the frittata itself. The strategic addition of wood to the fire imparts a smoke flavor that transports this Italian classic to the realm of barbecue. Note the use of a grilling grid, grill wok, or wire-mesh grill basket to grill the vegetables.

**YIELD** Serves 4

**METHOD** Direct grilling/ indirect grilling

**PREP TIME** 15 minutes

**GRILLING TIME** 6 to 10 minutes for the vegetables, plus about 20 minutes for the frittata

**GRILL/GEAR** Can be grilled over charcoal or gas. For even more flavor, you can grill the veggies over wood or a wood-enhanced fire. If you're enhancing a charcoal or gas fire, you'll need hardwood chunks or chips (unsoaked), see page 8. You'll also need a grill basket, grill wok, or grilling grid; a well-seasoned 10-inch cast-iron skillet (a 12-incher will work, too, but the frittata will be thinner).

## INGREDIENTS

### FOR THE VEGETABLES

4 cups diced vegetables (any or all of the following):

  Asparagus stalks, trimmed and cut into 1-inch pieces

  Mushrooms, trimmed, wiped clean, and quartered (halved if mushrooms are small)

  Zucchini, cut crosswise into ½-inch slices

  Yellow squash, cut crosswise into ½-inch slices

  Red or yellow bell pepper, stemmed, seeded, and cut into ½-inch dice

4 scallions, trimmed, white and green parts cut crosswise into ½-inch pieces

2 tablespoons extra virgin olive oil

Coarse salt (sea or kosher) and freshly ground black pepper

### FOR THE FRITTATA

8 large eggs, preferably organic

1¼ cups freshly grated Parmigiano-Reggiano or Pecorino Romano cheese (about 5 ounces)

3 tablespoons thinly slivered or chopped fresh herbs, such as basil, dill, tarragon, flat-leaf parsley, rosemary, sage, and/or other herbs (optional)

2 tablespoons unsalted butter or extra virgin olive oil

1. Set up your grill for direct grilling and heat to high (or build a wood fire). If using a grilling grid or grill wok, preheat it as well.

2. Prepare the vegetables: Place the veggies, including the scallions, in a mixing bowl and toss with the olive oil, salt, and pepper. Transfer to a grill basket or add to the preheated grill wok or grilling grid. Don't overcrowd the grill basket: You may need to work in several batches. Grill, stirring often, until the vegetables are darkly browned, 6 to 10 minutes. Set aside and let cool. The vegetables can be grilled ahead or at a previous grill session.

3. Make the frittata: Place the eggs in a large mixing bowl and lightly beat with a whisk or fork. Stir in 1 cup grated cheese, the herbs, grilled vegetables, and salt and pepper to taste.

4. Melt the 2 tablespoons of butter in the cast-iron skillet over the side burner on your grill or on your stovetop. Swirl the pan to butter the sides. Add the egg mixture and cook without stirring until the bottom starts to set, about 2 minutes.

5. Move the skillet off the burner and onto the grill grate, away from direct heat (you'll be indirect grilling from here on out). If enhancing a charcoal fire, add the wood chunks or chips to the coals; if enhancing a gas fire, place the chunks or chips in your grill's smoker box or place chunks under the grate directly over one or more burners. Reduce the heat to medium-high. Close the grill lid.

6. Cook the frittata until the eggs are set and the top is lightly browned, about 20 minutes. (To test for doneness, insert a bamboo skewer in the center of the frittata: It should come out clean.) Remove the skillet from the grill and let it rest for 3 minutes. Run the tip of a slender paring knife around the inside rim of the skillet. Place a large heatproof plate or platter on top. While holding the plate firmly against the skillet's rim, carefully invert the skillet and plate, giving the former a little shake to loosen the frittata. Lift the skillet: Ideally, the frittata will come loose on the plate. Sprinkle the remaining cheese on top. Cut into wedges and serve at once.

**WHAT ELSE** You'll want to use whatever vegetables are freshest and in season. I've made some suggestions for a summer frittata. You could also drill down to some classic veggie combinations, like asparagus and corn, mushroom and leek, or tomato and onion. In the cooler months, use winter vegetables like fennel, endive, broccoli or broccolini, and winter squash.

# GRILLED HALLOUMI
## WITH ROSEWATER AND HONEY

**YIELD** Serves 4 as an appetizer; 2 or 3 as a main course

**METHOD** Direct grilling

**PREP TIME** 15 minutes

**GRILLING TIME** 5 minutes

**GRILL/GEAR** Can be grilled over charcoal, gas, or wood. You'll also need bamboo skewers and heavy-duty aluminum foil.

**WHAT ELSE** Halloumi is available at Greek and Middle Eastern markets (and at a growing number of supermarkets and natural foods stores) and so is the other defining flavoring in this dish: rosewater (it smells perfumed—like roses). Noosh serves the cheese cubed and grilled on skewers, but I often grill the cheese in flat slabs, which is quicker and easier.

Attempt to grill most cheese and it melts (which is why it's so good for grilled cheese sandwiches). But not halloumi. For centuries, Greeks and Cypriots have put this white, semi-firm, salty cheese—dotted with nigella seeds (a black drop-shaped seed with a mild, herbaceous onion flavor)—on hot grills and skillets, where it softens and puffs without melting. You've probably had it the Greek way—grilled in a special frying pan called a saganaki, flambéed with brandy or ouzo. The trendy Eastern Mediterranean restaurant Noosh in San Francisco pairs it with honey and rosewater, creating a dish that's salty like an appetizer, perfumey-sweet like dessert, and perfectly appropriate as either. Serve with Your Basic Grilled Bread (page 98) or the Ember Flatbread (page 99).

## INGREDIENTS

1 pound halloumi cheese

1 bunch fresh mint

Extra virgin olive oil, for brushing

Vegetable oil for oiling the grill grate

Warmed honey, for drizzling

Rosewater, for sprinkling

¼ cup toasted shelled pistachio nuts (see Note)

**1.** Cut the cheese into small slabs 1½ inches square and ½ inch thick. Skewer them through the thin side on the bamboo skewers, placing fresh mint leaves between each. Alternatively, cut it through the narrow side into ½-inch-thick slabs. (In this case, omit the mint.) Lightly brush on both sides with olive oil.

**2.** Meanwhile, set up your grill for direct grilling and heat to high. Brush or scrape the grill grate clean and oil it well.

**3.** Arrange the cheese kebabs on the grate. (Slide a rectangle of folded aluminum foil under the exposed part of the bamboo skewers to keep them from burning.) Grill the cheese kebabs until sizzling and browned on both sides, 2 to 4 minutes per side.

**4.** To serve, transfer the grilled cheese kebabs to a platter. Drizzle with warmed honey and sprinkle with a few drops of rosewater. Top with toasted pistachio nuts and serve.

**NOTE:** To toast pistachio nuts, place in a dry skillet over medium-high heat. Cook until fragrant and just beginning to brown, about 2 minutes, shaking the pan so they toast evenly. Transfer the hot nuts to a bowl to cool.

# BRAZILIAN GRILLED CHEESE SKEWERS
## WITH COUNTRY SALSA

Queijo assado (baked cheese), aka queijo coalho (rennet cheese), turns up often at Brazilian barbecues and parties. Which pretty much means anywhere, from beachside grill stands to backyard barbecues, from noon to midnight and beyond. The cheese in question is a semi-firm, softly crisp, sweet-salty cheese from northeastern Brazil that squeaks on your teeth when you bite it. It's similar in texture and flavor to halloumi (facing page), which makes a fine substitute. The cheese is cut into rectangles or squares and grilled on bamboo or metal skewers. The seasonings are simple: maybe a sprinkling of oregano, maybe nothing. The fireworks come from a chile-stung country salsa—and from the sizzling golden cheese itself.

**YIELD** Serves 4

**METHOD** Direct grilling

**PREP TIME** 10 minutes

**GRILLING TIME** 10 minutes

**GRILL/GEAR** Can be grilled over charcoal, wood, or gas. (Traditionally, Brazilians grill over charcoal.) You'll also need bamboo skewers; a sheet of aluminum foil folded in thirds like a business letter to use as a grill shield (optional); and a grill fork (optional).

**WHAT ELSE** Look for queijo coalho at a Brazilian grocery store or find online (one source is the Wisconsin Cheese Mart). Alternatively, substitute another grilling cheese like halloumi or Rougette Bonfire Grilling Cheese.

## INGREDIENTS

1 pound Brazilian grilling cheese (queijo coalho) or halloumi

Extra virgin olive oil

Dried oregano flakes

Freshly ground black pepper

Vegetable oil for oiling the grill grate

Country Salsa (recipe follows), for serving

**1.** Cut the cheese into rectangles 4 to 6 inches long, 1 inch wide, and ½ inch thick. Skewer them lengthwise on bamboo skewers. Lightly brush on all sides with olive oil and sprinkle with oregano and pepper.

**2.** Set up your grill for direct grilling and heat to high. Brush or scrape the grill grate clean and oil it well.

**3.** Arrange the cheese skewers on the grate, running on a diagonal to or perpendicular to the bars of the grate. Slide the grill shield under the exposed parts of the bamboo skewers. Grill until sizzling and browned, turning with tongs, about 2 minutes per side. Move the kebabs as needed to keep them from sticking to the grate. You can use the prongs of a grill fork to pry the cheese off the grate if it sticks; don't overcook or the cheese will melt.

**4.** Transfer the kebabs to a platter or plates and serve with the Country Salsa spooned over them or served on the side.

# COUNTRY SALSA

**YIELD** Makes 2 cups

Molho à companha (country salsa) is Brazil's answer to Mexico's pico de gallo. The heat source of choice would be the pimenta malagueta—available pickled in Brazilian markets or in the form of a hot sauce called piri-piri. Substitute bird's-eye or other Thai chilies, serranos, or any hot pepper.

## INGREDIENTS

1 clove garlic, peeled and minced

½ teaspoon coarse salt (sea or kosher), plus extra as needed

3 tablespoons fresh lime juice, plus extra as needed

1 to 2 malagueta or other fresh hot peppers, seeded and minced (for a spicier salsa, leave the seeds in)

1 luscious ripe red tomato, cut into ¼-inch dice

½ green or yellow bell pepper, cut into ¼-inch dice (about ½ cup)

1 small sweet onion, cut into ¼-inch dice (about ½ cup)

¼ cup chopped fresh cilantro leaves or flat-leaf parsley leaves

¼ cup vegetable oil or extra virgin olive oil

Freshly ground black pepper

Mash the garlic and salt to a paste in the bottom of a mixing bowl with the back of a wooden spoon. Add the lime juice and stir until the salt crystals are dissolved. Stir in the malagueta, tomato, bell pepper, onion, cilantro, and oil. Stir in the black pepper and more salt or lime juice to taste: The salsa should be highly flavored. You can make the salsa up to 4 hours ahead and refrigerate; it is best when freshly made.

# INDIAN GRILLED CHEESE KEBABS
## WITH SAFFRON BUTTER

These sizzling, buttery grilled cheese and vegetable kebabs turn up across northern India where they're cooked on vertical skewers in India's distinctive charcoal-burning clay barbecue pit, the tandoor. Each of the four primary ingredients—salty cheese, sweet onion, tart tomato, and spicy poblano—brings an elemental flavor. But we're just getting started, because peppery fresh mint, nutty sesame seeds, and a hyper-aromatic saffron butter make this what may be the world's most flavorful grilled cheese.

**YIELD** Serves 8 as a starter; 4 as a main course

**METHOD** Direct grilling

**PREP TIME** 30 minutes

**GRILLING TIME** 8 to 12 minutes

**GRILL/GEAR** In India, these kebabs would be cooked in a tandoor, a cylindrical clay or ceramic barbecue pit that burns charcoal or wood. But conventional charcoal or gas grills work just fine. You'll also need metal or bamboo skewers (preferably flat ones to keep the ingredients from spinning) as well as a sheet of aluminum foil folded in thirds like a business letter to use as a grill shield (optional).

**WHAT ELSE** Paneer is a fresh Indian cheese not dissimilar to mozzarella. Once available only at Indian markets, it can now be found at Whole Foods and other supermarkets. Alternatively, use another firm grilling cheese, like Greek/Cypriot halloumi, scamorza (smoked mozzarella), fresh mozzarella, or Rougette Bonfire Grilling Cheese.

## INGREDIENTS

### FOR THE KEBABS

3 poblano peppers or 2 green bell peppers

3 luscious red ripe tomatoes

2 medium sweet onions, peeled

2 pounds Indian paneer or Greek halloumi cheese

1 bunch fresh mint, washed and shaken dry

### FOR THE SAFFRON BASTING BUTTER AND COATING

½ teaspoon saffron threads

1 tablespoon hot water

8 tablespoons (1 stick) salted butter

1 large shallot, peeled and minced

1 tablespoon minced peeled fresh ginger

½ teaspoon freshly ground black pepper

Vegetable oil for oiling the grill grate

½ cup sesame seeds

**1.** Cut the peppers into 1½-inch-square pieces, discarding the stems, ribs, and seeds. Cut each tomato in quarters from top to bottom. Cut the seeds and pulp off each quarter (save for stock); cut what remains of each quarter in half widthwise. Cut the onions in half widthwise and cut each half in sixths. Break each sixth into layers. Cut the large layers in half widthwise into 1½-inch pieces. (Save the smaller onion pieces for another use.) The idea is to cut each vegetable into 1½-inch pieces.

**2.** Cut the cheese into 1½-inch squares, each ½ inch thick. Stem the mint.

**3.** Assemble the kebabs: Skewer a piece of pepper through the flat side. Skewer a piece of tomato on top, followed by a layer of onion, a piece of cheese, and a mint leaf. All skewering should be done through the flat side. Repeat this sequence until all the ingredients are used up.

**4.** Make the basting mixture: Place the saffron threads in a small bowl, add the hot water, and soak for 5 minutes. Meanwhile, melt the butter in a small saucepan over medium heat. Add the shallot, ginger, and black pepper to the butter and cook until fragrant and just beginning to brown, about 2 minutes. Add the saffron with its soaking liquid and simmer for 30 seconds. Keep warm.

**5.** Set up your grill for direct grilling and preheat to high. Brush or scrape the grill grate clean and oil it well.

**6.** Brush the cheese kebabs on all sides with the basting mixture. Sprinkle lightly on all sides with the sesame seeds. Arrange the kebabs on the grill grate and grill until nicely browned on all sides, 2 to 3 minutes per side, turning as the cheese starts to melt and basting with the saffron butter.

**7.** Transfer the kebabs to a platter or plates. Serve the cheese kebabs at once, spooning any remaining saffron butter on top.

# PLANKED BRIE
## WITH FIG JAM AND WALNUTS

**YIELD** Serves 4

**METHOD** Indirect grilling

**PREP TIME** 5 minutes

**GRILLING TIME** 6 to 10 minutes

**GRILL/GEAR** Can be grilled over charcoal or gas. You'll also need an untreated cedar plank.

Plank grilling may seem new, but it's not. The technique dates back to before colonial times, when, for example, the Indigenous people living in what is now Connecticut would nail shad fillets to oak stakes to be roasted upright in front of a campfire. (The tradition continues to this day at the annual Shad Festival in Essex, Connecticut.) That's a lengthy prelude to this dish: Brie cheese grilled on a fire-charred cedar plank. In the old days, I advocated soaking the wood to keep it from burning; today I do the exact opposite. I char the plank directly over the fire to give it a smoke flavor, which transfers to the cheese. The fig jam adds a musky sweetness, while the walnuts provide a nutty crunch. It takes all of 5 minutes to assemble, and another 6 to 10 minutes to cook. The result looks terrific and tastes even better, with the cheese now oozy and smoky and just begging to be spread on grilled bread.

**WHAT ELSE** You'll need a soft-ripened cheese for this recipe, like Camembert or a small Brie. (Soft-ripened refers to a cheese that ripens from the outside in.) It should feel semi-firm but not hard when pressed. For an interesting variation, replace the fig jam with tapenade (olive paste) or pepper jelly or tomato jam. For nuts, you could use pecans or pistachios instead of walnuts.

## INGREDIENTS

1 small Brie or Camembert cheese (8 ounces), unwrapped

3 tablespoons fig jam, pepper jelly, or tomato jam

About 20 walnut halves

Your Basic Grilled Bread (page 98) or interesting crackers, for serving

**1.** Set up your grill for indirect grilling and heat to medium-high.

**2.** Place the plank directly over one of the fires and grill until singed on one side, about 2 minutes. Set aside and let cool.

**3.** Place the cheese in the center of the plank on the charred side. Spread the top with the fig jam using the back of a spoon. Arrange the walnuts on top in decorative concentric circles.

**4.** Place the plank on the grill away from the heat. Smoke-roast the cheese until the sides are soft, 6 to 10 minutes. Don't overcook or the cheese could collapse.

**5.** Serve the cheese on the plank hot off the grill. Spread it on the grilled bread.

# GRILLED CHEESE, PORTOBELLOS, AND COGNAC FLAMBÉ

**YIELD** Serves 4 as an appetizer; 2 as a light main course

**METHOD** Direct grilling

**PREP TIME** 15 minutes

**GRILLING TIME** 6 to 10 minutes

**GRILL/GEAR** Can be grilled over charcoal, gas, or wood. You'll also need a long-stemmed match.

Grilled cheese looms large in America's culinary vernacular, but true grilling cheeses are anything but common. Most cheese melts when heated. Grilling cheeses are designed to stay intact even when exposed to blistering fire. The most famous grilling cheese is halloumi, claimed with equal partisanship by both Greeks and Cypriots. (You'll find a halloumi recipe on page 258.) Another great grilling cheese is Paillasson from Île d'Orléans in the St. Lawrence River near Quebec City. The new kid on the block is Rougette Bonfire from the Rougette cheese company in Germany—a handsome white disk with a softly crisp texture and salty tang that puffs up like a souffle when you grill it. I like to serve it on a grilled portobello mushroom cap—milky cheese, earthy mushroom—a combination you take over the top by dousing it with flaming cognac.

## INGREDIENTS

4 large portobello mushrooms

Extra virgin olive oil for brushing and basting

Coarse salt (sea or kosher) and freshly ground black pepper

Dried oregano flakes

Hot red pepper flakes

4 Rougette Bonfire Grilling Cheeses or Paillassons (about 3.2 ounces each)

Vegetable oil for oiling the grill grate

2 tablespoons minced fresh chives

¼ cup cognac

Your Basic Grilled Bread (page 98), for serving (optional)

**1.** Stem the portobellos and wipe the caps clean with a damp paper towel. Brush each on both sides with olive oil. Season with salt, pepper, dried oregano, and hot red pepper flakes.

**2.** Brush the cheese on both sides with olive oil and sprinkle with pepper, dried oregano, and hot red pepper flakes.

**3.** Meanwhile, set up your grill for direct grilling and heat to high. Brush or scrape the grate clean and oil it well.

**4.** Grill the portobellos, gill sides down first, then cap sides down, until sizzling and tender, 2 to 4 minutes per side. Transfer to a heatproof platter gill sides up.

**5.** Arrange the cheeses on the grill and grill until puffed and lightly browned, about 2 minutes per side, giving each cheese a quarter turn after about 1 minute to lay on a handsome crosshatch of grill marks.

**6.** Arrange the grilled cheeses on top of the portobellos, one per mushroom. Sprinkle with the chives.

**7.** Gently warm the cognac in a small saucepan to body temperature. (Test it with your finger—it should feel warm but not hot.) Do not let it boil. Carefully ignite the cognac with a long-stemmed match and pour it over the cheese and mushrooms. Serve the cheese flambéed, but eat only after the flames have died out. Serve the bread (if using), for munching on the side.

**WHAT ELSE** Rougette Bonfire Grilling Cheese is available online or at select supermarkets, including Publix, Harris Teeter, Star Markets, and Fresh Market. For a source in your area visit Bonfirecheese.com. Or substitute another grilling cheese, like halloumi or queso panela, or if you live in Quebec, Paillasson from the Île d'Orléans (Orleans Island).

# VEGGIE AND CHEESE SHAWARMA
## WITH TWO SAUCES

**YIELD** Serves 4 and can be multiplied as desired

**METHOD** Direct grilling

**PREP TIME** 30 minutes

**GRILLING TIME** 8 to 12 minutes

**GRILL/GEAR** Can be grilled over charcoal, gas, or wood. You'll also need metal or bamboo skewers. If using the latter, fold a sheet of aluminum foil in thirds like a business letter to use as a grill shield (optional).

**WHAT ELSE** Shawarma is traditionally roasted on a vertical spit next to glowing coals tiered on vertical shelves. It's an ingenious setup found at food stalls the world over, and it guarantees a crisp end cut on every sandwich. Unfortunately, few of us have vertical rotisseries at home, so I've opted to grill the shawarma ingredients shish kebab–style on skewers. You get the same crusty edges, but without the need for special machinery.

Turks call it döner kebab, while Greeks prize it as gyro. In the Middle East, it's beloved as shawarma. There's even a Mexican version, tacos al pastor, made with chile-spiced pork. All are built around an ingenious premise: By carving the shawarma from the outside in, everyone gets a crispy end cut. You're probably familiar with the meat version: sliced or ground lamb in Islamic countries; the increasingly popular turkey in Israel; chile-slathered pork in the Yucatán. Here's a vegetable shawarma loaded with the eggplants, bell peppers, and onions beloved in the Middle East—plus shiitakes for extra umami flavor and halloumi cheese (optional) for protein. Equally integral to shawarma's appeal are the condiments—in this case, a cumin- and cardamom-scented rub; a piquant feta cheese sauce; and a salty-tart pickled mango sauce called amba—all specialties of my Israeli friend Eli Levy, who ran Atlantic Fish and Chop House on Martha's Vineyard. Consider this recipe a broad guide, not a precise blueprint.

## INGREDIENTS

**FOR THE KEBABS**

2 slender eggplants (about 1 pound)

1 large sweet onion, peeled

1 green or red bell pepper or poblano pepper

12 ounces fresh shiitakes

1 pound halloumi cheese (optional)

Vegetable oil for oiling the grill grate

**FOR THE RUB**

1 teaspoon ground cumin

1 teaspoon ground coriander

1 teaspoon ground turmeric

1 teaspoon coarse salt (sea or kosher)

1 teaspoon freshly ground black pepper

½ teaspoon ground cardamom

Extra virgin olive oil, for basting

**FOR SERVING**

Creamy Feta Sauce (recipe follows)

Spicy Amba Sauce (recipe follows)

1 cucumber, peeled, seeded, and thinly sliced (optional)

Pickled cabbage (available at Middle Eastern markets) or dill pickle slices (optional)

4 large pita breads, homemade (see page 102) or your favorite store-bought

**1.** Stem the eggplants and cut them in half lengthwise. (If using really bulbous eggplants, cut in quarters.) Cut each half widthwise into ½-inch-thick slices. Cut the onion in half widthwise, then cut each half in 6 wedges from top to bottom (rounded side to flat side). Break each wedge into layers. Use the large outside layers for the kebabs. (Save the smaller pieces for another use.) Cut the pepper into 1-inch pieces, discarding the stem, ribs, and seeds. Stem the shiitakes and cut any large caps in half or quarters. Cut the halloumi (if using) into 1-inch squares, each ¼ inch thick.

**2.** Assemble the kebabs: Thread a slice of eggplant onto a skewer followed by onion, pepper, mushroom, and cheese. Repeat this sequence until all the ingredients are used up.

**3.** Make the rub: Combine the cumin, coriander, turmeric, salt, pepper, and cardamom in a small bowl and mix well.

**4.** Brush the kebabs on all sides with olive oil and season all over with the rub. The shawarma can be prepared several hours ahead to this stage and refrigerated.

**5.** Place the Creamy Feta Sauce and Spicy Amba Sauce in serving bowls. Place the cucumber and pickled cabbage (if using) in separate serving bowls.

**6.** Just before serving, set up your grill for direct grilling and heat to high. Brush or scrape the grill grate clean and oil it well.

**7.** Slide the grill shield under the exposed parts of the bamboo skewers (if using). Grill the kebabs until the outside is charred and crispy and the center is cooked through, 2 to 3 minutes per side, 8 to 12 minutes in all. Baste the kebabs with olive oil as they grill.

**8.** Meanwhile, lightly brush the pita breads on both sides with olive oil and warm on a cooler section of the grill, 30 seconds to 1 minute per side.

**9.** To serve, place a veggie kebab on a pita bread. Using the pita as a sort of potholder, grasp the ingredients and pull out the skewer. Spoon the feta sauce and amba sauce over the veggies. Add the cucumber and pickled cabbage (if using). Fold up the pita and dig in.

# CREAMY FETA SAUCE

**YIELD** Makes about 1 cup

This feta sauce has a lot more flavor—piquant, sharp, salty—than the yogurt often served with shawarma. (You can substitute yogurt if you're pressed for time.) The sauce's creator, Eli Levy, likes the clean mild taste of feta from France. The sauce can be made up to 24 hours ahead, covered, and refrigerated.

## INGREDIENTS

6 ounces feta cheese
(preferably French), crumbled

6 tablespoons heavy cream

½ teaspoon dried oregano flakes

Coarse salt (sea or kosher) and freshly
ground black pepper

Puree the cheese in a food processor. Add the cream and oregano and pulse in short bursts to obtain a thick but pourable sauce. Add salt (just a little—you may not need any at all as feta is salty) and pepper to taste: The sauce should be highly seasoned.

# SPICY AMBA SAUCE

YIELD Makes about 1 cup

Amba is a pickled mango condiment popular in Israel, Iraq, and elsewhere in the Middle East. Look for it at Middle Eastern markets or order it online. Two common brands are Shemesh and Teta Foods.

## INGREDIENTS

½ cup amba (pickled mango sauce)

½ cup Thai sweet chili sauce, such as the Mae Ploy brand

2 tablespoons sriracha, or to taste

1 tablespoon Dijon mustard

½ teaspoon freshly and finely grated lemon zest

1 tablespoon fresh lemon juice

Combine the amba, chili sauce, sriracha, mustard, lemon zest, and lemon juice in a mixing bowl and whisk to mix. The sauce can be made up to 24 hours ahead, covered, and refrigerated.

# CHAPTER 10

# DESSERTS

**S**ome of our most popular "vegetables"—such as avocados and tomatoes—are, botanically speaking, actually fruits. Which brings me to a chapter that focuses on fruits you can and should grill: desserts. There's nothing like the high dry heat of the grill for caramelizing a fruit's natural sugars. Case in point, stone fruit kebabs smokily charred on fragrant cinnamon stick skewers. Or grilled tropical fruit reimagined as salsa, complete with cilantro and jalapeños—you'll be amazed how well the combination works. Apples get the hasselback treatment (remember hasselback potatoes?): thinly sliced, slathered with ginger rum butter, and grilled on a charred cedar plank. Live fire breathes new life into that old barbecue joint standby: banana pudding. And pineapples get a triple blast of fiery flavor: first from direct grilling on the rotisserie; then from caramelizing by blowtorch; and finally, from flaming rum. The result is a fiery volcano pineapple worthy of Trader Vic's tiki chic. Our final dessert contains no fruit, but it's loaded with barbecue goodness and wood smoke. French Canadians call it Grand-Pères ("grandfathers," literally)—I call it smoky, maple syrup–poached dumplings you'll grill and never forget.

# RECIPES

# HASSELBACK APPLES
## GRILLED ON CEDAR PLANKS

**YIELD** Makes 8 halves, enough to serve 4 to 8

**METHOD** Indirect grilling

**PREP TIME** 15 minutes

**GRILLING TIME** 30 to 40 minutes

**GRILL/GEAR** Can be grilled over charcoal or gas. You'll also need a melon baller; a hasselback potato cutter (optional); 2 untreated cedar planks (each at least 5 × 10 inches); a rimmed sheet pan; long-stemmed matches; a Microplane, for zesting (optional); a metal skewer.

**WHAT ELSE** You'll want a firm tart apple for this recipe—I recommend Honey Crisps or Fujis. For a variation—and to jump on the salted-every-kind-of-dessert bandwagon—you could grill the apples on a salt slab (just avoid doing this in cold weather as the salt slab could explode when you open the grill and expose it to the icy air). A hasselback potato slicer will help you make those thin parallel slices that are the hallmark of hasselback everything. But you can also do it by hand.

The hasselback potato started turning up on American grills a few years ago, and mania quickly ensued. So you might be surprised to learn that "hasselback-ing" actually originated in the 1950s at Restaurant Hasselbacken in Stockholm, Sweden. The process is simple enough—you make a series of thin parallel cuts in a rounded vegetable or fruit. When indirect grilled, the edges crisp like chips, while the center stays moist and tender. To this ingenious procedure we now add aromatic wood flavors from a fire-charred cedar plank, plus butter, ginger, and rum. Think of this as a turbocharged baked apple—with Scandinavian design.

## INGREDIENTS

### FOR THE APPLES

4 firm apples, like Honey Crisps, peeled

A cut lemon for rubbing

### FOR THE GINGER-RUM BUTTER

8 tablespoons (1 stick) unsalted butter

1 tablespoon freshly and finely grated peeled ginger (grate it on a Microplane)

2 tablespoons dark rum, plus ¼ cup for flambéing (the latter is optional)

½ cup turbinado sugar (such as Sugar in the Raw) or brown sugar

1 teaspoon ground cinnamon

### FOR SERVING (OPTIONAL)

Vanilla ice cream or whipped cream

Ground cinnamon, for garnish

**1.** Cut the apples in half from the blossom end to the stem end and scoop out the core and seeds with a melon baller. Place each apple half, rounded side up, in a hasselback cutting guide or between two wooden chopsticks, pencils, or skewers. Using a sharp slender knife, cut each apple into parallel ⅛-inch slices, but don't cut all the way through the flat side; you want to leave the bottom of the apple intact. Rub each apple with cut lemon to discourage browning.

**2.** Make the ginger-rum butter: Melt the butter in a small saucepan over medium heat. Add the ginger and cook until sizzling and fragrant, about 2 minutes. Remove the pan from the heat and stir in 2 tablespoons dark rum.

**3.** Place the sugar in a small bowl and stir in the cinnamon.

Use a pair of wooden skewers as a cutting guide.

**4.** Set up your grill for indirect grilling and heat to medium-high.

**5.** Position the cedar planks directly over one of the fires and grill until lightly charred on one side, about 2 minutes. Transfer to a rimmed sheet pan to cool.

**6.** Line up the apple halves, rounded sides up, on the charred sides of the planks. Brush with the ginger-rum butter, dabbing the basting brush to force the butter between the slices.

**7.** Place the apples on their cedar planks on the grill grate over the drip pan away from the heat. Close the grill lid and start indirect grilling. Brush the apples with ginger-rum butter every 10 minutes, again dabbing it between the slices. After 20 minutes, generously sprinkle each apple half with the cinnamon sugar. Continue indirect grilling until the tops of the apples are crusty and browned and the fruit is soft (test it with a metal skewer). Total cooking time will be 30 to 40 minutes.

**8.** Serve the apples hot off their cedar planks. For high drama, heat the remaining ¼ cup of dark rum in a small saucepan to body temperature (it should be finger-dip warm—do not let it boil). Light it with a long-stemmed match and spoon the flaming rum over the apples (being careful to avoid their cedar planks). For safety's sake, make sure your sleeves are rolled up and there's nothing else but the rum that can catch on fire. I wouldn't say no to adding a scoop of vanilla ice cream and a little sprinkle of cinnamon, but that would be gilding the lily.

**NOTE:** You can also use ¼ cup of 151-proof rum for flambéing, in which case there's no need to warm it before lighting.

# CINNAMON FRUIT SKEWERS
## WITH MINT JULEP GLAZE

**YIELD** Serves 4

**METHOD** Direct grilling

**PREP TIME** 15 minutes

**GRILLING TIME** 5 to 8 minutes

In most of the recipes in this book (and in the world of barbecue at large), we flavor foods from the outside in, using rubs, marinades, basting mixtures, barbecue sauces, and so on, applied to the surface. In these colorful kebabs, you flavor the fruit from the inside out thanks to the singular skewers: long sticks of fragrant cinnamon. A mint julep glaze adds more flavor, while chopped toasted pecans supply color and crunch. Awesome on their own, these kebabs would be even better served over vanilla or peach ice cream.

## INGREDIENTS

2 ripe peaches, preferably freestone

4 ripe plums

4 ripe apricots

1 bunch fresh mint, washed and shaken dry

2 lemons

Long slender cinnamon sticks (see What Else)

4 tablespoons (½ stick) unsalted butter

¼ cup brown sugar

¼ cup bourbon

Vegetable oil for oiling the grill grate

¼ cup toasted chopped pecans (see Note)

**1.** Cut small peaches in quarters; large peaches into 1½-inch wedges, discarding the stones. Cut the plums in quarters, the apricots in quarters or halves, discarding the stones—the fruit pieces should be about the same size.

**2.** Stem the mint leaves. Save the large leaves for the kebabs. Chop any small ones for the glaze.

**3.** Using a vegetable peeler, remove the zest from the lemons in ½-inch-wide strips. Using a paring knife, make ½-inch lengthwise slits in the lemon zest and large mint leaves. You'll thread the cinnamon sticks through these slits when you assemble the kebabs.

**4.** Thread the fruit onto the cinnamon sticks, alternating with mint leaves and lemon zest. Note: It helps to use a slender metal skewer to make starter holes in the fruit, through which you insert the cinnamon.

**5.** Make the glaze: Place the butter, brown sugar, bourbon, and 3 tablespoons of chopped mint in a small saucepan

over medium-high heat and boil until syrupy, whisking steadily, about 5 minutes.

**6.** Set up your grill for direct grilling and heat to high. Brush or scrape the grill grate clean and oil it well.

**7.** Brush the kebabs on all sides with the glaze and arrange on the grate. Grill until sizzling and browned on the outside, basting with the glaze, 1 to 2 minutes per side. Don't overcook—the fruit should remain cool and fresh in the center.

**8.** Transfer the kebabs to a platter or plates and spoon any remaining glaze over them. Sprinkle with the pecans and serve. (If the cinnamon sticks are not too charred, you can reuse them—scrub well with hot water and a stiff brush, then blot with a paper towel and let air dry completely.)

**NOTE:** To toast the pecans, place them in a dry skillet over medium-high heat. Cook until fragrant and just beginning to brown, shaking the pan, 1 to 2 minutes.

**GRILL/GEAR** Can be grilled over charcoal, gas, or wood. You'll thread the fruit on long cinnamon sticks (see What Else). You'll also need a slender metal skewer (optional).

**WHAT ELSE** You'll need long cinnamon sticks (technically speaking, cassia sticks—from a smooth-barked tree similar to true cinnamon). Six-inch sticks are readily available online; sometimes you can find 12-inch sticks at spice stores and craft shops (make sure any found at craft shops are food-safe). The number you need will depend on the length of the sticks—figure on about eight 6-inchers or four 12-inchers. For the best results, use ripe fruit. That means squeezable, soft, and very fragrant. And that means ripening at room temperature—ideally in a paper bag to hold in the fruit's ethylene (a natural ripening agent).

# THE GRILLED FRUIT SALAD
## THAT THINKS IT'S SALSA

**YIELD** Serves 6, and can be multiplied as desired

**METHOD** Direct grilling

**PREP TIME** 15 minutes

**GRILLING TIME** 6 to 8 minutes per fruit (you can do several at once), or as needed

**GRILL/GEAR** Can be grilled over charcoal or gas, but tastes best grilled over a wood or wood-enhanced fire. If you're enhancing a charcoal or gas fire, you'll need hardwood chunks or chips (unsoaked), see page 8.

It's hard to imagine a more refreshing dessert than fruit salad. And it's hard to imagine how to improve that salad, but I'm going to try—first by perfuming that fruit with wood smoke. Then by crusting the fruit with spiced sugar, which is transformed into luscious caramel by exposing it to a screaming hot fire. The flavorings are limited only by your imagination: Grand Marnier or Cointreau for the classicist; Scotch whisky or mezcal for the smokehead. Yes, I know cilantro seems like an odd herb to add to dessert—trust me: It works. Ditto for the jalapeños. If their presence makes you think of salsa, you're supposed to. And if it seems too weird, use fresh mint.

### INGREDIENTS

**FOR THE SPICED SUGAR**

2 cups granulated sugar or turbinado sugar (such as Sugar in the Raw)

2 tablespoons ground cinnamon

1 teaspoon ground cardamom or nutmeg (optional)

Vegetable oil for oiling the grill grate

**FOR THE GRILLED FRUIT (8 CUPS IN ALL), ANY COMBINATION OF THE FOLLOWING**

Oranges, cut crosswise into ½-inch slices, and seeded with a fork

Lemons, cut crosswise into ½-inch slices, and seeded with a fork

Pineapples, peeled, eyes removed, cored, and cut crosswise into ½-inch slices

Bananas, peeled and cut lengthwise in half

Peaches, pitted and cut into wedges

Plums, pitted and cut into wedges

Apricots, pitted and cut into quarters

Apples, cut into wedges, cored, and seeded

Mangos, pitted, peeled, and cut into ½-inch slices

Starfruit, cut crosswise into ½-inch slices

Strawberries (ideally, large ones), hulled and cut in half lengthwise

Grapes, cut into small bunches of 3 or 4 grapes each

**TO FINISH THE FRUIT SALAD**

1 bunch fresh cilantro or mint, stemmed and roughly chopped

1 to 2 jalapeño peppers, stemmed, seeded, and minced (optional)

1 teaspoon freshly and finely grated lemon or lime zest

1 to 2 tablespoons fresh lemon or lime juice, or to taste

1 to 2 tablespoons orange liqueur, such as Grand Marnier or Cointreau, or your spirit of choice such as mezcal, tequila, dark rum, or Scotch whisky (preferably single malt)

1 teaspoon pure vanilla extract (optional)

Gelato or ice cream, for serving (optional)

**1.** Set up your grill for direct grilling and heat to high (you want the fire screaming hot).

**2.** Place the sugar in a shallow bowl and stir in the cinnamon and cardamom (if using). Have this spiced sugar with its bowl grillside. While you're at it, have a large mixing bowl grillside, too.

**3.** Brush or scrape the grill grate clean and oil it well. If enhancing a charcoal fire, add the wood chunks or chips to the coals; if enhancing a gas fire, place the chunks or chips in your grill's smoker box or place chunks under the grate directly over one or more burners.

**4.** Using tongs, start dipping the fruit in the spiced sugar on all cut sides, then arrange it on the hot grill grate.

Grill until the sugar caramelizes (it will turn brown), 1 to 2 minutes per side. Work quickly, so you caramelize the outside of the fruit, but keep the center raw and fresh.

**5.** As each piece of fruit is ready, transfer it to the mixing bowl. Reserve any excess spiced sugar.

**6.** Let the fruit cool to room temperature. Cut any large pieces of fruit (like the bananas and mangos) into 1-inch pieces. Stir in the cilantro, jalapeños (if using), lemon zest, 1 tablespoon of lemon juice, liqueur, and vanilla (if using). Taste for seasoning, adding the reserved spiced sugar for sweetness or more lemon juice for acidity. Serve the fruit salad by itself, or over your favorite gelato or ice cream.

**WHAT ELSE** Consider this recipe a broad guide, adapting it to the fresh fruit that's in season and ripe in your area. I'm writing this in March in Miami, so my salad will contain starfruit, canistel (also called eggfruit), banana, papaya, and pineapple. In summer in New England, I'd use peaches, plums, and strawberries.

# VOLCANO PINEAPPLE

I've been grilling pineapple since the book that got me started in this crazy business, *The Barbecue! Bible*. I love how the high dry heat of the grill caramelizes the natural plant sugars. I love the texture and flavor contrast of caramel crust and fresh juicy center. In this dish, the pineapple gets brushed with molasses (the raw material for rum), then dredged in spiced sugar. If you get it right, the high heat lays on a candy-like crust. But you're not done yet. The final step takes the notion of fire to a whole new level—flambéing the grilled pineapple with 151-proof rum. Whipped cream or vanilla ice cream makes the perfect finish.

## INGREDIENTS

1½ cups turbinado sugar (such as Sugar in the Raw)

1 tablespoon ground cinnamon

1 teaspoon ground allspice

½ teaspoon ground cloves

1 peeled, cored ripe pineapple (see What Else)

¼ cup molasses (light or dark—your choice)

Vegetable oil for oiling the grill grate (if direct grilling)

1 cup 151-proof rum, or as needed

Ice cream or whipped cream, for serving (optional)

**1.** Set up your grill for spit-roasting and heat it as hot as it will go. On a charcoal grill, rake the coals under the spit (not just in front and back as we usually do for rotisserie grilling). On a gas grill, light the burners under the spit as well as behind it.

**2.** Make the spiced sugar: Combine the sugar, cinnamon, allspice, and cloves in a pie plate or other shallow dish large enough to accommodate the pineapple, and mix well with your fingertips.

**3.** Skewer the pineapple on the spit. The spit will pass right through the tunnel in the center. Use the prongs to hold the pineapple in place.

**4.** Using a basting brush, paint the pineapple on all sides with the molasses, then dredge it on all sides in the sugar mixture. Immediately put the pineapple on the grill, attaching the spit to the motor according to the manufacturer's directions.

**5.** Spit-roast the pineapple until the outside is darkly browned, 6 to 10 minutes. The sugar should cook to a dark caramel crust. You may need to help it brown with a blowtorch or

**YIELD** Serves 4

**METHOD** Spit-roasting

**PREP TIME** 10 minutes

**GRILLING TIME** 4 to 8 minutes, or as needed

**GRILL/GEAR** Can be grilled over charcoal, gas, or wood. You'll also need a rotisserie (optional); kitchen torch, blowtorch, or roofer's torch (optional); a rimmed sheet pan; a flameproof platter; and long-stemmed matches.

**WHAT ELSE** You'll need a peeled and cored pineapple for this, and as much as I'm a do-it-from-scratch sort of guy, fruit companies and supermarkets do a nice job of prepping these for you. Look for the darkest yellow pineapple you can find (or the deepest yellow peeled pineapple)—it will be sweeter. There are two ways to cook the pineapple: on a rotisserie or by direct grilling (see the variation that follows). Whichever you choose, start with the hottest possible fire: You want to caramelize the sugar on the exterior while leaving the fruit cool and fresh in the center. A blowtorch helps you achieve this quickly and easily. A roofer's torch does the job even faster! Note: If using a roofer's torch, work with extreme caution. Wear heavy-duty grill gloves or welder's gloves. Make sure there's nothing behind the grill or the flame that could catch fire. Remember, the metal burner head will be hot, so set it down on a heatproof surface.

Spit-roasting the pineapple. Note the lit burner directly under the fruit.

roofer's torch. The idea is to sear the exterior while keeping the fruit cool and moist in the center.

**6.** Carefully unskewer the pineapple on a rimmed sheet pan and stand it upright on a round flameproof serving platter. Pour the 151-proof rum in the center where the core was. Light it with a long-stemmed match. Let it burn for a while (there's your volcano), then cut the pineapple in 4 pieces, either crosswise or lengthwise. Serve in heatproof bowls with ice cream or whipped cream on the side if you like, spooning the rum (flaming or not) over the fruit.

## VARIATION

**DIRECT GRILL METHOD**

Set up your grill for direct grilling and heat it as hot as it will go. Brush or scrape the grill grate clean and oil it well. Arrange the molasses-brushed, sugar-dredged pineapple on the grill, long side running the same direction as the bars of the grate. Grill, turning with tongs, until the outside is sizzling and the sugar coating is browned and caramelized, 2 to 3 minutes per side, 8 to 12 minutes in all. Finish as described in Step 6.

# GRILLED BANANA PUDDING

**YIELD** Serves 4

**METHOD** Direct grilling

**PREP TIME** 20 minutes

**GRILLING TIME** 4 minutes

**GRILL/GEAR** Can be grilled over charcoal, gas, or wood.

Banana pudding is a de rigueur dessert at barbecue joints across the country, especially in the American South. That set me thinking about a banana pudding that actually took advantage of the flavor-amplifying power of grilling. And *that* led me to crust the bananas with sugar and grill them over a raging hot fire. Stir them into the custard, or take a modernist approach by building the dessert in layers: cookies on the bottom, custard in the center, and caramelized banana on top. Nabisco Nilla Wafers appeal to the kid in all of us, but gingersnap cookies or the now-ubiquitous speculoos cookies from Belgium and the Netherlands have a more interesting flavor and crunch (you can find them at Trader Joe's and other supermarkets).

## INGREDIENTS

### FOR THE CUSTARD

3 cups whole milk

½ cup heavy cream (or more milk)

⅓ cup granulated sugar

⅓ cup cornstarch or all-purpose flour

Pinch of salt

3 egg yolks, preferably organic

1 teaspoon pure vanilla extract

1 tablespoon Scotch whisky, preferably single malt, or mezcal (optional)

### FOR THE BANANAS

Vegetable oil for oiling the grill grate

4 ripe (but still firm) bananas

1½ cups granulated sugar

### TO PUT IT ALL TOGETHER

12 Nabisco Nilla Wafers, gingersnaps, speculoos or other favorite cookie

Whipped cream (plain, or make it smoky by adding a few drops of mezcal or single-malt Scotch)

Ground cinnamon or freshly grated nutmeg, for serving

**WHAT ELSE** My goal in this recipe was to create a dessert truly worthy of the barbecue that precedes it. There are several ways to get there. At the very least, you want to grill the bananas over a screaming-hot fire to caramelize the sugar. To up the smoke flavor, I suggest adding a tablespoon of single-malt Scotch whisky or mezcal.

**1. Make the custard:** Place the milk and cream in a medium-size heavy saucepan and bring to a simmer over medium-high heat.

**2.** Meanwhile, place the sugar, cornstarch, and salt in a heatproof mixing bowl and whisk to mix. Add the egg yolks and whisk to mix. Slowly whisk in the hot milk in a thin stream. Do this gradually so you don't scramble the eggs. Whisk well, then return the mixture to the saucepan. Gradually bring to a boil over medium-high heat, whisking steadily until thick and custard-like, about 2 minutes. Continue simmering the custard for 2 minutes, then return it to the mixing bowl. Whisk in the vanilla and Scotch whisky (if using). Press a sheet of plastic wrap directly on top of the custard to prevent a skin from forming. (Alternatively, rub a tablespoon of butter at the end of a fork across the top of the custard—again to keep a skin from forming.) Let the custard cool to room temperature, then

refrigerate. The custard can be prepared several hours ahead to this stage.

**3.** Grill the bananas: Set up your grill for direct grilling and heat it as hot as it will go. Brush or scrape the grill grate clean and oil it well. Peel each banana and cut in half lengthwise. Spread the sugar on a plate. Dip each banana in the sugar to coat both sides, then arrange the bananas cut sides down on the grate on a diagonal. Grill until darkly browned on both sides, 1 to 2 minutes per side. Transfer the bananas to a plate to cool.

**4.** Put it all together: Remove the custard from the refrigerator and uncover it. Cut the bananas crosswise into ¾-inch slices. Gently stir them into the custard. Place a layer of cookies on the bottom of a glass serving bowl, such as a trifle bowl. Spoon in half of the custard mixture. Add a second layer of cookies and the remaining custard. Pipe or spoon the whipped cream (if using) on top. Sprinkle with cinnamon and dig in.

# GRANDS-PÈRES
## (SMOKY DESSERT DUMPLINGS POACHED IN MAPLE SYRUP WITH BACON)

**YIELD** Serves 4 to 6

**METHOD** Direct grilling

**PREP TIME** 15 minutes, plus 20 minutes for resting the dough

**GRILLING TIME** About 30 minutes

Flour dumplings poached in maple syrup. It's a dessert that could only have originated in Quebec. But I first experienced it at the Eggtoberfest in Atlanta, Georgia—the handiwork of Big Green Egg rep and Montreal grill master Simon Daoust. Simon had the genial idea to cook the Grands-Pères ("grandfathers," literally) on a Big Green Egg, and the even more genial idea to balance the sweet maple syrup with salty grilled bacon. The only thing missing? Wood smoke, of course, which you'll add by interspersing the coals with maple chunks. The addition of orange and cinnamon may make you think of super-moist cinnamon buns.

## INGREDIENTS

### FOR THE DUMPLINGS

2 cups unbleached all-purpose flour, plus extra for your hands and work surface

¼ cup granulated sugar

2 teaspoons baking powder

½ teaspoon ground cinnamon

½ teaspoon coarse salt (sea or kosher)

4 tablespoons (½ stick) cold unsalted butter, cut into ½-inch pieces

1 cup milk or half-and-half

1 teaspoon pure vanilla extract

Vegetable oil for oiling the grill grate

### FOR THE BACON

3 strips thick-cut artisanal bacon

### FOR POACHING THE DUMPLINGS

2 cups pure maple syrup

1 cinnamon stick (3 inches long)

1 clove

1 strip orange zest (½ by 1½ inches)

### FOR SERVING

Vanilla or maple ice cream (optional)

**1.** Combine the flour, sugar, baking powder, cinnamon, and salt in a mixing bowl. Cut in the butter using two knives, a pastry blender, or a fork, until the mixture feels crumbly, like sand. Stir in the milk and vanilla to make a moist dough thick enough to roll into balls. Cover the dough and refrigerate for 20 minutes.

**2.** Flour your hands and divide the dough into 12 equal pieces, then roll into balls on a lightly floured surface.

**3.** Meanwhile, set up your grill for direct grilling and heat to medium-high. Brush or scrape the grill grate clean.

**4.** Place the cast-iron skillet on the grill. Add the bacon and fry until crisp and browned on both sides, 3 to 4 minutes per side. Transfer the bacon to a wire rack or paper towel–lined plate to drain and cool. Pour off the bacon fat (save it for another use). Wipe the pan clean with a paper towel.

**5.** Return the cast-iron skillet to the grill. Pour in the maple syrup and 2 cups of water, and add the cinnamon stick. Pin the clove to the orange zest and add it as well. Bring the mixture to a boil (this will take 3 to 5 minutes).

**6.** If enhancing a charcoal fire, add the wood chunks or chips to the coals; if enhancing a gas fire, place the chunks or chips in your grill's smoker box or place chunks under the grate directly over one or more burners.

**7.** Carefully drop the dough balls into the boiling maple syrup mixture and close the grill lid to hold in the smoke. Poach until doubled in size and cooked through, 10 to 15 minutes, turning once with a slotted spoon so both sides cook evenly. Insert a metal skewer to test doneness—it should come out clean.

**8.** Transfer the dumplings to bowls. Spoon some of the poaching liquid over them. Crumble the bacon on top. I wouldn't say no to a scoop of maple or vanilla ice cream. Sweet. Salty. Soft and crisp. Who doesn't love that?

**GRILL/GEAR** Best cooked on a charcoal grill, but can also be grilled on wood or gas. You'll also need a wire rack (or paper towel–lined plate); a large, deep cast-iron skillet; a slotted spoon; and hardwood chunks or chips (preferably maple, unsoaked), see page 8.

**WHAT ELSE** You must use real maple syrup for this recipe—preferably from Quebec. In keeping with the theme, I'd use maple wood for smoking.

# APPENDICES

# SAUCES, CONDIMENTS & SEASONINGS

One of the secrets of great barbecue is a process called layering flavors. You start with a rub—a soulful amalgam of salt, pepper, paprika, and brown sugar, for example, or an herb-scented dry chimichurri. Next might come a basting of ember oil, or apple cider spritzed from a spray bottle. As you approach the end of cooking, you might slather on a sweet and sticky barbecue sauce. Or a fiery glaze of sweet Thai chili sauce and sriracha. But you're not done yet, because you'll continue to add layers of flavor in the form of salsas, relishes, cremas, and alliolis—each vigorously dosed with spice, smoke, and fire. And don't forget smoked tomato sauce—my secret weapon for grilled eggplant parmigiana (not to mention for breathing a barbecue soul into pasta). The recipes in these pages are all you need to make good barbecue great and take great barbecue to the stratosphere.

# SALSA THREE WAYS

Mexicans have been grilling salsa for longer than there's been a Mexico, roasting New World ingredients such as tomatoes, poblanos, and jalapeños on a fire-heated grill called a comal. Today, we achieve even more flavor using wood smoke and direct fire. Here's your straightforward salsa transformed by direct grilling, followed by variations for ember-grilling and smoking. Each method produces a different texture and flavor, but all take commonplace salsa over the top. Serve this vibrant salsa with chips like the Grilled Chia Seed Totopos on page 47 or spoon it over quesadillas, grilled eggs, grilled cheese, grilled mushrooms, and other vegetables.

**YIELD** Serves 4

**METHOD** Direct grilling, ember-grilling (caveman grilling) or smoking

**PREP TIME** 15 minutes

**GRILLING TIME** 15 minutes for grilling; 10 minutes for ember-grilling (caveman grilling); 30 minutes for smoking

**GRILL/GEAR** Can be grilled over charcoal or gas, but ideally, you'll be working over a wood or wood-enhanced fire. If you're enhancing a charcoal or gas fire, you'll need hardwood chunks or wood chips (unsoaked), see page 8. You'll also need a rimmed sheet pan; a toothpick; and a food processor or molcajete with a tejolote (a Mexican lava stone mortar and pestle; optional).

**WHAT ELSE** Use this recipe as a roadmap, not a specific itinerary. Substitute plum tomatoes for the heirlooms. Add a slice of grilled pineapple. Replace the jalapeños with habaneros or a dried pepper, such as ancho or pasilla. Add a shot of mezcal or tequila. You get the idea.

## INGREDIENTS

Vegetable oil for oiling the grill grate

1 small onion, peeled and quartered, or 1 bunch scallions, trimmed

1 clove garlic, peeled and skewered on a toothpick

1 poblano pepper

4 tomatoes, preferably heirloom (total of 2 to 2½ pounds)

2 large tomatillos, husked and rinsed (or another tomato)

2 large jalapeño or serrano peppers

2 limes, cut in half crosswise

1 canned chipotle in adobo, minced, with 1 teaspoon can juices (optional—it reinforces the smoke flavor)

½ cup chopped fresh cilantro leaves

Coarse salt (sea or kosher) and freshly ground black pepper

**1.** Set up your grill for direct grilling and heat to high. Brush or scrape the grill grate clean and oil it well. If enhancing a charcoal fire, add the wood chunks or chips to the coals; if enhancing a gas fire, place the wood chunks or chips in the smoker box or under the grate directly over one or more burners.

**2.** Arrange the onion, garlic, poblano, tomatoes, tomatillos, jalapeños, and limes on the grate. Grill until darkly browned, even charred, on the outside, 2 to 10 minutes (the onion will take the longest), turning with tongs. Don't overcook: The tomatoes and tomatillos should remain cool and raw in the center. Transfer the veggies to a rimmed sheet pan to cool.

**3.** To finish the salsa, scrape any really burnt parts off the veggies with a paring knife. Don't worry about removing every last bit of charred skin—a few black spots add color and flavor. Remove the toothpick from the garlic and discard. Roughly chop the garlic. Set aside the limes for Step 5. Seed and core the poblano if you haven't already done so. For a milder salsa, seed the jalapeños.

**4.** Cut the charred veggies into 1-inch pieces, then grind to a coarse puree in a food processor, running the machine in short bursts. Do not overprocess. Alternatively, coarsely chop the charred vegetables by hand or grind in a molcajete with a tejolote. Work in the canned chipotle with its juices (if using).

**5.** Squeeze in the juice from the charred limes, then add the cilantro and salt and pepper to taste: The salsa should be highly seasoned. Note: You can prepare the salsa up to 4 hours ahead (refrigerate until serving), but I like the freshness of eating it within 15 minutes of making it.

# VARIATIONS

### EMBER-GRILLED SALSA

Set up your grill for ember-grilling (caveman grilling). You'll be working over a charcoal or wood fire. Arrange the veggies and limes on the embers (wrap the garlic in aluminum foil so it doesn't burn) and grill until charred on all sides, but still raw in the center, 2 to 6 minutes, or as needed, turning with tongs. Proceed with the recipe from Step 3.

### SMOKED SALSA

Set up your smoker following the manufacturer's instructions and heat to medium-low. Cut the onion in quarters. Cut the poblano in half lengthwise and seed. Place the garlic in one of the poblano halves. Cut the tomatoes and tomatillos in half widthwise. Cut the jalapeños in half lengthwise and seed or not, depending on your affection for heat. Cut the lime in half widthwise. Set the vegetables and lime, cut sides up, on a wire rack over an aluminum foil drip pan filled with ice (this keeps them cool and raw) and smoke until bronzed with smoke, but still raw in the center, 15 to 30 minutes. Proceed with the recipe from Step 3.

# AJVAR
# (BALKAN FIRE-ROASTED PEPPER AND EGGPLANT PASTE)

**V**isit a grill parlor in Belgrade (and elsewhere in the Balkans and Asia Minor), and you'll be offered a condiment that's thicker than a sauce and looser than a chopped salad, and that handily doubles as both. Serbs call it ajvar (from the Turkish word *havyar*), and if that sounds familiar, think of a salted fish roe with a similar name: caviar. So you could think of ajvar as vegetable caviar, and however you serve it—as a spread, as a condiment, as a salad, or as a dip for grilled pita bread (see page 102)—your meal will be immeasurably enriched.

**YIELD** Makes 3½ to 4 cups, enough to serve 4 to 8

**METHOD** Ember-grilling (caveman grilling) or direct grilling

**PREP TIME** 10 minutes

**GRILLING TIME** 8 to 15 minutes

**GRILL/GEAR** Can be grilled over charcoal, gas, or wood. You'll also need a small bamboo skewer; a rimmed sheet pan; heavy-duty aluminum foil; and a food processor.

**WHAT ELSE** There are two ways to cook the vegetables: by direct grilling or by ember-grilling. The latter gives you a more soulful, smokier flavor. Guess which I prefer. Ajvar comes in varying degrees of spiciness, so I've made the horn peppers (or serranos or jalapeños) optional. I've made the dill optional, too, but I love how it rounds out the flavor. Note: Some people like to add grilled onion to the ajvar. Just FYI.

## INGREDIENTS

4 horn peppers or 2 serrano or jalapeño peppers (optional)

3 red bell peppers

2 medium eggplants (about 1 pound each)

5 cloves garlic, peeled

½ cup extra virgin olive oil

1 teaspoon freshly and finely grated lemon zest

1 to 2 tablespoons fresh lemon juice

3 tablespoons chopped fresh dill (optional)

Coarse salt (sea or kosher) and freshly ground black pepper

**1.** Set up your grill for ember-grilling. Rake out the coals and fan off any loose ash. Alternatively, set up your grill for direct grilling and heat to high. Brush or scrape the grill grate clean (there's no need to oil it).

**2.** Lay the horn peppers (if using), and the bell peppers and eggplants on the embers (or place on the grate if direct grilling). Grill, turning with tongs, until the veggies are charred on all sides and very tender (use a slender metal skewer to check for doneness—it should pierce the veggies easily). This will take 2 to 4 minutes for the horn peppers and

6 to 10 minutes for the bell peppers and eggplants (a little longer if direct grilling). Transfer the charred vegetables to a rimmed sheet pan to cool.

**3.** Meanwhile, skewer the garlic on a small bamboo skewer and loosely wrap in foil. Place the foil-wrapped garlic on the embers (or on the grill, if direct grilling). Grill until browned, about 2 minutes, turning with tongs. Transfer to the sheet pan to cool.

**4.** Scrape the burnt skins off the eggplants, stem them, and cut into 1-inch dice. Scrape the burnt skins off the peppers, cut in half, and remove and discard the stems, veins, and seeds. Cut into 1-inch dice. Unwrap and unskewer the garlic.

**5.** Coarsely puree the ingredients in a food processor. Work in the olive oil, lemon zest, lemon juice, dill (if using), and salt and pepper to taste. The ajvar should be highly seasoned. This will give you a great spread or sauce. If not serving right away, store in a covered jar in the refrigerator. The ajvar will keep for at least 3 days. Serve it chilled or at room temperature.

## VARIATION

To make this as a salad, cut the eggplants and peppers into ½-inch dice. Mince the garlic. Place in a bowl and stir in the olive oil, lemon zest, lemon juice, dill (if using), and salt and pepper to taste.

# SMOKED TOMATO SAUCE

**YIELD** Makes 3½ to 4 cups

**METHOD** Smoke-roasting (indirect grilling with wood smoke) or smoking

**PREP TIME** 10 minutes, plus 5 to 10 minutes for simmering the sauce

**GRILLING TIME** 12 to 20 minutes for smoke-roasting (indirect grilling with wood smoke); 1 hour for smoking

Tomato sauce is so elemental, so essential to human happiness, of course you'll want to have a few smoked and grilled versions in your repertory. Spread atop grilled pizza (see pages 109 and 111). Use to make Cedar-Planked Eggplant Parmigiana (page 188). Spoon it over your favorite pasta. I always keep a quart handy in my freezer.

## INGREDIENTS

4 to 5 luscious ripe red tomatoes (about 2½ pounds), cut in half widthwise

½ green bell or poblano pepper (optional)

1 small onion, peeled and cut into 6 wedges

1 clove garlic or 1 small shallot, peeled

1 rib celery, washed (optional)

2 tablespoons extra virgin olive oil, plus extra for drizzling

Coarse salt (sea or kosher) and freshly ground black pepper

1 tablespoon tomato paste

¼ cup dry white vermouth or white wine

6 fresh basil leaves, slivered

2 fresh sage leaves, slivered, or more basil

1 teaspoon granulated sugar, or to taste (optional)

2 tablespoons unsalted butter, or more olive oil

**1.** Set up your grill for indirect grilling and heat to medium.

**2.** Arrange the tomatoes, bell pepper (if using), onion, garlic, and celery (if using), in a large aluminum foil drip pan. Drizzle with olive oil and season with salt and black pepper.

**3.** Place the vegetables in their pan on the grill away from the heat. If enhancing a charcoal fire, add the wood chunks or chips to the coals; if enhancing a gas grill, place the chunks or chips in your grill's smoker box or place chunks under the grate directly over one or more burners. Close the grill lid. Smoke the veggies until the tomatoes are soft and smoky, 12 to 20 minutes. Note: You can also smoke the veggies low and slow in a smoker following the manufacturer's instructions: You'll need about 1 hour.

**4.** Remove the pan from the heat and let the vegetables cool, then transfer to a cutting board. Some people like to remove the tomato skins—I don't bother. Finely chop the tomatoes and set them aside. Finely chop the pepper (if using), onion, garlic, and celery (if using).

**5.** Heat 2 tablespoons of olive oil in a large saucepan. Add the grilled pepper (if using), onion, garlic, and celery (if using), and cook over medium-high heat until golden brown, about 3 minutes, stirring often. Add the tomato paste and fry until fragrant, about 1 minute. Stir in the vermouth and boil until mostly evaporated, about 1 minute.

**6.** Stir in the chopped tomatoes with their juices and the basil and sage. Gently simmer the sauce until richly flavored, 5 to 10 minutes. Add the sugar if you'd like the sauce to be a little sweeter. Stir in the butter at the end.

Correct the seasoning, adding salt and pepper to taste: The tomato sauce should be highly seasoned. If not serving right away, let cool to room temperature, then refrigerate in a sealed container for up to 3 days, or freeze.

**NOTE:** This gives you a fairly coarse tomato sauce, which is how I like it. For a finer sauce, you could puree it with an immersion blender or in a food processor.

# VARIATION

## GRILLED TOMATO SAUCE

In this version, you add smoky caramelized flavors by grilling the tomatoes and other vegetables over a hot fire (ideally a wood fire or wood-enhanced fire; see page 8).

**1.** Set up your grill for direct grilling and heat to high. If enhancing a charcoal fire, add the wood chunks or chips to the coals; if enhancing a gas fire, place the wood chunks or chips in your grill's smoker box or place chunks under the grate directly over one or more burners.

**2.** Lightly brush the tomatoes, bell pepper (if using), onion, garlic, and celery (if using) with the olive oil and season with salt and black pepper.

**3.** Arrange the vegetables on the grate and grill until blistered and browned, 1 to 2 minutes per side. Transfer to a cutting board and let cool. Finish the sauce following the instructions from Step 4.

**GRILL/GEAR** Can be smoked in a charcoal grill or in a smoker; can be direct grilled over charcoal, gas, or wood. You'll also need a large aluminum foil drip pan and hardwood chunks or wood chips (unsoaked), see page 8.

**WHAT ELSE** There are several ways to cook this tomato sauce—all smoke-driven and all delectable. You could hot-smoke the tomatoes by indirect grilling. Or smoke them cold or low and slow in a smoker. Or blister them directly over a hot fire—preferably wood or wood-enhanced—as directed in the variation.

# SALSA BRAVA

**YIELD** Makes 2½ to 3 cups

**METHOD** Direct grilling

**PREP TIME** 15 to 20 minutes

**GRILLING TIME** About 2 minutes

**GRILL/GEAR** Can be grilled over charcoal or gas, but for the best flavor grill over a wood fire or a wood-enhanced fire. If you're enhancing a charcoal or gas fire, you'll need hardwood chunks or wood chips (unsoaked), see page 8.

**WHAT ELSE** I call for grilling the tomatoes here, and if you work over a wood or wood-enhanced fire, you'll get a wood smoke flavor that transforms this tapas bar staple into a condiment you'll want to eat by the spoonful. Alternatively, smoke the tomatoes following the instructions in Step 3 of Smoked Tomato Sauce (page 290). For both methods, source luscious vine-ripened tomatoes. If these are out of season, use a good fire-roasted canned brand, like Muir Glen, available at most supermarkets. (You'll need a 14.5-ounce can.)

This spicy tomato sauce accompanies Spain's popular papas bravas, those crisply fried potatoes served at tapas bars around the world. Most tapas bars start with canned tomatoes, but you, grill fanatic that you are, will make the sauce with fresh tomatoes charred over a smoky wood fire. While you're at it, why not smoke-roast some new potatoes (start with them cut in half—see page 236); it beats the pants off deep-frying. Salsa brava makes a great dip or sauce for any imaginable grilled vegetable, from asparagus to zucchini. My latest fave is the Sunchokes Bravas on page 157.

## INGREDIENTS

Vegetable oil for oiling the grill grate

4 to 5 luscious ripe red tomatoes (about 2½ pounds)

1 medium onion, peeled and quartered lengthwise (leave the root end intact so the wedges hold together)

3 tablespoons extra virgin olive oil

1 teaspoon granulated sugar, or to taste

1½ teaspoons pimentón (Spanish smoked paprika) or sweet paprika

¼ teaspoon cayenne pepper, or to taste

1 to 2 tablespoons sherry vinegar, preferably Spanish, or red wine vinegar

Coarse salt (sea or kosher) and freshly ground black pepper

**1.** Set up your grill for direct grilling and heat to high. Brush or scrape the grill grate clean and oil it well.

**2.** Arrange the tomatoes on the grate and grill until the skins are blistered, but the flesh is still cool and raw in the center, about 2 minutes. Grill the onion the same way, turning to cook the quarters on each side, 1 to 2 minutes per side. Transfer the vegetables to a platter to cool.

**3.** Heat 2 tablespoons of the olive oil in a medium saucepan. Finely chop the grilled onion and add it to the oil. Cook over medium heat until just beginning to brown (discard the root end), about 3 minutes. Remove the pan from the heat.

**4.** Pull the skins off the tomatoes and discard. Finely chop the tomatoes by hand or in a food processor. Add them to the onion mixture in the pan along with the sugar, pimentón, and cayenne. Simmer the sauce over medium-high heat until concentrated and rich-tasting, 5 to 8 minutes. The last 2 minutes, stir in the vinegar, the remaining tablespoon of olive oil, and salt and pepper. Correct the seasoning, adding salt or vinegar to taste: The sauce should be highly seasoned. If not using right away, store the salsa brava in a covered jar in the refrigerator. It will keep for several days.

# CHARRED POBLANO CREMA

Miami barbecue buffs uttered cries of jubilation when Brooklyn smoke master Billy Durney brought Hometown Bar-B-Que from Red Hook to an industrial neighborhood called Allapattah. But it's not his pitch-perfect brisket, his forearm-size beef ribs, or his textbook pulled pork that earn a place in this book. No, it's broccoli. Broccoli! Crisply seared over a wood-burning fire on a plancha and served with a creamy white sauce that doles out a double dose of smoke and fire. Durney calls the latter poblano crema—based on fire-roasted poblanos. I call it the poblano's Second Coming, and it's heaven-sent for grilled vegetables, tacos, quesadillas, and more.

**YIELD** Makes 1½ cups

**METHOD** Ember-grilling (caveman grilling) or direct grilling

**PREP TIME** 10 minutes

**GRILLING TIME** 9 to 12 minutes

**GRILL/GEAR** Can be grilled over charcoal, gas, or wood. You'll also need a rimmed sheet pan and a food processor.

**WHAT ELSE** As with all pepper recipes in this book, there are two possible ways to grill them. The first is ember-grilling (caveman grilling), which gives you an incomparable smoke flavor. The second is direct grilling: Crank up your grill's heat as hot as it will go. You could even char the peppers directly on the grill's side burner or one of your gas stove burners. Note: I call for sour cream in this recipe, but you could also use Mexican crema (more tart than American sour cream) or French crème fraîche.

## INGREDIENTS

2 to 3 poblano peppers (enough to make ½ cup roasted, peeled, seeded, and diced)

1 cup sour cream

3 tablespoons chopped fresh cilantro leaves

¼ teaspoon ground cumin, or to taste

1 tablespoon fresh lime juice, or to taste

Coarse salt (sea or kosher) and freshly ground black pepper

**1.** Set up your grill for ember-grilling. Rake out the embers in a single layer and fan off any loose ash. Lay the poblanos on the embers and roast, turning with tongs, until the skins are black on all sides, about 2 minutes per side. Alternatively, if direct grilling, heat your grill as hot as it will go and brush or scrape the grill grate clean (no need to oil it). Arrange the poblanos on the grate and grill until charred on all sides, 2 to 3 minutes per side, 9 to 12 minutes in all.

**2.** Transfer the poblanos to a rimmed sheet pan to cool. Cut them in half lengthwise. Remove the stems and scrape out and discard the veins and seeds. Chop the poblanos. You should have about ½ cup. Place in a food processor and puree.

**3.** Add the sour cream, cilantro, cumin, lime juice, and salt and pepper to taste. Puree until smooth. If not serving right away, store in a sealed jar in the refrigerator. The crema will keep for at least 3 days.

# PIQUILLO AND EMBER-GRILLED PEPPER RELISH

**YIELD** Makes 2 cups, enough to serve 4 to 8

**METHOD** Ember-grilling (caveman grilling) or direct grilling

**PREP TIME** 15 minutes

**GRILLING TIME** 20 minutes

**GRILL/GEAR** Charcoal or wood for ember-grilling; gas for direct grilling (see variation). You'll also need a rimmed sheet pan and a cast-iron skillet.

Of all the vegetables you can grill in the embers, none delivers the payoff of peppers. The charred skins impart an intoxicating smoke flavor, making the peppers sweeter than you would ever expect a vegetable to be. Add buttery jarred Spanish piquillo peppers and ember-grilled onions (additional sources of sweetness) and wine vinegar to offset the plant sugars, and you'll understand why I serve this simple relish atop grilled bread, scooped up with grilled pita chips or tortilla chips, and as a relish for grilled cheese, meats, or vegetables. Hell, enjoy it straight off the spoon.

## INGREDIENTS

2 red bell peppers

2 yellow bell peppers

1 sweet onion

¼ cup pine nuts, pistachios, slivered almonds, or other nuts

1 jar (7 ounces) piquillo peppers, drained and cut into ½-inch strips

2 tablespoons red wine vinegar, or to taste

2 tablespoons extra virgin olive oil

Coarse salt (sea or kosher) and freshly ground black pepper

¼ cup chopped fresh flat-leaf parsley leaves, or other fresh herb

**1.** Set up your grill for ember-grilling. Rake out the coals in an even layer and fan off any loose ash.

**2.** Lay the bell peppers and onion on the embers. Grill until the peppers are charred black on all sides, 2 to 3 minutes per side, 8 to 12 minutes in all, turning with tongs. Transfer the peppers to a rimmed sheet pan to cool.

**3.** Grill the onion until charred black on all sides and soft in the center, 15 to 20 minutes, turning with tongs. Transfer the onion to the sheet pan to cool.

**4.** Meanwhile, place the nuts in a dry cast-iron skillet on the embers or your grill's side burner. Toast until browned and fragrant, 1 to 2 minutes. Transfer the nuts to a bowl.

**5.** Using a paring knife, scrape the burnt skin off the peppers and onion. Transfer the peppers to a cutting board and cut in half. Remove the stems and scrape out and discard the veins and seeds. Cut the peppers into ½-inch strips.

**6.** Cut the onion in half, then cut each half lengthwise into pieces the size of the peppers. Place in a mixing bowl.

**7.** Stir in the piquillo peppers, vinegar, olive oil, and salt and pepper to taste: The relish should be highly seasoned.

**8.** Right before serving, stir in the parsley and pine nuts.

**NOTE:** A relish this elemental lends itself to a myriad of embellishments. For a Sicilian touch, add currants and capers. Or shave ricotta salata cheese on top.

# VARIATION

### DIRECT GRILLING

Set up your grill for direct grilling and heat as hot as it will go. Brush or scrape the grill grate clean (there's no need to oil it). Grill the bell peppers and onions until charred, or at least dark brown, on all sides. (This will take a little longer than ember-grilling and you may not actually be able to char the peppers black on a gas grill.) Prepare the relish as described in Steps 4 through 8.

**WHAT ELSE** Piquillo peppers are small red peppers grown in Basque country in northern Spain—sweet to begin with and positively dulcet when roasted. Piquillo means "little beak." Look for them in jars or canned at Spanish markets or online (a good source is Latienda.com). In a perfect world, you'd ember-grill the bell peppers and onions on charcoal. But gas grillers can achieve a similar effect by cranking up the heat as hot as their grills will go (see the variation). I like the sharpness of red wine vinegar, but you could also go for an Asian-inspired flavor with rice vinegar, Spanish-inspired with sherry vinegar, or Italian-inspired with balsamic. Likewise, you can vary the toasted nuts, from almonds or pine nuts to pistachios or macadamias.

# SMOKED ALLIOLI
## (SPANISH GARLIC MAYONNAISE)

**YIELD** Makes 2 cups

**METHOD** Indirect grilling or smoking

**PREP TIME** 15 minutes

**GRILLING TIME** 6 minutes

**GRILL/GEAR** Can be grilled over charcoal, gas or wood. You'll also need a food processor.

**WHAT ELSE** What follows is a smoked allioli, but you could certainly make the traditional version by using fresh garlic instead of smoked. The lemon isn't strictly traditional, but I like how it brightens the sauce. Serve allioli as a dip for grilled artichokes, asparagus, or other vegetables. Or slather it on grilled bread, which you then top with grilled peppers or other vegetables to make Spanish crostini. Note: Some people like to use pasteurized eggs when making allioli (or mayonnaise) to eliminate any risk of bacterial contamination.

Allioli is the Spanish answer to French aioli, Greek skordalia, and the other thick creamy garlic sauces served with grilled veggies and seafood around the Mediterranean. The twist here is using smoked garlic, which gives it an otherworldly flavor. Note: I give you two versions. One is a traditional raw egg version; the other starts with store-bought mayonnaise.

## INGREDIENTS

1 whole large egg and 1 egg yolk (preferably organic; see What Else)

3 to 5 cloves smoked garlic (see page 299), peeled and roughly chopped

1 teaspoon coarse salt (sea or kosher), or to taste

½ teaspoon Espelette pepper or cayenne pepper (optional—if you like your allioli with a kick)

¾ cup extra virgin olive oil

¾ cup canola or other vegetable oil (or more olive oil)

1 teaspoon freshly and finely grated lemon zest

2 tablespoons fresh lemon juice, or to taste

Crack the whole egg and egg yolks into a food processor fitted with a chopping blade. Add the garlic, salt, and Espelette pepper (if using), and process to puree the garlic. With the machine running, add the oils in a very thin stream through the feed tube:

The mixture will thicken. Work in the lemon zest and lemon juice. Correct the seasoning, adding lemon juice or salt as needed: The allioli should be highly seasoned. Store in a covered jar in the refrigerator; it will keep for at least 3 days.

# VARIATION

## SMOKED ALLIOLI MADE WITH STORE-BOUGHT MAYONNAISE

If you have a food processor, allioli is easy to make from scratch at home. It's even easier to start with store-bought mayonnaise. Yes, I sometimes take this shortcut myself.

**INGREDIENTS**

3 to 5 cloves smoked garlic (see page 299), peeled and minced

½ teaspoon sea salt

½ teaspoon Espelette pepper or cayenne pepper (optional—if you like your allioli with a kick)

1½ cups mayonnaise, preferably Hellmann's or Best Foods, or vegan mayonnaise

1 teaspoon freshly and finely grated lemon zest

2 tablespoons fresh lemon juice, or to taste

2 tablespoons extra virgin olive oil

Place the garlic, salt, and Espelette pepper (if using) in the bottom of a mixing bowl and mash well with the back of a spoon. Whisk in the mayonnaise, lemon zest, lemon juice, and olive oil. Correct the seasoning, adding lemon juice or salt to taste: The allioli should be highly seasoned. Store in a covered jar in the refrigerator; it will keep for at least 3 days.

# YOGURT SMOKED OR GRILLED

**YIELD** Makes 2 cups

**METHOD** Indirect grilling/ smoking

**PREP TIME** None

**GRILLING TIME** 5 to 8 minutes, or as needed, in a grill; 40 to 60 minutes in a smoker

**GRILL/GEAR** You'll need a charcoal grill for this one. Or any sort of smoker. You'll also need hardwood chunks or wood chips (unsoaked), see page 8; and 2 large aluminum foil drip pans (one filled with ice).

**WHAT ELSE** Yogurt is an indispensable part of barbecue— used in marinades in India; as a condiment for grilled meats in Greece and the Middle East; mixed with rosewater and seltzer to make dugh, the beverage that accompanies barbecue in Afghanistan and Iraq. What you may not know is that elsewhere on Planet Barbecue, the yogurt itself becomes barbecue—either by smoking it (as they do in Lebanon) or by enhancing it with flame-charred squash (page 314).

For millennia, shepherds in the Middle East have hung fresh yogurt in cloth bags to drain off the excess water. That's the origin of "hung" or strained yogurt, which most Americans know today as Greek- or Turkish- style yogurt. (Hang it even longer and it becomes a soft tangy cheese called labneh.) In parts of Lebanon, the cloth is hung next to a wood fire to speed up draining and drying, with the happy result that the wood smoke actually flavors the yogurt. This smoked yogurt is simultaneously familiar and otherworldly—spectacular when consumed by itself and a revelation when served with other grilled fare.

## INGREDIENTS

1 pint Greek-style yogurt (whole milk for the richest flavor, but low-fat or no-fat makes great smoked yogurt, too; see Note)

**1.** Set up your grill for indirect grilling and heat to medium. If enhancing a charcoal fire, add the wood chunks or chips to the coals; if enhancing a gas fire, place the chunks or chips in your grill's smoker box or place chunks under the grate directly over one or more burners.

**2.** Meanwhile, spread out the yogurt in a large foil pan and place it in another foil pan filled with ice. Place both pans on the grill away from the heat. Close the grill lid and smoke the yogurt until bronzed with a light patina of smoke, 5 to 8 minutes.

**3.** Transfer the yogurt to a bowl and whisk to mix. Serve it as is. Or stir 1 minced garlic clove, 1 cup grated cucumber, and ¼ cup chopped fresh mint or parsley into it to make a smoky tzatziki.

**NOTE:** If you like your smoked yogurt thick and creamy, start with Greek- style yogurt. For a thinner, wetter consistency, use regular yogurt. You can also smoke the yogurt in a smoker low and slow, that is, at 250°F for 40 to 60 minutes. Again, keep the yogurt over ice.

# SMOKED GARLIC AND OTHER ALLIUMS

If I were to name the single most important flavoring on the world's barbecue trail, it would be garlic. From Buenos Aires to Baku to Bali, it's hard to imagine a dish that isn't scented in some way with this aromatic bulb. Smoking transforms garlic in two ways: The heat mellows its pungency while bringing out the bulb's sweetness. The smoke adds a dimension of flavor you'd never suspect garlic could possess. So what can you do with smoked garlic? Spread it on bread to make bruschetta or garlic bread. Puree it with chickpeas to make an unbelievably flavorful hummus (see page 53). Mash it with mayonnaise to make a smoked garlic allioli (see page 296). Soak a few cloves in olive oil to make a fabulous oil for salads or basting. (Food safety calls for refrigerating the resulting oil and using it within 72 hours.) Impale a few cloves on a toothpick and add to your favorite martini. And that's just for starters!

## INGREDIENTS

1 head garlic

**1.** Break up the garlic into cloves. Cut the stem ends off each and peel. Skewer the garlic crosswise on toothpicks, 4 cloves per toothpick.

**2.** Set up your grill for indirect grilling and heat to medium. Add the wood chunks or chips to the coals.

**3.** Arrange the garlic skewers on the grill grate away from the heat. Lower the lid and smoke the garlic until bronzed and tender (squeeze it between your thumb and forefinger), 15 to 20 minutes, or as needed.

**4.** Transfer the garlic to a wire rack to cool. Store smoked garlic in a sealed container in the refrigerator. It will keep for at least 3 days.

**YIELD** Makes 8 to 12 cloves of garlic

**METHOD** Smoke-roasting (indirect grilling with wood smoke)

**PREP TIME** 5 minutes

**SMOKING TIME** 15 to 20 minutes (or as needed)

**GRILL/GEAR** If smoke-roasting, work over charcoal. If smoking, any sort of smoker will do—outdoor or indoor. You'll also need wooden toothpicks; hardwood chunks or wood chips (unsoaked), see page 8; and a wire rack.

**WHAT ELSE** When buying garlic, look for heads or cloves that are free of green shoots. A green shoot in the center indicates garlic that's past its prime. One easy way to peel garlic is to lightly flatten a clove with the side of a cleaver or chef's knife, then slip off the skin. Alternatively, roll it in a garlic peeler—a flexible plastic tube. But the coolest method of all is to place the cloves in a large jar, attach the lid, and shake for all you're worth. You'll shake the skins right off.

## VARIATIONS

### SMOKED SHALLOTS

For me, shallots are the most elegant member of the allium family—with a flavor that triangulates onion, garlic, and leek, but manages to transcend all three.

Smoke 4 shallots, peeled and cut in half lengthwise as described on page 299. The cooking time will be 20 to 30 minutes.

### SMOKED ONIONS

The last and largest of our triumvirate of alliums. To save time, I like to cut the onions lengthwise in quarters for smoking (leave the stem end intact). Use a sweet onion like a Vidalia or Walla Walla.

Peel and quarter 1 large sweet onion. Secure each quarter with a toothpick to keep the layers together. Lightly brush the cut parts of the onion with olive oil. (This keeps them from drying out.) Smoke as described on page 299, Step 3. The smoking time will be 40 to 60 minutes.

# EMBER OIL

**YIELD** Makes 2 cups

**METHOD** Ember-grilling (caveman grilling)

**PREP TIME** Just the time it takes to light the charcoal

**GRILLING TIME** 3 minutes

**GRILL/GEAR** Charcoal; you'll also need tongs and a fine-mesh strainer.

**WHAT ELSE** There's no need to use a costly extra virgin olive oil for this (but of course, you can if you want to). Store the Ember Oil in a covered jar away from heat and light. Try to use it within 3 days.

This preparation is so simple, I almost hate to put it in this book. But its charcoal flavor is so uncanny, its uses so diverse, I would be remiss if I didn't share it. In a nutshell, you plunge a glowing charcoal ember into a pan of oil. The resulting Vesuvian hiss and boil transfer the charcoal flavor from the ember to the oil. Use any way you would use a flavored oil—for sautéing, in vinaigrettes, for drizzling, and more.

## INGREDIENTS

2 cups olive oil, grapeseed oil, canola oil, or other mild-flavored oil

1 to 2 lit embers of natural lump charcoal

**1.** Place the oil in a small, deep saucepan. Using tongs, grab a glowing orange coal from your grill or smoker's fire box. Gently blow on it to dislodge any loose ash. Plunge the ember in the oil—it will bubble and hiss and generally look like the oil is about to boil over. (If you use a deep enough pot, it won't.)

**2.** Let the ember burn out in the oil and let the oil cool to room temperature. Strain it through a fine-mesh strainer into a jar and store at room temperature. It will keep for at least 3 days. When the charcoal flavor begins to fade, it's time to prepare a new batch.

## VARIATION

**EMBER BUTTER**

Here's a richer version of the Ember Oil. Great for dipping grilled artichokes (see page 132), asparagus (page 28), or Smashed Potatoes (see page 236).

Melt 1 cup (2 sticks) of unsalted butter in a deep saucepan. Prepare as described in Ember Oil and store in the refrigerator.

# ALL-PURPOSE BARBECUE RUB

If you've read my books or watched my TV shows over the years, you're surely familiar with this rub. It's my basic barbecue rub—sweet with sugar, spicy with black pepper, tangy with sea salt, and aromatic with paprika and celery seed. And wondrously customizable. It adds an instant barbecue flavor to any food to which it's applied.

**YIELD** Makes 1 cup

**PREP TIME** 5 minutes

**WHAT ELSE** Make sure your spices are of recent vintage. If the jar has been on your stove for 3 years and the spice inside has no smell, it won't taste like much either. Figure on 2 to 3 teaspoons of rub per pound of vegetable or protein. Feel free to customize, substituting any of the ingredients in parentheses.

## INGREDIENTS

¼ cup coarse salt (sea or kosher)

¼ cup freshly ground black pepper (or white pepper or lemon pepper)

¼ cup sweet paprika (or hot paprika, Spanish pimentón, or chile powder)

¼ cup brown sugar (light, dark, white, turbinado, maple, Sucanat, or other dry sweetener)

1½ teaspoons granulated onion

1½ teaspoons granulated garlic

1 to 3 teaspoons hot red pepper flakes (depending on your heat tolerance)

1 teaspoon celery seeds

Combine the salt, pepper, paprika, brown sugar, granulated onion and garlic, hot red pepper flakes, and celery seeds in a bowl or jar and mix with a fork or your fingers, breaking any lumps in the brown sugar. Cover and store away from heat and light. The rub will keep for several weeks.

# DRY CHIMICHURRI RUB

**YIELD** Makes 1 cup

**PREP TIME** 5 minutes

**WHAT ELSE** Yes, I call for dried herbs here, not fresh, but make sure they're still kicking before you use them. Not sure? Open the jar and sniff: If the contents don't smell like much, they won't taste like much either. Figure on 2 to 3 teaspoons of rub per pound of vegetable or protein.

This is it. The original Argentinean chimichurri. No olive oil. No vinegar. No fresh garlic or parsley. Just the dry seasonings light enough and nonperishable enough to fit in a gaucho's saddlebag. Works great on most vegetables, especially tomatoes and mushrooms, as well as grilling cheeses like provoleta—brush with olive oil and sprinkle with rub. That's all there is to it.

## INGREDIENTS

¼ cup dried oregano

¼ cup dried basil

¼ cup dried parsley

1 tablespoon dried thyme

3 tablespoons coarse salt (sea or kosher)

2 tablespoons cracked black peppercorns

2 tablespoons granulated garlic

1 tablespoon hot red pepper flakes

Combine the oregano, basil, parsley, thyme, salt, pepper, granulated garlic, and hot red pepper flakes in a bowl or jar and stir with a fork to mix. Cover and store away from heat and light. The rub will keep for several weeks.

# A VEGETABLE ABECEDARIUM

**A**lmost all vegetables can be grilled and benefit immeasurably from live fire. But you don't grill all vegetables the same way. Here's an alphabetical list of the key players and the best ways to grill them.

**NOTE:** Prior to grilling any vegetable, brush or scrape the grill grate clean (just as you would for any food). Oil the grill grate well when grilling sliced or stick-prone vegetables. It is not necessary to oil the grate when grilling whole smooth-skinned vegetables, such as artichokes, eggplants, and bell peppers.

**ARTICHOKES:** Despite their firm thistly texture, artichokes rock when grilled. They're so popular, grill cultures around the world have devised at least four methods for grilling them.

**Prep:** Using kitchen scissors, snip the barbed tips off the leaves. Use a chef's knife to cut ¾ inch off the top (the crown) and cut the bottom ¼ inch off the stem (the rest of the stem is edible). Then, depending on the recipe, grill whole, halved, quartered, or in wedges. Remove the fibrous choke with a melon baller, then rub the cut parts with half a lemon to keep them from discoloring. Sicilians have a singular way to prepare and grill artichokes: They smash the artichoke (top side down) against a hard surface a half dozen times to spread apart the leaves before griling.

**Direct grill:** Cut small artichokes in half or large ones into wedges, brush with olive oil, and direct grill over high heat until browned and tender. Be sure to baste with plenty of extra virgin olive oil or melted butter during grilling. Note: Italians and Spaniards often direct grill artichokes whole. In this case, use plenty of oil or melted butter (dab it between the leaves) and work over a moderate fire. Grill until the outside leaves are crisp and the heart is tender (test it with a slender skewer).

**Blanch and direct grill:** Cut the artichoke in half from top to bottom. Using a melon baller, scoop out and discard the fibrous choke. Blanch (parboil) the artichokes in rapidly boiling salted water with a squeeze of lemon juice until almost tender, 3 to 6 minutes for small artichokes, 10 to 15 minutes for large artichokes. Drain well in a colander, rinse with cold water to chill, and drain again. (Draining is best done on a wire rack—place the artichokes cut sides down on the rack.) Then blot dry, brush the artichoke with olive oil or melted butter, and direct grill until sizzling, browned, and tender.

**Indirect grill (caveman grill):** Drizzle olive oil or melted butter over the artichokes and between the leaves. Stuff seasonings, such as garlic and chopped mint, between the leaves. Arrange the artichokes stem side down on the grate and indirect grill until tender enough to pierce easily with a slender skewer, 30 to 50 minutes.

**Ember-grill:** Artichokes can also be roasted in the embers. See my recipe for Sicilian-style artichokes on page 214.

**ASPARAGUS:** From Japan to the United States, asparagus is one of the most popular vegetables for grilling.

**Prep:** Snap or cut the fibrous bottom ends off the asparagus stalks and discard. (Some people like to peel the lower part of the stem with a vegetable peeler to remove any fibrous sheath.) Lay 4 or 5 stalks side by side, then pin into a raft with wooden toothpicks. Brush the rafts on all sides with oil (olive, sesame, walnut) or melted butter. Note: It's a lot easier to grill and turn 4 asparagus rafts than 20 individual stalks.

**Direct grill:** Grill over high heat until blistered and browned on both sides.

**Pan-grill:** Grill the loose stalks in an aluminum foil drip pan with a little olive oil directly over a hot fire.

**AVOCADOS:** Yes, you can grill this fruit (botanically speaking, avocado is a fruit, not a vegetable).

Do so over a wood or wood-enhanced fire, and you'll add a dimension of flavor most of us have never dreamed an avocado capable of possessing. (You can also smoke avocados—see page 44.)

**Prep:** Let avocados ripen at room temperature until gently yielding when pressed with your thumb. Then, using a sharp knife, cut the avocado in half lengthwise to the pit. Twist the halves in opposite directions to separate. Carefully embed the knife blade in the pit with a flick of the wrist, then twist the knife to remove the pit.

**Direct grill:** Arrange the avocado halves cut sides down over a wood or wood-enhanced fire. Grill until browned and the flesh is infused with wood smoke.

**BEETS:** Like most hard, dense vegetables, beets do best with indirect grilling, smoke-roasting, or ember-grilling (caveman grilling). Some chefs like to steam or parboil them first to make them more tender.

**Prep:** Trim off any stringy roots and leafy tops (you can cook the latter like collard greens). Scrub the beet with a stiff-bristled vegetable brush.

**Indirect grill:** Indirect grill the beets at moderate heat until soft enough to pierce with a slender skewer, 30 to 60 minutes (depending on the size of the beet). Or direct grill over moderate heat, turning often with tongs.

**Ember-grill (caveman grill):** This ancient method gives beets a haunting smoke flavor. Roast until the exterior is completely charred and the beet is tender (test with a slender metal skewer), 30 to 45 minutes. Cut off and discard the burnt exterior.

**BOK CHOY:** A high water content makes this an excellent vegetable for grilling.

**Prep:** Grill small ones whole or cut in half lengthwise; cut larger ones lengthwise in quarters and brush with sesame oil or olive oil.

**Direct grill:** Start cut sides down and grill over a hot fire until browned. Then invert and grill the rounded sides until tender, but still a little crisp. Do not overcook. You can also grill bok choy on a hot plancha.

**BROCCOLI:** There are two schools of thought on this popular brassica. The first is direct grilling. (Some people blanch it first.) The second is plancha grilling.

**Prep:** Trim off the stem end. (Peel the bottom inch or so of the stem with a vegetable peeler if the outside feels tough.) Cut the broccoli lengthwise, stems and all, into quarters or ½-inch-thick steaks.

**Direct grill:** Brush with olive oil or melted butter and work over a medium-high fire. Grill until browned on the outside and crisp-tender.

**Plancha grill:** Heat the plancha on a hot grill. Brush the broccoli with olive or sesame oil and grill until browned and tender on all sides.

**BROCCOLINI/BROCCOLI RABE:** With slender stems and delicate florets, these broccoli cousins are perfect for direct grilling. You'll love how they char and crisp.

**Prep:** Cut off the ends of the stems and separate into individual stalks.

**Direct grill:** Brush with oil (olive or sesame) or melted butter and direct grill over a medium-high fire until browned and tender. Fabulous grilled over a wood fire.

**BRUSSELS SPROUTS:** These tiny cabbages turn up everywhere—how did we ever grill without them?

**Prep:** Cut the bottom ⅛ inch off the stem end. Some people like to cut an X into the bottom stem to help the sprouts roast more evenly. If the brussels sprouts are large, cut them in half through the stem. Remove and discard any blemished leaves.

**Direct grill:** Skewer the brussels sprouts kebab style (I like to place squares of bacon between them). Brush with melted butter or olive oil and direct grill over a medium-hot fire until browned and tender.

**Pan-grill:** Place whole or halved brussels sprouts in an aluminum foil drip pan and indirect grill at high heat until sizzling, browned, and tender. Move the pan directly over the heat at the end to crisp the exterior. (You can also direct grill the sprouts from start to finish in a foil pan—but in this case, you have to stir often.) Optional—add wood chunks or chips to generate smoke.

**Spit-roast:** In late fall, you can buy whole stalks of brussels sprouts. I like to attach them to the rotisserie spit and spit-roast (see page 178).

**CABBAGE:** Popular at New Wave grill restaurants where cabbage often comes grilled caveman-style on the embers. Savoy cabbage, with its crenelated leaves, is particularly well suited to grilling.

**Prep:** Pull off and discard any wilted leaves. Leave whole or cut in half through the stem end for ember-grilling (caveman grilling). Cut into quarters or wedges for direct grilling.

**Direct grill:** Brush cabbage quarters or wedges with olive oil or melted butter and direct grill over a medium-high fire until browned and tender.

**Ember-grill (caveman grill):** Endows the cabbage with an irresistible smoke flavor. Grill small cabbages whole. Cut larger ones in half. Nestle in charcoal or wood embers and grill until tender (test with a metal skewer). Trim off the burnt exterior.

**CARROTS:** Another darling of new school grilling, fire-roasted carrots turn up at cutting-edge restaurants around the world. Grill whole or in chunks.

**Prep:** Trim off the greens (you can save them to make pesto; see page 142) and scrub the exterior with a stiff-bristled vegetable brush. (I no longer bother with peeling.) I like to grill carrots whole, or cut crosswise into 3-inch sections. So they cook evenly, cut any large sections lengthwise in half or quarters so all are about the same size.

**Direct grill:** Lightly brush whole carrots with olive oil or butter and direct grill over medium to medium-high heat. This works especially well over a wood or wood-enhanced fire.

**Pan-grill:** This is my favorite way to grill carrots. Place in an aluminum foil drip pan with olive oil or butter and indirect grill at high heat until sizzling, browned, and tender. Move the pan directly over the heat the last couple minutes to crisp the exterior. (You can also direct grill the carrots from start to finish in a foil pan—but in that case, you have to stir more often.) Optional but highly recommended: Add wood chunks or chips to the fire to generate smoke.

**CAULIFLOWER:** Its size and shape make it the Boston butt (pork shoulder) of the vegetable kingdom. Grill and serve whole. Note: Romanesco (see page 174) would be grilled the same way.

**Prep:** Pull off and discard any green leaves. I usually grill cauliflower raw—sometimes whole, sometimes cut into florets. Some people like to blanch (parboil) it prior to grilling: Cook until half tender (test with a skewer) in boiling salted water to cover. Rinse under cold water, then drain well. Blot dry, oil, and you're ready for grilling.

**Steam-grill:** Tightly wrap the cauliflower with 3 to 4 tablespoons water in aluminum foil. Indirect grill in the foil until the cauliflower is almost tender (about 45 minutes or so). The water turns to steam, which cooks the cauliflower. Wearing insulated food gloves (steam is hot), unwrap the cauliflower. Then brush with olive oil or melted butter and direct grill until browned and tender.

**Indirect grill:** Oil and season the cauliflower and indirect grill until browned and tender. Wood smoke would be most welcome.

**Spit-roast:** My favorite way to grill cauliflower. Thread onto a rotisserie spit and spit-roast until browned and tender. (This takes 1 to 1½ hours.)

**CELERY ROOT/CELERY:** London superstar chef Yotam Ottolenghi roasts celery root on a wood-burning hearth to make a meatless shawarma. Note: Celery stalks should be direct grilled like zucchini (see page 314).

**Prep:** If ember-grilling (caveman grilling), scrub the exterior with a stiff-bristled vegetable brush. If indirect grilling, pare off the skin. If pan-grilling, peel and cut into 1-inch wedges or chunks.

**Ember-grill (caveman grill):** Nestle the celery root in the embers. Roast, turning with tongs, until tender (test with a metal skewer). Cut off the burnt part before serving.

**Indirect grill:** Peel and roast on a medium-high grill as for cauliflower (see page 188). Wood smoke welcome.

**Pan-grill:** Prepare as pan-grilled carrots described on page 306.

**CORN:** One of the world's all-time best vegetables to grill, enjoyed from Mexico to Japan and beyond. You need to grill corn naked (sans husk) to achieve the proper smoky caramel flavors—grilling in the husk is simply steaming.

**Prep:** Husk the corn. If you plan to serve it on the cob, strip back the husk from the top to the stem end as though you're peeling a banana, but leave the husk attached. Tie the husk together with butcher's string below the ear of corn. This forms a convenient handle. Note: Be sure to pull back the husk completely, including the often-forgotten last inch.

**Direct grill:** Brush the corn with olive oil or melted butter and season with salt and pepper. Direct grill over high heat. Slide a folded sheet of aluminum foil under the husk to keep it from burning.

**Ember-grill (caveman grill):** Okay, this method is the one exception to the husk-off rule. Lay the corn in its husk directly on a bed of glowing embers. Grill until the husk burns off and the kernels are golden brown, turning with long-handled tongs and protecting your hands with grill gloves. Added advantage: The burning husk drives a smoke flavor into the corn. Brush off any loose ash or burnt silk with a vegetable brush, then butter and season the corn. It doesn't get better than this.

**COLLARD GREENS:** Yes, you can grill collards and other leafy vegetables, like Swiss chard and kale.

**Prep:** Trim off the tough stems. Make a V-shaped cut to remove them from the center of the leaves.

**Direct grill:** Brush the leaves with olive oil or melted butter and season well. Direct grill until browned and crisp, a couple minutes per side.

**EDAMAME:** Usually served steamed, but fresh soybean pods can also be charred over a hot fire.

**Prep:** Leave the edamame in the pods. If direct grilling, lightly toss with oil (I like sesame) and season with salt and pepper. If ember-grilling (caveman grilling), leave plain.

**Direct grill:** Heat a vegetable grate or grid over a hot fire. Place the edamame on it and grill until sizzling and browned, a few minutes per side, turning with a spatula. Alternatively, place the edamame in a wire-mesh grill basket and direct grill, tossing or stirring so all brown evenly.

**Ember-grill (caveman grill):** This is a fantastic way to grill edamame and other pod vegetables, like snap peas. Place in a wire-mesh grill basket and place the basket directly on the embers. Grill until browned and charred, stirring with tongs.

**EGGPLANT:** This bulbous fruit (botanically speaking, it's a berry) is the world's most popular veggie for grilling. In Japan, the small slender Asian eggplants are grilled on hibachis and served with sweet-salty miso sauce. In Turkey, it's grilled shish kebab–style—often with minced lamb between the slices. Throughout the Middle East, eggplant is flame- or ember-grilled (caveman grilled) in the skin to make the smoky dip baba ghanoush (see page 55). Two attributes make eggplant perfect for grilling: the skin, which emits a fragrant and delectable smoke when charred; and the porous flesh, which absorbs that smoke—and other flavorings, such as olive oil and lemon juice—like a sponge. When buying eggplants, choose the small, slender fruits (1 to 2½ inches in diameter)—the flavor is milder and sweeter than jumbos, and you get a higher ratio of charred smoky skin to flesh.

**Prep:** The easiest way to grill eggplant is whole and right in the skin. Alternatively, cut the eggplant widthwise or lengthwise into ¼- to ½-inch-thick slices. Brush with olive or sesame oil, season well, and direct grill over a hot fire. Note: When I went to cooking school in Paris, we were taught to salt eggplant slices to draw out the bitter juices. You'd rinse off those juices after an hour and blot dry. Today's eggplant varieties aren't bitter, so I don't bother.

**Direct grill:** To grill eggplants whole, heat your grill as hot as it will go. Grill until the skins are charred and the flesh is soft (test it with a metal skewer). When direct grilling eggplant slices, work over a hot, but not screaming hot, fire.

**Ember-grill (caveman grill):** This the best way to grill eggplants for baba ghanoush (see page 55) and other dips. Lay whole eggplants on the hot coals. Grill until charred on all sides and very tender. Apartment dwellers take note: In the Middle East, people who lack

grills char eggplants directly on the burners of their stoves, delivering the same smoky flavor you'd get on a grill.

**ENDIVE (Belgian):** Firm, crisp, and pleasingly bitter, Belgian endive makes a great vegetable for grilling. Treviso (an endive cousin—this one with purplish leaves) and radicchio would be grilled the same way.

**Prep:** Cut the endive in half lengthwise. (Cut large ones in quarters.) Brush with olive oil and season well.

**Direct grill:** Grill over high heat until browned on all sides and tender. Do not overcook; you want the endives to stay raw in the center.

**ESCAROLE (see Lettuce/Frisée/ Escarole/Broccoli Di Ciccio)**

**FAVA BEANS:** Come springtime, you'll find jumbo green pods of fresh fava beans in the produce section—especially in Italian markets.

**Prep:** No special prep needed.

**Direct grill:** Fire up your grill as hot as it will go. Arrange the fava pods on the grate and grill until charred on both sides, 4 to 6 minutes per side, 8 to 12 minutes in all. Open the pod and enjoy the sweet smoky beans.

**Ember-grill (caveman grill):** Lay the pods directly on the embers, or place in a wire-mesh grill basket directly on the embers. When charred on both sides, they're ready.

**FENNEL:** This anise-flavored bulb delivers a double blast of flavor. Toss the stems and feathery fronds on the fire to generate fennel-scented smoke. (That's how people in the South of France grill sea bass.) You can also chop the feathery parts and use them as a fresh herb. The grilled bulbs (see page 155) taste like a cross between anise and celery.

**Prep:** Trim off the stalks and fronds, saving them to add to your fire. Cut ⅛ inch off the stem end. Cut the bulb in half (through the narrow side) or in quarters, or cut lengthwise through the stem end into ¼-inch-thick slices.

**Direct grill:** Brush the fennel pieces with olive oil and season with salt and pepper. Grill until browned and crisp-tender, 5 to 8 minutes.

**Ember-grill (caveman grill):** Place the bulbs directly on the coals. Grill until charred on the outside and tender inside (test with a slender skewer). Scrape off any burnt parts prior to serving.

**GARLIC:** Grilling and smoking mellow garlic's odiferous bite—not to mention adding an amazing, unexpected dimension of flavor. A number of recipes in this book call for grilled or smoked garlic.

**Prep:** To grill a whole garlic head, loosely wrap in foil and direct or indirect grill over medium heat. Alternatively, cut the garlic head in half crosswise through the side. Brush the cut sides with olive oil and season with salt and pepper. Direct grill over a medium-high fire. To grill individual cloves, peel and skewer lengthwise on wooden toothpicks.

**Direct grill:** Work over a medium fire. If cloves start to burn before they're tender, loosely wrap in foil.

**Indirect grill:** Use for whole heads of garlic. Wood smoke is optional, but welcomed.

**Ember-grill (caveman grill):** Loosely wrap the peeled and skewered cloves in foil and lay on the embers. Great for ember-grilled salsa (see page 288).

**GREEN BEANS/HARICOTS VERTS/SNAP PEAS:** At first glance, you might think these skinny green veggies are too small to grill, but with a little ingenuity (and a vegetable grid or wire-mesh grill basket), you can radically transform their flavor using live fire.

**Prep:** Snap off the ends and pull out the strings running the length of a green bean or snap pea. If direct grilling, toss with olive or sesame oil and season with coarse salt and pepper.

**Direct grill:** Place the beans in a wire-mesh grill basket or grill wok or on a hot vegetable grid. Grill over a hot fire until blistered and browned.

**Pan-grill:** Place the beans in an aluminum foil drip pan with a little olive or sesame oil. Direct grill over a hot fire, turning with tongs, until the beans are sizzling and browned.

**Ember-grill (caveman grill):** Place the beans (they should be dry) in

a wire-mesh grill basket and lay it right on the glowing embers. Turn the beans with tongs so they cook and brown evenly.

**KALE:** One normally doesn't grill leaves, but grilled kale crisps like a potato chip (see page 38)—especially the lacinato variety, aka dinosaur kale.

**Prep:** Using a paring knife, make sharp V-shaped cuts in the center of the leaf to remove any thick stems. Lightly brush the kale on both sides with olive or sesame oil and season well.

**Direct grill:** Direct grill over a medium to medium-high fire until browned. Transfer to a wire rack: The leaves will crisp on cooling.

**LEEKS:** Leeks (or more accurately, their small cousins, calçots) are one of Spain's national grilled treasures—roasted in the embers and served rolled in newspapers or on clay roofing tiles with Romesco Sauce (see page 176) for dipping.

**Prep:** Cut off and discard the dark green leaves. If the white part is sandy, make 2 lengthwise cuts to within 2 inches of the furry root end (one at 90 degrees to the other), then plunge the stalks up and down in a deep bowl of cold water to wash them. Some people like to blanch large leeks in boiling salted water for a couple of minutes prior to grilling.

**Direct grill:** There are several ways to grill leeks. Grill large leeks whole over high heat until charred on the outside and tender inside (test with a slender skewer). Discard the charred exterior and enjoy the soft creamy interior. Or cut them in half lengthwise, brush with olive oil, and grill until browned and soft. Or grill small leeks whole.

**Ember-grill (caveman grill):** This is how the Spanish grill their small leek-like calçots.

**LETTUCE/FRISÉE/ESCAROLE/ BROCCOLI DI CICCIO:** Yes, you can grill crisp lettuces, like romaine, not to mention lettuce-like members of the chicory family, like radicchio, escarole, frisée, and Belgian endive.

**Prep:** Halve or quarter the heads (cutting from top to stem) and rinse in a bowl of cold water to remove any grit. Shake or spin dry. Brush with oil, or not. Los Angeles restaurant diva Nancy Silverton grills broccoli di ciccio (a chicory-like green in the brassica family) dry to char the slender leaves, then tosses them with olive oil and lemon juice.

**Direct grill:** Direct grill romaine, frisée, and escarole over a hot fire—ideally wood, so you put a little smoke on the leaves. Serve cool or at room temperature.

**Cold-smoke or hay-smoke:** This is how I like to smoke delicate lettuces, like Boston or Bibb (see page 72).

**MUSHROOMS:** If ever there was a vegetable for grilling, it's the mushroom. The spongy texture absorbs marinades, bastes, and smoke flavor. Depending on the variety, it can be steak-like (think portobello), oyster-like (think oyster mushrooms), or even crisp and smoky, like bacon (see the Shiitakes Channeling Bacon recipe, page 26). Beloved by vegetarians, vegans, and omnivores alike,

grilled mushrooms pair well with bacon, pancetta, and other cured meats.

**Prep:** Wipe clean with a damp paper towel, as needed. Trim ¼ inch off the stems, or if working with shiitakes, remove the stem entirely. Grill small mushrooms on skewers kebab-style. Or use a vegetable grilling grid or wire-mesh grill basket. Grill larger mushrooms, like portobellos, as you would a burger or steak. Brush with olive or sesame oil, melted butter, or other fat-rich basting mixture.

**Direct grill:** Over medium-high to high heat. Marinades and bastes welcome.

**Hobo pack–style:** Great for bunches of cluster mushrooms, like beech mushrooms or hen-of-the-woods.

**OKRA:** Often associated with the American South, where it's usually served stewed, okra is totally awesome grilled. Added advantage: Grilling okra whole dramatically minimizes the slime factor.

**Prep:** Leave whole: Cutting an okra pod and exposing the inside to air increases its sliminess. I like to skewer okra pods side by side to form rafts, then grill as you would asparagus.

**Direct grill:** Over high heat, brushed with melted butter or sesame oil.

## ONIONS AND SHALLOTS:

Onions contain a lot of sugar (14 grams for a large onion), and nothing brings out their natural sweetness like grilling. Talk about versatile: Onions can be direct grilled, indirect grilled, smoked, spit-roasted, and ember-grilled.

**Prep:** To grill onion slices, peel and cut crosswise into ½-inch-thick rounds and pin crosswise with a toothpick or small skewer to hold them together. To grill onion wedges, cut from tip to root and pin with a wooden toothpick. To stuff an onion, cut out the root end in an inverted cone-shaped plug and fill with your favorite stuffing.

**Direct grill:** Brush onion slices or wedges with olive oil and season well. Grill until darkly browned over a medium-high fire. You can also direct grill a whole onion: Leave the skin on and grill over a medium fire until darkly browned on the outside and very soft inside (test with a slender skewer).

**Indirect grill:** Remove the skin of the onion and grill whole or stuffed—set atop a ring of crumpled aluminum foil—over medium heat. Wood smoke optional, and certainly welcome. Test for doneness with a slender skewer.

**Spit-roast (rotisserie-grill):** Brazilians thread large peeled onions onto flat skewers for spit-roasting over a medium-high charcoal fire.

**Ember-grill (caveman grill):** A wonderful way to grill onions. Nestle, skin and all, in the embers and grill until charred on the outside and soft inside (test with a skewer). Split them open at the top with a knife. Add butter, mascarpone, balsamic syrup, etc.

**PARSNIPS:** Grilling makes this cream-colored, carrot-shaped root even sweeter.

**Prep:** Scrub or peel. Because parsnips are so much wider at the top than the bottom, you'll want to cut in half crosswise, then cut the top (fatter) part lengthwise in halves or quarters so all the pieces are the same size.

**Pan-grill:** Indirect grill in a foil pan with olive oil or butter at medium-high heat as you would carrots (see page 143). Move the pan directly over the heat the last few minutes to sear the exterior.

## PEAS (Sugar Snap or Snow):

Not the first vegetables you'd think of grilling, but live fire adds an intriguing smoke flavor and sweetness.

**Prep:** Snap off the ends and pull out the strings.

**Direct grill:** On a grilling grid or in a wire-mesh grill basket, turning with tongs.

**Ember-grill (caveman grill):** Grill in a wire-mesh grill basket directly in the embers. Amazing!

## PEPPERS (Bell, Horn, Poblano, Shishito, Padrón, and so on):

Another vegetable that seems expressly put on earth for grilling. You can grill peppers until darkly browned, in which case, peeling is not necessary. Or you can char the skins, imparting a haunting smoke flavor, in which case the pepper must be peeled before serving. Apartment dwellers note: In the Middle East, people who lack grills char the peppers directly on their stovetop burners.

**Prep:** Leave them whole, or cut into 1-inch triangles or squares and thread onto skewers for grilling kebab-style.

**Direct grill:** Grill over high heat until darkly browned.

**Indirect grill:** Cut the tops off bell peppers and remove the seeds and ribs. Stuff with grated cheese, grilled bread, roasted mushrooms or other vegetables, rice, or other favorite filling and indirect grill until the sides are soft.

**Ember-grill (caveman grill):** By far my favorite way to grill peppers. Lay on the embers and grill until completely charred on all sides, turning often with tongs. Transfer to a metal platter or bowl to cool, then scrape off the burnt skin. There is nothing sweeter, smokier, or better than an ember-grilled pepper.

**POTATOES:** Grilling potatoes always makes me think of the Vincent van Gogh painting *The Potato Eaters*, in which the subjects eat potatoes roasted in the fireplace. Grilling adds a smoke flavor you simply can't achieve in the oven.

**Prep:** When grilling whole, simply wash and scrub the skins. Or cut into slices, wedges, or chunks.

**Direct grill:** Direct grill Yukon Gold or small baking potatoes in the skin over a medium fire. Armenians thread sliced potatoes on skewers, which they direct grill over charcoal (see page 167).

**Pan-grill:** My favorite way to grill fingerling potatoes, baby potatoes, or 1-inch chunks. Indirect grill in an aluminum foil pan with butter or olive oil. Move directly over the heat the last few minutes to crisp the exterior. For even more flavor, add wood chunks or chips to the coals.

**Indirect grill:** Like baking a potato in the oven, but you get to perfume it with wood smoke.

**RUTABAGAS AND TURNIPS:** Grilling intensifies their intrinsic sweetness.

**Prep:** Wash turnips with a stiff-bristled vegetable brush. Cook small ones whole; halve or quarter large ones. Peel rutabagas to remove the waxy skin. Indirect grill whole or cut into 1- or 2-inch wedges or chunks.

**Indirect grill:** On a crumpled foil ring as for an onion. Wood smoke always welcome.

**Pan-grill:** Indirect grill in an aluminum foil pan with olive oil or butter, moving the pan directly over the heat to crisp the edges for the last few minutes. Stir often while grilling.

**SCALLIONS AND RAMPS:** Great as a vegetable, accompaniment, or flavoring.

**Prep:** Brush with a little olive oil and season with salt and pepper. Leave the furry roots intact—they'll help hold the alliums together.

**Direct grill:** Grill over a hot fire until browned and the fat part is tender. Scallions and ramps are also excellent grilled on a plancha.

**SUNCHOKES (aka Jerusalem artichokes):** One of my favorite tubers for grilling, with a creamy texture and a flavor reminiscent of artichokes.

**Prep:** Wash and scrub with a stiff-bristled vegetable brush.

**Pan-grill:** Place in an aluminum foil pan with a little olive oil or butter and season with salt and pepper. Indirect grill at high heat until tender (test with a skewer). Move directly over the fire for the last few minutes to brown and crisp the exterior.

**Ember-grill (caveman grill):** Roast the Jerusalem artichokes in a wire-mesh grill basket on the embers, or directly on the embers, turning with tongs. This delivers a haunting smoky flavor. Josiah Citrin, chef-owner of Charcoal Venice, makes a wonderful ember-grilled Jerusalem artichoke puree that he serves by way of a sauce.

**SWEET POTATOES AND YAMS:** These sweet moist tubers are among my favorite veggies for grilling—direct, indirect, smoked, ember-grilled—all raise the humble sweet potato to the realm of gustatory wonderment. Korean cooks grill them in the skins to be served with sweet soy sauce and sesame. Nancy Silverton pairs them with spiced yogurt. At my house, we ember-grill them to make a sweet potato casserole for Thanksgiving (see page 225).

**Prep:** Wash and scrub well with a stiff-bristled vegetable brush.

**Direct grill:** Grill right in the skins over a moderate fire. Or slice on the diagonal or lengthwise into steak fries, brush with butter or oil, and direct grill.

**Indirect grill:** Lightly brush the outsides of the sweet potatoes with melted butter, olive oil, or bacon fat. Indirect grill at medium-high heat until crisp on the outside and soft inside (test with a skewer). Wood smoke always welcome.

**Pan-grill:** Slice, wedge, or dice the potatoes and roast in a foil pan with olive oil or melted butter. Work over a medium-high fire. Move the pan directly over the fire the last few minutes to brown and crisp the edges.

**Ember-grill (caveman grill):** Lay the sweet potatoes in their skins on the embers and roast until charred on the outside and tender (test with a skewer). Delectable with melted butter and cinnamon, maple syrup, or yogurt spiced with paprika, salt, and pepper.

**TOMATOES:** Like all vegetables with a high water content, tomatoes are excellent for grilling—especially over a wood or wood-enhanced fire. Direct grilled, indirect grilled, smoked, ember-grilled—whenever live fire is involved, tomatoes benefit big-time.

**Prep:** Grill cherry tomatoes whole; plum tomatoes, whole or cut in half lengthwise. Cut beefsteaks into thick slices for grilling (or leave whole for ember-grilling).

**Direct grill:** Brush thick tomato slices with olive or sesame oil and liberally season, then grill over a screaming hot fire. Blister plum and cherry tomatoes whole directly over that hot fire. (Skewer cherry tomatoes or use a vegetable grate or wire-mesh grill basket).

**Indirect grill:** Remove the stem end in an inverted cone-shaped plug. Stuff with ricotta or other favorite cheese or breadcrumbs and anchovies. Indirect grill at a medium-high to high heat. Wood smoke welcome.

**Smoke:** Cut the tomatoes in half and smoke (at 250°F) or cold smoke (at less than 100°F). Makes awesome gazpacho and tomato vinaigrette.

**Ember-grill (caveman grill):** Char plum and beefsteak tomatoes directly on the embers. (While you're at it, ember-grill an onion, poblano, jalapeño, and a couple of garlic cloves to make an unforgettable salsa; see page 287.)

## WINTER SQUASH
**(Acorn, Butternut, Delicata, Hubbard, Kabocha, Pumpkin, Spaghetti, Sweet Dumpling, Turban):** Dense-textured, rich-flavored, with abundant natural sweetness; grilling makes winter squash even more amazing.

**Prep:** Cut butternut squash in half lengthwise. Cut smaller round squashes, like acorn, delicata, spaghetti, sweet dumpling, etc., in half widthwise. Scrape out the seeds (which you can clean and roast with olive oil, salt, and pepper until browned and crisp). Alternatively, cut the squash into 1- to 2-inch wedges or chunks for direct grilling or plancha grilling. Similarly, cut large squash, such as Hubbard, kabocha, etc., into 1- to 2-inch wedges or chunks for direct grilling or plancha grilling. Cut round squash, like acorns and delicatas, crosswise into ½-inch-thick rings for grilling. Brush with melted butter or oil before grilling.

**Direct grill:** Direct grill squash rings, chunks, or wedges over medium-high heat. Also excellent grilled on a plancha or in a skillet or aluminum foil pan.

**Indirect grill:** Indirect grill round half squashes and butternuts cut sides up (generously baste with butter or olive oil). Alternatively, grill cut sides down on a salt slab or plancha. Test for doneness with a bamboo skewer.

**Ember-grill (caveman grill):** Lay the whole squash (e.g., butternut, pumpkin) directly on the embers and roast until the outside is charred and the flesh is tender (test with a skewer). Ember-grilled pumpkin makes an amazing Thanksgiving pie.

**ZUCCHINI AND SUMMER SQUASH:** Grilling is one of the best ways to cook these abundant (dare I say, overabundant) summer veggies. Because of their high water content, you'll want to work quickly over a hot fire. The idea is to sear the zucchini before it has a chance to stew and become soggy.

**Prep:** Choose small zucchini (6 to 8 inches long). Thinly slice lengthwise (not more than ¼ inch thick)—a mandoline works well for this.

**Direct grill:** Grill sliced zucchini over a screaming hot fire. (A wire-mesh grill basket makes your life easier when grilling a lot of slices.) Or use the ribbon and skewer grilling method on page 231.

**Indirect grill:** This works well for stuffed zucchini, like the braciole on page 203. Again, work over a hot fire.

**Ember-grill (caveman grill):** Char the zucchini to impart smoke and tenderness. Great in a smoky tzatziki (see page 298).

# CONVERSION TABLES

Please note that all conversions are approximate but close enough to be useful when converting from one system to another.

## OVEN TEMPERATURES

| FAHRENHEIT | GAS MARK | CELSIUS |
|---|---|---|
| 250 | ½ | 120 |
| 275 | 1 | 140 |
| 300 | 2 | 150 |
| 325 | 3 | 160 |
| 350 | 4 | 180 |
| 375 | 5 | 190 |
| 400 | 6 | 200 |
| 425 | 7 | 220 |
| 450 | 8 | 230 |
| 475 | 9 | 240 |
| 500 | 10 | 260 |

**NOTE:** Reduce the temperature by 20°C (68°F) for fan-assisted ovens.

## APPROXIMATE EQUIVALENTS

1 stick butter = 8 tbs = 4 oz = ½ cup = 115 g

1 cup all-purpose presifted flour = 4.7 oz

1 cup granulated sugar = 8 oz = 220 g

1 cup (firmly packed) brown sugar = 6 oz = 220 g to 230 g

1 cup confectioners' sugar = 4½ oz = 115 g

1 cup honey or syrup = 12 oz = 350 g

1 cup grated cheese = 4 oz = 125 g

1 cup dried beans = 6 oz = 175 g

1 large egg = about 2 oz or about 3 tbs

1 egg yolk = about 1 tbs

1 egg white = about 2 tbs

## LIQUID CONVERSIONS

| U.S. | IMPERIAL | METRIC |
|---|---|---|
| 2 tbs | 1 fl oz | 30 ml |
| 3 tbs | 1½ fl oz | 45 ml |
| ¼ cup | 2 fl oz | 60 ml |
| ⅓ cup | 2½ fl oz | 75 ml |
| ⅓ cup + 1 tbs | 3 fl oz | 90 ml |
| ⅓ cup + 2 tbs | 3½ fl oz | 100 ml |
| ⅓ cup | 4 fl oz | 125 ml |
| ⅔ cup | 5 fl oz | 150 ml |
| ¾ cup | 6 fl oz | 175 ml |
| ¾ cup + 2 tbs | 7 fl oz | 200 ml |
| 1 cup | 8 fl oz | 250 ml |
| 1 cup + 2 tbs | 9 fl oz | 275 ml |
| 1¼ cups | 10 fl oz | 300 ml |
| 1⅓ cups | 11 fl oz | 325 ml |
| 1½ cups | 12 fl oz | 350 ml |
| 1⅔ cups | 13 fl oz | 375 ml |
| 1¾ cups | 14 fl oz | 400 ml |
| 1¾ cups + 2 tbs | 15 fl oz | 450 ml |
| 2 cups (1 pint) | 16 fl oz | 500 ml |
| 2½ cups | 20 fl oz (1 pint) | 600 ml |
| 3¾ cups | 1½ pints | 900 ml |
| 4 cups | 1¾ pints | 1 liter |

## WEIGHT CONVERSIONS

| US/UK | METRIC | US/UK | METRIC |
|---|---|---|---|
| ½ oz | 15 g | 7 oz | 200 g |
| 1 oz | 30 g | 8 oz | 250 g |
| 1½ oz | 45 g | 9 oz | 275 g |
| 2 oz | 60 g | 10 oz | 300 g |
| 2½ oz | 75 g | 11 oz | 325 g |
| 3 oz | 90 g | 12 oz | 350 g |
| 3½ oz | 100 g | 13 oz | 375 g |
| 4 oz | 125 g | 14 oz | 400 g |
| 5 oz | 150 g | 15 oz | 450 g |
| 6 oz | 175 g | 1 lb | 500 g |

# INDEX

Note: Page references in *italics* indicate photographs.

# ABOUT THE AUTHOR

**S**teven Raichlen is a journalist, lecturer, TV host, and *New York Times* bestselling author whose 31 books have more than 5 million copies in print and include the international blockbusters *The Barbecue! Bible*, *Planet Barbecue*, and *Project Smoke*. The five-time James Beard Award winner also hosts the popular *Project Fire* and *Project Smoke* TV shows on public television and stars in several French- and Italian-language TV shows. An award-winning journalist, Raichlen has written for the *New York Times*, *Wall Street Journal*, *Esquire*, *GQ*, and all the major food magazines. In 2015, he was inducted into the Barbecue Hall of Fame.

Raichlen holds a degree in French literature from Reed College in Portland, Oregon, and studied medieval cooking in Europe on a Thomas J. Watson Foundation Fellowship. (He also won a Fulbright Scholarship.) He and his wife, Barbara, live in Miami and Martha's Vineyard.